Clear Grammar 1

2nd Edition

Keys to Grammar for
English Language Learners

Keith S. Folse

Ann Arbor
University of Michigan Press

ISBN-13: 978-0-472-03241-9

2013   2012   2011   2010   4   3   2   1

Contents

To the Teacher

The purpose of a grammar book for English language learners (ELLs) is to help our students acquire the patterns of English. Simply put, grammar is nothing more than patterns. Some of these patterns are relatively easy (e.g., adjectives precede nouns), while others are more difficult (e.g., prepositions or articles). To help our students acquire these patterns, the four books in the *Clear Grammar* series feature a unique combination of useful grammar information written in simple language with activities that promote more accurate and fluent writing, speaking, reading, and vocabulary.

Clear Grammar 1 offers students and teachers a solid introduction to beginning level grammar. It is part of a four-volume series of grammar books for all levels of students of English as a second or foreign language. Book 1 covers grammar points for beginning non-native speakers of English, including simple present, possessive and demonstrative adjectives, descriptive adjectives, simple past, *wh-* questions, present progressive, count and non-count nouns, prepositions, *be going to*, and a brief introduction of present perfect.

Clear Grammar 2 continues with more difficult points, including irregular past, articles, and modals. *Clear Grammar 3* continues with grammar points such as present perfect, infinitives vs. gerunds, and relative clauses. *Clear Grammar 4* concludes the series with advanced topics such as reductions of clauses, past modals, and past perfect.

Clear Grammar 1 contains exercises that provide relevant practice in basic grammar points for ELLs at the beginning level. It assumes that the students have at least a fair reading and writing ability with the English alphabet. It is designed to be used by adult learners—high school age and up. It is suitable for either intensive or non-intensive programs.

Important features of all four new editions of *Clear Grammar* include:

1. clear grammar explanations with user-friendly charts
2. a grammar discovery task using students' inductive learning skills
3. a large number of activities: more than 220 in the book
4. a wide variety of activities: fill in the blank, sentence completion, scrambled sentences, matching, error ID, editing, original writing, reading, and vocabulary
5. many more grammar activities at the longer discourse level
6. reading skills: each unit includes a critical reading activity and a sentence-reading exercise in which the target grammar is featured.
7. writing skills: each unit concludes with two writing activities, one on editing student writing and the other for original student writing
8. vocabulary skills: each unit includes at least two vocabulary practices, one of which focuses on collocations
9. communication skills: each unit includes one or two speaking activities that require students to speak and listen to each other while using the target grammar
10. extra practice activities online that are indicated within each unit

The books in the *Clear Grammar* series have eight main goals:

1. to teach the basic grammar points necessary for ESL students
2. to expose students to a substantial amount of useful, high-frequency vocabulary that is related to the grammar point being studied, including words, phrases, and idioms
3. to provide ample written practice in these structures at the multisentence and dialogue levels
4. to provide practice at varying cognitive levels (i.e., not just knowledge and comprehension but also synthesis and evaluation)
5. to engage ELLs through a variety of activities and games
6. to improve students' writing, speaking, reading, and listening
7. to provide ample opportunities for students to check their progress while studying these structures
8. to serve as a grammar reference that is written with language and terms that a beginning-level ESL student can understand without teacher assistance.

The units may be done in any order. However, it is recommended that the general sequencing of the units be followed whenever possible. An attempt has been made to recycle material from one unit into following units where appropriate. For example, once past tense for irregular verbs has been covered, many of the sentences in subsequent exercises in other units include irregular past tense for further reinforcement.

Though a great deal of variety of material exists in the book, there is a general pattern within each unit.

Unit Organization

1. **Discover Grammar Task.** In many grammar classes, the teacher simply explains the grammar lesson to the students. Another effective technique is to involve the students in a grammar discovery task that begins each unit.

   Students work together to read a short passage or conversation of one to two paragraphs that is rich in examples of the target grammar and then answer a series of questions about the structures in the text. These questions focus on grammar and meaning.

   Students may or may not be able to actually figure out the grammar issue, but this creates a teachable moment in response to the learners' need to know. Your goal is to pique the students' curiosity about the lesson's grammar. After completing the task in their books, students should discuss their answers as a class before beginning the actual lesson. Some students are better able to remember information that they themselves have worked with, so involving students in this kind of discovery task may benefit their ultimate learning.

2. **Grammar Presentation Charts.** Simple, easy-to-follow charts explain the target grammar, which often features corpus-based vocabulary connected to the grammar point.

3. **List of Potential Errors with Corrections.** This section of the unit includes a list of several of the most common errors made by learners. Following each error is the corrected form so that students can see not only what they should avoid but how it should be corrected. Our students represent a wide range of linguistic groups, and every effort has been made to take this into account in selecting which kinds of errors to include here.

4. **Written (as opposed to speaking) Exercises.** Teachers and students want a large number of written exercises to allow for ample practice of the newly learned structure. The exercises have been sequenced so that the early exercises require only passive knowledge of the grammar point. For example, students circle one of two answers or put a check mark by the correct word. These exercises are followed by others that are more cognitively demanding and require active production of the language structure. In this way, students can comfortably move from passive knowledge to active production of a structure.

    The written exercises in this book are short enough to be done in a small amount of time, yet they are thorough enough to provide sufficient practice for the structure in question. These exercises may be done in class or as homework. Furthermore, they may be checked quickly either by individual students or by the class.

5. **Grammar at the Discource Level.** As often as possible, the written exercises in this book consist of connected sentences related to a single topic. The title of the material is indicated just before the grammar activity. This connected discourse helps ELLs improve their overall English fluency while focusing on the target grammar items.

6. **Extra Online Practice.** After students have practiced a structure, they are directed to do corresponding interactive activities on the website that accompanies this series. Students record their scores for these activities in their books, which gives teachers who so desire an opportunity to see how students are doing on a particular grammar item.

7. **Mini-Conversations.** Instead of unconnected single-sentence exercises, this written exercise consists of dialogues that require students to recognize or use the target grammar in a broader context than single sentences.

8. **Editing.** Students need to become proficient at editing their own grammar. To that end, a special activity in each unit allows ELLs to be the judge of whether or not a given sentence does or does not contain an error with the target grammar items.

9. **Sentence Study for Critical Reading.** In this activity, students read a sentence that contains the target grammar and then must choose which of four other sentences are true based on the information in the original sentence. To improve critical-thinking skills, all four of the statements may be true, so students must read all four and carefully consider their veracity.

10. **Speaking Exercises.** Each unit has at least one interactive speaking activity that provides an opportunity for students to practice the grammar and build fluency.

11. Two **Review Tests.** Equally as important as the teaching of a given grammar point is the measurement of the learning that has taken place. Near the end of every unit are two review tests. These review tests have various kinds of questions to assess learners' ability in different ways.

    Review Test 1 contains multiple choice questions. It is important to discuss not only why the correct answers are correct but also why the distractors are not correct. Review Test 2 is Production and Evaluation. Part 1 of this review test requires production of the grammar, usually through a fill in the blank activity. Because editing grammar is such an important student skill, Part 2 requires students to edit material that contains typical ELL errors.

12. **Reading Practice.** This longer reading activity generally consists of 200–400 words of text followed by several comprehension questions. The target grammar has been underlined to reinforce students' knowledge and awareness of the grammar.

13. **Two Vocabulary Practices.** Grammar knowledge without expanding vocabulary knowledge is useless, so vocabulary must be practiced and learned. The units overtly present new vocabulary to help students increase their vocabulary as much as possible. To this end, two vocabulary practice activities help solidify students' knowledge of vocabulary.

    Word Knowledge features 25–35 key words from the unit and two answer options. Students should select the one word that is clearly related to the target vocabulary word.

    Collocations features 25–40 key phrases or word combinations that are used frequently. Here students choose the one word that best completes the phrase. Examples include *a* _____ *menu* with *sauce* and *special* as answer choices, and *in* _____ with *fact* and *menu*.

14. **Writing Practice.** The writing practice at the end of each unit has two parts. In Part 1, students must edit a student writing according to a list of errors that have been identified. These errors represent the most typical ELL errors for this level and grammar point. In Part 2, students are to write a short assignment based on something similar to the passage written for Part 1. Teachers may elect to have their students write sentences or paragraphs depending on the curriculum in their program.

15. **One-Minute Lesson Notes.** A unique feature of this series is the inclusion of numerous student notes, which appear as small shaded boxes throughout the chapters. These notes contain important information on an array of language areas, including grammar, vocabulary, pronunciation, capitalization, punctuation, and learning strategies, which teachers may discuss with the whole class or just point out to students for additional information.

Using this Book

This book will help you to improve your English speaking, writing, reading, and listening. You will learn useful grammar and important vocabulary. Be sure to do every exercise. If you do not understand the correct answer to any question, ask your teacher or a classmate.

 Grammar Lesson

These charts have useful grammar information. Learn this information. Ask your teacher if there is anything you do not understand.

 BE CAREFUL!

These mistakes are common. Do you make these same mistakes? Study these mistakes and the corrections very carefully.

Speaking Practice

Doing exercises on paper is not enough. In these conversations and speaking activities, you must try to use your new grammar as much as possible. Listen to other students' grammar.

 Reading Practice

As you do this practice, be sure to notice the underlined grammar examples in the reading.

 Vocabulary Practice

Grammar is important, but you need to have a big vocabulary. Pay careful attention to the two vocabulary practices.

Writing Practice

Part 1 works on editing. You need to be able to write correctly, so Part 1 works on editing. In Part 2, you can write original work.

 One-Minute Lesson

These boxes have important information about grammar, vocabulary, spelling, or language usage.

 Review Tests

Each unit has two review tests. The first one has multiple choice questions, and the second has other kinds of questions.

 Online Exercise

This symbol means that there is an extra practice activity online. Be sure to write your score in your book.

1

Unit 1

Simple Present Tense of *Be*

Discover the Grammar

Read the information about Jaime Sandoval, and then answer the seven questions.

Line	
1	Hello! My name is Jaime Sandoval. I am from Mexico originally. My new
2	home is in Providence, Rhode Island. Rhode Island is a small state in the
3	northeastern part of the United States. It is near New York and Boston. They
4	are more famous than Providence. This place is not very large, but Providence
5	is a nice city. The winters in Providence are cold, but the summers are beautiful.
6	In fall, the leaves are so pretty! Providence is great. My wife and I like this
7	place. We think that it is an excellent place for our family. Our house is old, and
8	it is not very large. That is OK because my family and I are happy here in
9	Providence. I am glad that we live in Providence.

1. Underline the two examples of *am*. Write the line number and the word before *am*.
   a. Line ___: _____ am
   b. Line ___: _____ am

2. Study these examples of *is* and *are* from page 2.

is	*are*
a. Line 1: My name is Jaime Sandoval. b. Line 2: My new home is in Providence. c. Line 2: Rhode Island is a small state. d. Line 4: This city is not very large. e. Line 7: It is an excellent place . . . f. Line 7: Our house is old.	g. Line 5: The winters in Providence are cold. h. Line 5: The summer are beautiful. i. Line 6: The leaves are so beautiful. j. Line 8: My family and I are happy.

   When do we use *is*? When do we use *are*? What is the difference?

   _____

   _____

3. Line 1 says *I am*, but Line 8 says *I are*. Can you explain the difference?

   _____

4. After *am/is/are*, sometimes we find a noun. A noun is the name of a person (teacher), place (school), or thing (book). Write the nouns from page 2.

   a. Line 1:   My name   is   _____

   b. Line 2:   Rhode Island is   a small _____

   c. Lines 4–5:   Providence   is   a nice _____

   d. Line 7:   It   is   an excellent _____

5. After *am/is/are*, sometimes we find an adjective. An adjective is a word that describes: *happy, big, good, green, hungry, beautiful*. Write the adjectives from page 2.

   a. Line 5:   The winters   are   _____

   b. Line 5:   The summers   are   _____

   c. Line 6:   The leaves   are   so _____

   d. Line 6:   Providence   is   _____

   e. Line 7:   Our house   is   _____

   f. Line 8:   It   is not   very _____

   g. Line 8:   My family and I are   _____

   h. Line 9:   I   am   _____

6. After *am/is/are*, sometimes we find a place. Write the place from page 2.

    a. Line 1:   I   am   _____ _____

    b. Line 1–2:   My new home is   _____ _____

    c. Line 3:   It   is   _____ _____

7. What questions do you have about *am/is/are*?

_____

_____

_____

Grammar Lesson

KEY
1

Simple Present Tense of *Be*: Affirmative

Singular	Plural
I am in class now.	Jo and I are in class. We are in class.
You are Mike's friend.	You and Mike are friends. You are friends.
Mike is hungry. He is in the kitchen.	Mike and Pam are hungry. They are in the kitchen.
Pam is a good swimmer. She is very fast.	Pam and Hank are good swimmers. They are very fast.
The car is red. It is new.	The cars are red. They are new.

<u>Rule 1.</u> In the simple present tense, be has three forms: am, is, are.

<u>Rule 2.</u> We use am with *I*; is with *he, she, it*; are with *you, we, they.*

<u>Rule 3.</u> I, you, he, she, it, we and they are called **subject pronouns**. It is necessary to include a subject (noun or pronoun) with am, is, are. A **pronoun** takes the place of a **noun**: *The book is green. <u>It</u> is green.*

⚠ BE CAREFUL!

Common Learner Errors	Explanation
1. Joseph and Mark ~~is~~ are in the kitchen.	Use is with singular subjects and are with plural subjects.
2. A and E ~~vowels~~ are vowels.	Remember to use am, is, or are.
3. Juan is from Venezuela. ~~Is~~ He is from Caracas.	Use a subject with am, is, and are.

EXERCISE 1. Affirmative *am/is/are*

For each subject, fill in the blanks with the correct forms of **be**: *am, is, are.*

1. you ____are____
2. Emily _____
3. you and Emily_____
4. your wife _____
5. the man and I _____
6. this computer _____
7. Bob, Jose, and Sue _____
8. my brother _____
9. my brothers _____
10. Flight 227 _____
11. we _____
12. the answer to Number 11_____
13. the book _____
14. the chapter _____
15. the chapters _____
16. the chapters in this book _____
17. Anna and Lee _____
18. Ted, Ron, and I _____
19. Ted and Ken _____
20. the people _____

EXERCISE 2. Affirmative *am/is/are* in Context

Fill in the blanks with the correct forms of **be**: *am, is, are.*

World Cities

1. Four of the five largest cities ____are____ in Asia. These cities _____ Tokyo, Jakarta, New York, Seoul, and Manila.

2. Tokyo _____ in Japan. The population of the Tokyo area _____ more than 30,000,000.

3. Canada _____ a big country. The capital _____ Ottawa. The largest cities _____ Toronto, Montreal, and Vancouver.

4. Greece and Italy _____ in Europe. The capital of Greece _____ Athens. The capital of Italy _____ Rome, but other famous cities in Italy _____ Venice and Milan.

5. South America's biggest cities _____ Buenos Aires, Lima, and Bogota. Buenos Aires _____ in Argentina. Lima _____ in Peru. Bogota _____ in Colombia. These three cities _____ also capitals of their countries.

Nouns

	Common Noun (name of a person, place, or thing)	Proper Noun (name of a specific person, a specific place, or a specific thing)
person	*a girl*	*Susan*
	a boy	*Matt*
	a teacher	*Mrs. Currier*
place	*a country*	*Canada*
	a university	*the University of California*
	a hotel	*the Wellborn Hotel*
thing	*a day*	*Friday*
	an airline	*Southern Airlines*
	a test	*TOEFL*®

Rule 1. A **common noun** is the name of a person, place, or thing. Examples are *a teacher, a country,* and a *day*.

Rule 2. Common nouns are not usually capitalized. However, if a common noun is the first word of a sentence (*Teachers are important.*) or in a title ("*Life in Mexico City*"), we capitalize it.

Rule 3. A **proper noun** is the name of a specific person, place, or thing. Examples are *Mrs. Currier, Canada,* and *Friday*.

Rule 4. Proper nouns are capitalized.

EXERCISE 3. *Be* Sentences with Capitalization and Punctuation

Add capital letters to the proper nouns in these sentences. Write your new sentences on the lines.

The Students in My Class

1. There are ten students in my class at the english language institute.

   There are ten students in my class at the English Language Institute.

2. Three of the students are from mexico.

3. maria and pablo are from mexico city.

4. teresa is from acapulco.

5. Five of the students are from the middle east.

6. ahmed is from saudi arabia.

7. mohamed is from the united arab emirates.

8. lofti is from egypt.

9. mansour is from yemen, and fatimah is from Jordan.

10. Finally, two students are from asia.

11. najmuddin is from malaysia.

12. pom is from thailand.

Do Online Exercise 1.1. My score: ____/10. ____% correct.

EXERCISE 4. *am/is/are* in a Postcard

Read the postcard from Richard to his mother. Fill in the blanks with the correct form of the verb *be*.

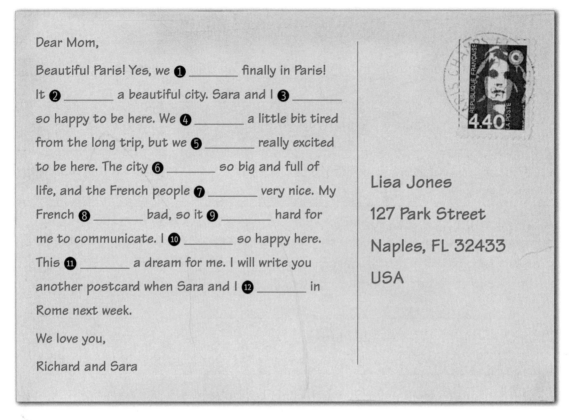

Dear Mom,

Beautiful Paris! Yes, we ❶ _____ finally in Paris! It ❷ _____ a beautiful city. Sara and I ❸ _____ so happy to be here. We ❹ _____ a little bit tired from the long trip, but we ❺ _____ really excited to be here. The city ❻ _____ so big and full of life, and the French people ❼ _____ very nice. My French ❽ _____ bad, so it ❾ _____ hard for me to communicate. I ❿ _____ so happy here. This ⓫ _____ a dream for me. I will write you another postcard when Sara and I ⓬ _____ in Rome next week.

We love you,

Richard and Sara

Lisa Jones

127 Park Street

Naples, FL 32433

USA

![checkmark] **EXERCISE 5. Editing: Is It Correct?**

If the sentence is correct, write a check mark (✔) on the line. If it is not correct, write X on the line and circle the mistake. Then change the sentence to make it correct. Write the change above the sentence. (*Hint:* There are eight sentences. Two are correct, but six have mistakes.)

Examples: __✓__ Mrs. Kim is a good teacher.

                                                         are

    __X__ The students in Mrs. Kim's (classroom from) ten countries.

My Favorite Things

_____ 1. My favorite class this year is grammar.

_____ 2. My favorite color for shoes are black.

_____ 3. I like Anthea. She my favorite friend.

_____ 4. I like spaghetti. Is my favorite food.

_____ 5. I have two dictionaries. The small one has only important words, but the big one has more than three thousand words. I think a dictionary with a lot of words are good for students.

_____ 6. I like to travel. My favorite country is Canada. Canada between the Atlantic Ocean, the Arctic Ocean, and the Pacific Ocean.

_____ 7. Everyone in my family loves Chinese food. Fried rice are my favorite dish.

_____ 8. The name of the singer on the radio right now is Paola Sanchez. She is a great singer.

ONE-MINUTE LESSON

We use **a** or **an** with professions: *She is **a** great singer* or *He is **an** actor*. A common mistake is *My father is doctor*. The name of a profession usually has **a** or **an** before it. (For more information, see Unit 10.)

EXERCISE 6. Pair Speaking: Talking about People, Places, and Things

Step 1. Work with a partner. Decide who is Student A and who is Student B. Work only in the box.

Step 2. Number the boxes from 1 to 10 in any order. Do not number them in order.

Step 2. Fill in the blanks with *am, is,* or *are* to make the correct sentences. Check your answers with another student who did the same part (A or B) as you.

Step 3. Now work with a partner with a different letter. Student B will close his or her book. Student A will read out all ten items in numerical order. Student B must complete Student A's items correctly. Say the word *blank* for the line. For example, Student A will say, "You blank here" and Student B must say, "You are here." If this is correct, Student A says, "That's correct." If this is not correct, Student A says, "That isn't correct. Try again" and Student repeats the item. When all of the items are finished, Student B will read out his or her ten items, and Student A will answer them.

Student A

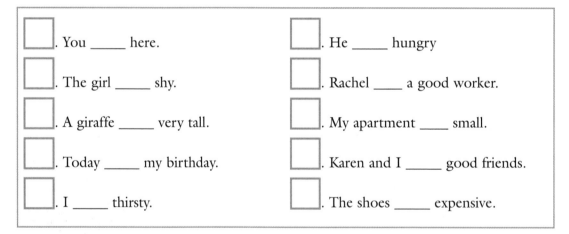

	. You _____ here.		. He _____ hungry
	. The girl _____ shy.		. Rachel _____ a good worker.
	. A giraffe _____ very tall.		. My apartment _____ small.
	. Today _____ my birthday.		. Karen and I _____ good friends.
	. I _____ thirsty.		. The shoes _____ expensive.

Student B

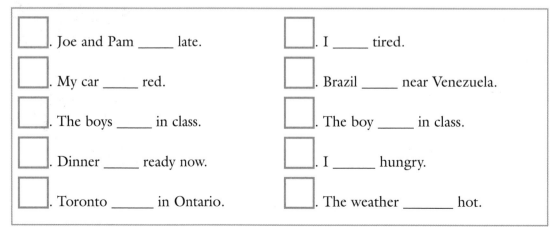

	. Joe and Pam _____ late.		. I _____ tired.
	. My car _____ red.		. Brazil _____ near Venezuela.
	. The boys _____ in class.		. The boy _____ in class.
	. Dinner _____ ready now.		. I _____ hungry.
	. Toronto _____ in Ontario.		. The weather _____ hot.

🔑 Contractions with *am, is, are*

am	I am tired.	→	I'm tired.
is	He is a singer.	→	He's a writer.
	She is a doctor.	→	He's a doctor.
	It is a hard word.	→	It's a hard word.
are	You are late.	→	You're late.
	We are late.	→	We're late
	They are late	→	They're late.

Rule 1. You can use a contraction for a pronoun and am, is, are: 'm, 's, 're.

Rule 2. In spoken language, we often use a contraction with a noun: *Kevin's* here.

Rule 3. Contractions are not used in formal writing.

Rule 4. You cannot use a contraction in a short affirmative answer. *A: Are you hungry? B: Yes, I **am**. NOT: Yes I'm.*

EXERCISE 7. Contractions in Context

Complete these sentences by using a contraction with a pronoun.

Favorite Things to Eat

1. My favorite <u>vegetable</u> is celery. ___It's___ really delicious.

2. These <u>cookies</u> are great. _____ homemade.

3. My mother makes <u>really good vegetable soup</u>. _____ my favorite thing to eat.

4. For lunch, we usually eat <u>a salad</u>. _____ just right for the middle of the day.

5. <u>My sister and I</u> like to cook. _____ really good cooks.

6. Paolo likes <u>carrots</u>. He thinks that _____ good for your eyes.

7. Sue's two favorite foods are <u>shrimp and turkey</u>. _____ very delicious.

8. <u>Tacos</u> are my favorite food. _____ easy to make.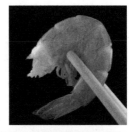

9. <u>Fried chicken</u> is delicious, but _____ not good for you because it has so much oil.

10. Mario likes <u>spinach</u>. He says that _____ better than any other vegetable.

🖱 **Do Online Exercise 1.2. My score: ____ /10. ____ % correct.**

Simple Present Tense of *Be*: Negative

Making a negative statement with verb *be* is easy. Study these two steps:	
Step 1 Check for verb **be**.	Colombia and Brazil **are** in Africa.
Step 2 Put **not** after **be**.	Colombia and Brazil **are not** in Africa.
Contractions are possible: is not → isn't are not → aren't	

Other examples:

Statement		Negative
I am in your class.	→	I am **not** in your class.
You are Mike's friend.	→	You **aren't** Mike's friend.
Maria is hungry.	→	Maria is **not** hungry.
		Maria **isn't** hungry.
		Maria's **not** hungry.

<u>Rule 1</u>. We use the word **not** to make a negative sentence with the verb be: am not, is not, are not.

<u>Rule 2</u>. There is no contraction for **am not**. It is possible to use contractions for is not **and** are not: isn't, aren't.

<u>Rule 3</u>. It is also possible to make a contraction with the subject and be before the word not: I'm not, she's not (she isn't), you're not (you aren't), etc. There is no difference in meaning between these two forms of contractions.

BE CAREFUL!

Common Learner Errors	Explanation
1. The food at that restaurant ~~no is~~ is not delicious.	Do not use no am, no is, or no are.
2. California, Texas, and Alaska ~~not~~ are not small states.	Remember to include am, is, or are.

EXERCISE 8. Negative *am/is/are* in Context

The information in these statements is not true. Make the information correct by changing each verb to a negative. Follow the example.

Some Facts about Food

1. Spaghetti ~~is~~ *isn't* from Greece.

2. Tuna fish is very high in fat.

3. Sushi and sashimi are from China.

4. Strawberries are usually purple.

5. A watermelon is yellow on the inside and red on the outside.

6. A large amount of salt is good for your body.

7. Chocolate is from the leaves of a tropical plant.

8. Butter and cream are from goats.

Extra Practice: Give the correct information about the food items. Example: *Spaghetti isn't from Greece. Spaghetti is from Italy.*

Do Online Exercise 1.3. My score: _____ /10. _____ % correct.

EXERCISE 9. Affirmative/Negative of *am/is/are* in a Dialogue

Complete the sentences with *am, am not, is, isn't, are,* or *aren't.*

Matt Dean: Good morning, viewers! My name ❶ _____ Matt Dean, and welcome to our show! Our show ❷ _____ "Cooking with Great Cooks," and our guest chef today ❸ _____ Carol Lim. Good morning, Carol.

Carol Lim: Good morning, Matt. Thank you for having me on your show today.

Matt Dean: You ❹ _____ welcome! It ❺ _____ a pleasure to have a great chef like you on our show. Carol, you ❻ _____ a chef at Ocean View Restaurant, right?

Carol Lim: Yes, that ❼ _____ where I work. We have a very good restaurant there with lots of excellent food. Our seafood dishes ❽ _____ outstanding.

Matt Dean: So what dish ❾ _____ on your special menu for us today?

Carol Lim: Well, my special dish for today ❿ _____ Spicy Shrimp Pasta. It ⓫ _____ a very easy dish, and I know that your TV audience will like it a lot.

Matt Dean: It sounds good, but I don't like really hot food. How spicy is it?

Carol Lim: Oh, don't worry! It ⓬ _____ really very hot. It just looks hot.

Matt Dean: Is it difficult to make?

Carol Lim: No, it ⓭ _____ difficult. It ⓮ _____ so easy that you can make it in about 30 minutes.

Matt Dean: OK. What ⓯ _____ the ingredients?

Carol Lim: Matt, the ingredients ⓰ _____ 2 cups of cooked spaghetti, 1 dozen shrimp tails, 1 cup of chopped onions, 4 tablespoons of butter, a little salt, and a little pepper.

Matt Dean: Ok, tell me what to do.

Carol Lim: Heat a frying pan. Add the butter. When the butter ⓱ _____ hot, add the onions. When the onions ⓲ _____ brown, add the shrimp tails. When the shrimp tails ⓳ _____ red (or bright pink or orange) on one side, turn them over. Cook everything for about 2 more minutes. Then add the spaghetti all at once. Add the salt and pepper. Mix everything together very carefully. When the spaghetti ⓴ _____ covered with the butter sauce, your Spicy Shrimp Pasta ㉑ _____ ready to eat!

Matt Dean: Carol, I can't cook well. I ㉒ _____ a good cook. This recipe sounds easy, so maybe I really can cook this dish for dinner tonight.

Carol Lim: Guests at our restaurant ㉓ _____ crazy about this dish! They love it! In fact, this ㉔ _____ probably the most popular dish at our restaurant. Here you go. Taste this!

Matt Dean: Mmmmm. . . . This ㉕ _____ really delicious. I ㉖ _____ surprised because it ㉗ _____ spicy. I mean, the shrimp tails ㉘ _____ red, and the dish looks spicy, but it ㉙ _____ hot. Great job, Carol!

Four Sentence Patterns with *Be*

1. subject + *be* + adjective	This book is very interesting. Your new shoes are very beautiful.
2. subject + *be* + noun	My best classes are grammar and reading. Mrs. Jones is a nurse.
3. subject + *be* + place	The best computers are over there. The meeting is in Room 221.
4. subject + *be* + time	My job interview is tomorrow. Our local rock concerts are always at night.

EXERCISE 10. Identifying Sentence Patterns with *Be*

For each sentence, place a check mark (✔) in the correct column to identify the underlined words as adjective, noun, place, or time.

My Job

Sentences with **be**	adj.	noun	place	time
1. I am a <u>secretary</u>.	☑	☐	☐	☐
2. My company is <u>Brighton Corporation</u>.	☐	☑	☑	☐
3. Brighton Corporation is <u>huge</u>.	☐	☐	☐	☐
4. The office where I work is <u>new</u>.	☐	☑	☐	☐
5. My office is <u>in Room 816</u>.	☐	☐	☑	☐
6. It is <u>on the eighth floor</u>.	☐	☐	☑	☐
7. My first meeting each day is <u>at 9 AM</u>.	☐	☐	☐	☑
8. Each meeting is <u>different</u>.	☐	☑	☐	☐
9. Each client is <u>unique</u>.	☑	☐	☐	☐
10. In my opinion, most clients are pretty <u>nice</u>.	☑	☐	☐	☐
11. However, some clients are difficult <u>people</u>.	☑	☐	☐	☐
12. At Brighton Corporation, I am really very <u>happy</u>.	☑	☐	☐	☐
13. From time to time, the work in my office is <u>difficult</u>.	☐	☑	☐	☐
14. Most of the time, my job is a <u>piece of cake</u>.	☐	☑	☐	☐

Simple Present Tense of *Be*: Making a Question

Making a question with verb be is easy. Study these three steps:		
Step 1	Check for verb be.	Colombia and Brazil are in Africa.
Step 2	Move be to the front of the sentence.	are Colombia and Brazil in Africa.
Step 3	Use a capital letter for the first word of the question, and change the period (.) to a question mark (?).	Are Colombia and Brazil in Africa?

Other examples:

Statement		Question
I am in your chair.	→	Am I in your chair?
You are late.	→	Are you late?
We are late.	→	Are we late?
The shoes are $60.	→	Are the shoes $60?
He is a writer.	→	Is he a writer?
Sarah is a doctor.	→	Is Sarah a doctor?
Earth is a hard word to spell.	→	Is *earth* a hard word to spell?

Rule 1. To make a question with am, is, or are, begin the question with am, is, or are.

Rule 2. In a question, the word after am, is, or are is a noun or pronoun (the subject).

BE CAREFUL!

Common Learner Errors	Explanation
1. Are ~~absent Marco and Lena~~ Marco and Lena absent ?	Move the subject just after am, is, or are. Do not move the subject to the end of the question.
2. ~~Do~~ Are you hungry?	Do not begin am/is/are questions with do or does.

EXERCISE 11. Scrambled Sentences

Read the words, and then make a question. Don't forget to add the question mark (?).

1. very busy Smith is Ms. today   *Is Ms. Smith very busy today?*

2. cats now thirsty the are   _____

3. Paul in and Naomi class today are   _____

4. is Robert day early to class every   _____

5. homework his correct is   _____

6. day you late class to are every   _____

7. Venezuela Caracas capital is the of   _____

8. open Ben on the Street now is bank   _____

9. Saturday park crowded is on the   _____

10. sleepy today Sam and Victor are   _____

   Do Online Exercise 1.4. My score: ____ /10. ____% correct.

EXERCISE 12. Mini-Conversations

Circle the correct words in these eight mini-conversations.

1. A: Who (am, is, are) your best friend?

   B: I have many really good friends, but my best friend (am, is, are) Yolanda.

2. A: How old (am, is, are) your car?

   B: It (am, is, are) five years old. Why do you ask?

3. A: (Am, Is, Are) you good at math?

   B: Yes, I (am, is, are). I like math a lot. It (am, is, are) easy for me.

4. A: How (am, is, are) your new apartment?

   B: It (am, is, are) great. My apartment is a little small. It has two bedrooms, and they (am, is, are) really nice.

5. A: What (am, is, are) the current population of Canada?

   B: Canada (am, is, are) a really big country, but the population (am, is, are) not so big. It (am, is, are) approximately 34,000,000.

6. A: Where (am, is, are) you from?

   B: I (am, is, are) from Panama.

7. A: In some countries, the name of the capital city (am, is, are) the same as the name of the country.

   B: Yes, that (am, is, are) right. For example, Mexico City (am, is, are) the capital of Mexico, and Panama City is the capital of Panama.

8. A: (Am, Is, Are) your reading class hard?

   B: Well, it (am, is, are) not very easy, but I don't think that it (am, is, are) so hard.

ONE-MINUTE LESSON

I don't think that math is so hard. After expressions such as *I think* or *We hope*, you can put the word **that** before the next part of the sentence or not. In other words, the word **that** as a connector is optional. You can say *I think that John is at work* or *I think John is at work*. Both forms are correct.

EXERCISE 13. Speaking Practice: An Interview

This family survey is missing the verbs. Write the correct form of the verb be in the space. Then ask a classmate these questions, and write his or her answers.

FAMILY SURVEY

1. What _____ your full name?   _____

2. What _____ your nationality?   _____

3. What _____ your current address?   _____

                                               _____

4. _____ you a full-time student?   _____

5. _____ you an only child?   _____

6. What _____ your parents' names?   _____

                                               _____

7. _____ you married now?   _____

8. If yes, what is your spouse's first name?   _____

Simple Present Tense of *Be*: Questions with Full and Short Answers

Answering a *be* question with a short answer is easy. Study these four steps:		
Step 1	Listen for a question that begins with a form of be.	Are Colombia and Brazil in South America?
Step 2	Decide if the answer is yes or no.	Yes
Step 3	Use a pronoun for the noun subject.	Yes, they
Step 4	Repeat the form of be that is in the question. (Add not for negative.)	Yes, they are.

Other examples:

Questions	Full Answers	Short Answers
Are you hungry now?	Yes, I am hungry now. (OR: Yes, I'm hungry now.) No, I am not hungry now.	Yes, I am. No, I am not.
Are the apples fresh?	Yes, the apples are fresh. No, the apples aren't fresh.	Yes, they are. No, they aren't.
Is today your birthday?	Yes, today is my birthday. No, today isn't my birthday.	Yes, it is. No, it isn't.

<u>Rule 1</u>. In short answers with be, use the correct form of be (am, is, are) for the subject.

<u>Rule 2</u>. In an affirmative short answer, do not use a contraction.

BE CAREFUL!

Common Learner Errors	Explanation
1. Are the students happy about their scores? No, they ~~not~~ aren't.	Do not forget am, is, or are in the short answer for am/is/are questions.
2. Is that book interesting? Yes, ~~it's~~ it is.	Contractions are not possible in short answers in the affirmative with am/is/are.

EXERCISE 14. Giving Short Answers

Write two possible short answers for each question.

Example: Is your reading class easy?

Yes, it is. **OR** No, it isn't.

1. Are cats good pets for children?

   _____ OR _____

2. Are Sam, Mark, and Rachel in the same class this year?

   _____ OR _____

3. Are you sleepy?

   _____ OR _____

4. Is the food at that restaurant delicious?

   _____ OR _____

5. Are you and Gina on different softball teams?

   _____ OR _____

6. Are coffee and tea good for your health?

   _____ OR _____

7. Is the teacher the tallest person in the classroom?

   _____ OR _____

8. Is China the richest country in the world today?

   _____ OR _____

ONE-MINUTE LESSON

Adjectives that end in –est are called superlatives. These words show the highest level of a group. For example, in a group of 10 friends, John is the **tallest** person, Mary is the **smartest** student, and Susan is the **busiest** mother. We add –est to one-syllable words and to two-syllables words that end in –y. (For more information on comparatives, see page 105.)

Do Online Exercise 1.5. My score: ____ /10. ____ % correct.

Simple Present Tense of *Be*: *There is / There are*

Affirmative Statements

	There is	a rug	in the middle of the room.
	There are	two shoes	on the rug.
	There are	some newspapers	on the floor.

Negative Statements

	There isn't	a CD player	in the room.
	There is	no CD player	in the room.
	There aren't	any people	in the room.
	There are	no people	in the room.

Yes-No Questions

	Is there	a flight to Boston	for under $300?
	Are there	many people	in your class?

Information Questions

How many people	are there		in your class?
How much sugar	is there		in one glass of soft drink?

Rule 1. We use there is and there are to describe the things in a place.

Rule 2. We use there is for singular nouns (*flight, book, problem*) or non-count nouns (*sugar, salt, water*). If the word is singular, we use a or an in front of it.

Rule 3. We use there are for plural nouns. We often use some with affirmative and **any** for negative.

Rule 4. The question form is is there or are there: Are there any tickets?

BE CAREFUL!

Common Learner Errors	Explanation
1. ~~Are~~ There are many people in Thailand.	Do not forget to use there.
2. In Thailand, ~~have~~ there are many people.	Do not use have. Use is or are.

EXERCISE 15. *There is/There are* Practice

Fill in the blank with *there is*, *there are*, *is there*, or *are there*.

1. _____ 26 letters in the English alphabet.

2. _____ 50 states in the United States.

3. _____ just one reason that I want to learn English.

4. _____ some forks and spoons in the top drawer.

5. _____ a special website for pet owners.

6. _____ a CD that goes with that book?

7. _____ more than ten students in your class?

8. _____ some ice cream in the freezer?

9. How many books _____ on your desk?

10. How many people _____ in your family?

11. How much money _____ in the envelope?

12. How much orange juice _____ in the refrigerator?

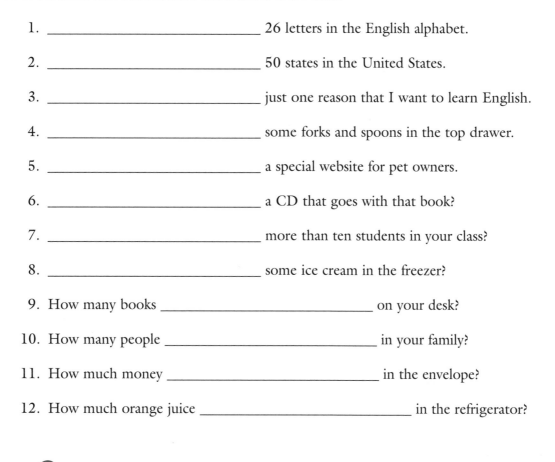

Do Online Exercise 1.6. My score: _____/10. _____% correct.

EXERCISE 16. Speaking Practice: Describing What You See

Part 1.

Write eight sentences to describe what you see in this picture. Write four true sentences and four false sentences. (Use affirmative sentences only.)

True Sentences	False Sentences
1.	1.
2.	2.
3.	3.
4.	4.

Part 2.

Now work with a partner or in small groups. Take turns reading one of your sentences. Other students will listen to your statement and then say if your statement is true or false.

EXERCISE 17. Making Yes-No Questions in Conversations

Make yes-no questions from the statements in parentheses. Add question marks.

Example: A. Shopping makes me tired!

B. <u>Are you really tired?</u> (You are really tired.)

A. Yes, I want to sit down! My feet hurt!

Conversation 1

A: Read, read, read . . . _____ (❶ That is all you do.)

B: Well, I like to read, so I read a lot.

A. What is that book?

B: It's called *The Red River.*

A: _____ (❷ It is a good book.)

B: Yes, it's very good.

A: *The Red River.* . . . That sounds familiar. _____
_____ (❸ There is a movie for that book, too.)

B: Yes, there is.

A: _____ (❹ The movie is good.)

B: The movie is OK, but I think the book is much better.

Conversation 2

A: Where is Nancy?

B: She's in the hospital.

A: What? _____ (❺ She's in the hospital again.)

B: Yes, she is. It's her second time in less than ten days.

A: _____ (❻ She's OK.)

B: She's all right, but she's in a lot of pain.

A: _____ (❼ She's really sick.)

B: Well, she has a broken leg. The doctor says that she is going to be in the hospital for
two or three days.

Conversation 3

A: Oceania Airlines. May I help you?

B: Yes, please. Do you fly to Cairo?

A: Yes, twice a week. When do you want to travel?

B: Next week. _____ (❽ There is a flight on Monday.)

A: Yes, there is.

B: _____ (❾ It's in the morning.)

A: Yes, it is. You leave at 8 AM and arrive in Cairo at 6 PM. How is that?

B: That sounds great. I'd like to make a reservation.

A: Oh, I'm sorry, but that's not possible.

B: Why? _____ (❿ The flight is full.)

A: Yes, it is. I'm afraid there aren't any seats right now. Can I check another day for you?

ONE-MINUTE LESSON

When you say *I'm afraid of snakes*, **afraid** has a negative meaning, and this means you don't like snakes and don't want to be near them. However, **afraid** sometimes has a polite meaning. In *I'm afraid there aren't any seats right now*, the word **afraid** means that you are sorry that there are no more seats now. Use **I'm afraid** before a sentence when you want to express you are sorry about something in a more formal, less direct way.

EXERCISE 18. Sentence Study for Critical Reading

Read the numbered sentences. Then read the three answer choices, and place a check mark in the yes or no boxes in front of each sentence to show if that answer is true based on the information in the original sentence. If there is not enough information to mark something as yes, then mark it as no. More than one true answer is possible.

1. Everyone thinks that Bob and Gary are brothers, but they aren't. They're just good friends.
   - [ ] yes [ ] no a. Bob and Gary have the same parents.
   - [ ] yes [ ] no b. Bob and Gary are good friends, but they are not brothers.
   - [ ] yes [ ] no c. Bob is the same age as Gary.

2. All the grammar books are on the desk, and the dictionaries are on the table.
   - [ ] yes [ ] no a. There are more grammar books than dictionaries.
   - [ ] yes [ ] no b. There is more than one grammar book.
   - [ ] yes [ ] no c. The dictionaries and the grammar books are in the same place.

3. Victor is in his kitchen.

   ☐ yes ☐ no   a. He is at home.

   ☐ yes ☐ no   b. There is a sofa in the room.

   ☐ yes ☐ no   c. He isn't in the bathroom.

4. Carla is a student in high school. She is an excellent student.

   ☐ yes ☐ no   a. Carla has three or four good friends.

   ☐ yes ☐ no   b. Carla is not a teacher.

   ☐ yes ☐ no   c. Her test scores are very good.

5. The white cats and the gray cat are in the dining room.

   ☐ yes ☐ no   a. They are in the refrigerator.

   ☐ yes ☐ no   b. They are not in the living room.

   ☐ yes ☐ no   c. They are inside the house.

6. Mr. Lee is an elementary school teacher, and his wife is a high school teacher.

   ☐ yes ☐ no   a. Mrs. Lee is a teacher.

   ☐ yes ☐ no   b. Mrs. Lee's husband is a teacher.

   ☐ yes ☐ no   c. Mrs. Lee's school is near their house, but Mr. Lee's school isn't.

7. The blue car is $18,000, but the white car is $16,000.

   ☐ yes ☐ no   a. The blue car is more expensive than the white car.

   ☐ yes ☐ no   b. The white car is more expensive than the black car.

   ☐ yes ☐ no   c. The price of the white car is $2,000 less than the price of the blue car.

8. On Monday, Wednesday, and Friday, our English class is in Room 212. On Tuesday, we are in Room 221, and we are in Room 201 on Thursday.

   ☐ yes ☐ no   a. We have English class on five days.

   ☐ yes ☐ no   b. Room 212 is our classroom on Monday, Tuesday, and Wednesday.

   ☐ yes ☐ no   c. On Friday, our English class is in Room 201.

EXERCISE 19. Speaking Practice: Identifying Your Mystery Friend

Step 1. Work with a partner. Each student chooses one "mystery friend." Your job is to guess the name of your partner's mystery friend.

Step 2. Take turns asking yes-no questions about the mystery friend. Use *is* or *are* when possible. If the answer is yes, the questioner continues asking questions. If the answer is no, the partner can ask questions. The first person to guess the partner's mystery friend is the winner.

Examples: "Is your friend a woman?" or "Is your friend short?"

Kevin	*Carl*	*Melissa*	*Ashley*
a man	a man	a woman	a woman
tall	short	tall	short
from Florida	from Florida	from Florida	from Florida
a bus driver	a taxi driver	a bus driver	a taxi driver
Alan	*Mark*	*Terri*	*Jeanine*
a man	a man	a woman	a woman
tall	short	tall	short
from Florida	from Florida	from Florida	from Florida
a bus driver	a bus driver	a taxi driver	a bus driver
Mario	*Victor*	*Chanda*	*Theresa*
a man	a man	a woman	a woman
tall	short	tall	short
from New York	from New York	from New York	from New York
a bus driver	a taxi driver	a bus driver	a taxi driver
Scott	*Ryan*	*Shelley*	*Liz*
a man	a man	a woman	a woman
tall	short	tall	short
from New York	from New York	from New York	from New York
a taxi driver	a bus driver	a taxi driver	a bus driver

More practice: Do this activity again with another student. This game has some luck, but some students are good players.

REVIEW   **EXERCISE 20. Review Test 1: Multiple Choice**

Circle the letter of the correct answer in these conversations.

1. "Where are the books?"

   "Well, the grammar book is on the sofa, and the vocabulary book and the reading book _____ on the table."

       a. is   b. are   c. isn't   d. aren't

2. "Whose books are these?"

   "The name on all the books _____ Mary D. Smith."

       a. is   b. am   c. are   d. not

3. "Are you and Mike friends?"

   "Yes, _____."

       a. I am   b. we are   c. you are   d. he is

4. "The questions are difficult."

   "Yes, _____ very hard."

       a. are   b. is   c. they are   d. it is

5. "Where are the boys?"

   "Joseph and Mark _____ in the kitchen."

       a. is   b. no is   c. are   d. no are

6. "Do you think grammar class is difficult?"

   "No, it isn't. The most difficult _____."

       a. reading class   b. class is reading   c. class reading   d. reading is class

7. "_____ cheap in your country?"

   "No, they aren't. They're very expensive."

       a. Cars are   b. Gasoline is   c. Is gasoline   d. Are cars

8. "Are you from Asia?"

   "No, _____."

       a. you are   b. we are   c. you aren't   d. we aren't

REVIEW ▶ **EXERCISE 21. Review Test 2: Production and Evaluation**

Part 1.

Read this short passage. Fill in the blanks with *am, is,* or *are.*

This ❶ _____ a map of North America. The country to the north of the

United States ❷ _____ Canada. Canada ❸ _____ a very large country,

but not so many people live there. The population ❹ _____ 34,000,000.

(The population of the United States ❺ _____ 265,000,000.)

Canada has two official languages. These two languages ❻ _____

English and French. Most of the people who speak French live in Quebec.

Quebec ❼ _____ a large province in Canada. (In case you do not know,

a province ❽ _____ similar to a state.)

The capital of Canada ❾ _____ Ottawa. The largest cities ❿ _____

Toronto, Montreal, and Vancouver. Vancouver ⓫ _____ in the west, but

Toronto and Montreal ⓬ _____ not in the west. Montreal ⓭ _____

in the eastern part of the country, and Toronto ⓮ _____ in the central

part of Canada.

Part 2.

Read the short passage. There are five mistakes. Circle the mistakes, and write the correction
above each mistake.

My son's name is Chris. Chris ten years old. He is in the fifth grade in

elementary school. He likes to study. Is a good student.

My daughter's name Jenny. Jenny is seven years old. She in the second grade

in school elementary. Chris and Jenny is in the same school, but they are in

different grades.

> ⏰ **ONE-MINUTE LESSON**
> Common words are common because they have multiple meanings. The word
> **grade**, for example, can be the number on your test (*What was your grade?*), a year
> in school (*She is in 10th grade*), or what happens with tests (The teacher has to
> *grade* the papers now). Be sure to learn different meanings for common words,
> not just one meaning.

EXERCISE 22. Reading Practice: Three Different Countries

Read the information about three countries. Then fill in the chart, and answer the seven questions on page 32. The grammar from this unit is underlined for you.

A South American Country

Ecuador <u>is</u> a country in South America. The name *Ecuador* comes from the location of the country. Ecuador <u>is</u> located near the Equator. The capital of Ecuador <u>is</u> Quito, but Quito <u>isn't</u> the largest city. The largest city <u>is</u> Guayaquil. The population of Ecuador <u>is</u> fourteen million. The Ecuadorian flag colors <u>are</u> yellow, blue, and red.

A European Country

Switzerland <u>is</u> a small country in central Europe. The three largest cities <u>are</u> Zurich, Geneva, and Basel, and the capital city <u>is</u> Bern. The four official languages in Switzerland <u>are</u> French, German, Italian, and Romansch. The population of Switzerland <u>is</u> eight million. The Swiss flag <u>is</u> red and white.

An Asian Country

Vietnam <u>is</u> a country in southeast Asia. The population of Vietnam <u>is</u> slightly more than eighty-six million. The largest cities <u>are</u> Ho Chi Minh City and Hanoi. Ho Chi Minh City <u>is</u> the largest city in the country, but Hanoi <u>is</u> the capital. The Vietnamese flag <u>is</u> red with a yellow star in the middle.

Country	Capital	Largest City	Population	Flag Colors
Ecuador				
Switzerland				
Vietnam				

1. How many colors are in the Swiss flag?

   _____

2. Is the population of Ecuador larger than the population of Vietnam?

   _____

3. Which of these three countries is in South America?

   _____

4. Which flag is possible for Vietnam?

   _____

   a.   b.   c.   d.

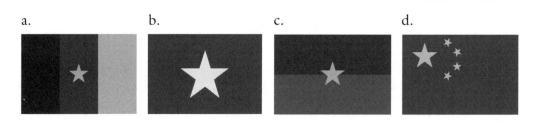

5. Circle the two statements that are true.
   a. The population of Switzerland is greater than the population of Ecuador.
   b. The population of Vietnam is greater than the population of Ecuador and
      Switzerland together.
   c. The capital of Ecuador is also the largest city in that country.
   d. The largest city of Vietnam is not the capital city.

6. Of these three countries, circle the one that is the smallest in size.
   a. Ecuador
   b. Vietnam
   c. Switzerland
   d. We don't have enough information to answer.

7. If you could visit one of these three countries, which one would you like to visit
   and why?

   _____

   _____

   _____

   _____

   _____

EXERCISE 23. Vocabulary Practice: Word Knowledge

Circle the word or phrase that is most closely related to the word or phrase on the left. Use a dictionary to check the meaning of words you do not know.

Vocabulary	Answer Choices	
1. summer	hot	cold
2. glad	fresh	happy
3. leaves	fall	winter
4. swim	in the kitchen	in the ocean
5. a chapter	of a book	of a family
6. population	a country	a postcard
7. a giraffe	short	tall
8. hard	delicious	difficult
9. vegetables	shrimp and turkey	spinach and celery
10. special	unique	usual
11. ingredients	cities	parts
12. the audience	drivers	viewers
13. outstanding	excellent	favorite
14. a recipe	cooking	swimming
15. popular	people like it	people don't like it
16. an interview	questions + answers	tests + scores
17. huge	very big	very small
18. a piece of cake	very easy	very difficult
19. absent	present	not present
20. crowded	many people	not many people
21. a spouse	husband or wife	salt or pepper
22. a score	a job	a number
23. a team	offices	sports
24. a rug	on the floor	on the table
25. a drawer	a part of a desk	a part of a floor
26. however	and	but
27. twice	two times	two weeks
28. slightly less than 100	98 or 99	60 or 80
29. middle	central	problem
30. a star	in the ocean	in the sky
31. originally	in the beginning	at the end
32. a dozen	10	12
33. about	approximately	the same

EXERCISE 24. Vocabulary Practice: Collocations

Fill in each blank with the answer on the right that most naturally completes the phrase on the left. If necessary, use a dictionary to check the meaning of words you do not know.

Phrase	Answer Choices	
1. the eastern _____	live	part
2. in the _____	floor	kitchen
3. the _____ population	current	famous
4. a little _____	bit	some
5. is full _____	by	of
6. fried _____	answer	rice
7. _____ the radio	in	on
8. in numerical _____	order	list
9. _____ soup	strong	vegetable
10. so _____ oil	many	much
11. I'm _____ right	all	many
12. how _____	age	old
13. thank you _____	by	for
14. a _____ menu	sauce	special
15. _____ worry	don't	isn't
16. a dozen _____	cookies	person
17. are _____ at math	good	nice
18. easy _____ me to do	for	to
19. in the _____ drawer	north	top
20. _____ now	left	right
21. a bus _____	driver	writer
22. is similar _____	to	with
23. _____ yellow	bright	shy
24. all at _____	once	twice
25. _____ apples	fresh	glad
26. covered _____ chocolate	for	with
27. _____ my opinion	for	in
28. brand _____	new	old
29. from time to _____	there	time
30. that _____ familiar	listens	sounds
31. a broken _____	book	leg
32. a little _____	of salt	salt
33. he is crazy about _____	absent	football
34. _____ of the time	many	most
35. about _____	home	five
36. chopped _____	onions	places
37. between A _____ B	and	but
38. the _____ of a car	price	recipe
39. more expensive _____	of	than
40. in _____	fact	true

EXERCISE 25. Writing Practice: Introducing the Students in Your Class

Part 1. Editing Student Writing

Read these sentences about one student's class. Circle the 14 errors. Then write the number of the sentence with the error next to the type of error. (Some sentences have more than one error.)

_____ a. no subject   _____ e. singular-plural

_____ b. *am/is/are* (wrong form)   _____ f. word order

_____ c. no verb   _____ g. no *a*

_____ d. short answer   _____ h. capital letter

My Class
1. There are 12 student in my class.
2. five students from Saudi Arabia.
3. My teacher's name is Mr. Kerlin. Is very nice man and a good teacher.
4. Three students is from Colombia.
5. One man are from Vietnam. He is very smart. His English really excellent.
6. One woman is from Senegal. Is a very interesting person.
7. One man is from Korea. In Korea, he a taxi driver, but now he is student.
8. My name is Carlos. Am I a good student? Yes, I'm. I'm in class every day, and I do all my homework.
9. I like the people in my class. are very interesting the students in my class.

Part 2. Original Student Writing

Now write some sentences about the students in your class.

 Unit 2

Possessive Adjectives (*my, your, his, her, its, our, their*) and Demonstrative Words (*this, that, these, those*)

Discover the Grammar

Read the information about Tim Wilson's family, and then answer the eight questions.

Line	
1	I'm Tom. My name is Thomas, but everyone calls me Tom.
2	I'd like to introduce you to my family.
3	This my wife. Her name is Karen.
4	This is our daughter. Her name is Anna.
5	This is our son. His name is Zachary, but his nickname is Zack.
6	These are our cats. Their names are Smokey and Ebony.

1. Underline three examples of *my*. What do you think *my* means? _____

   _____

2. When do you use *my* and when do you use *I*? _____

   _____

3. Circle the three examples of *our*. What do you think the difference between *my* and *our* is? _____

4. Now underline *his* and *her*. When do you think we use *his* and *her*? _____

   _____

5. Put a box around *their*. When do you think we use *their*? Can we use *their* for only animals? What about for people? _____

   _____

6. Write M, W, or B to tell if the word is used for **men, women,** or **both men and women.**

   a. my _____   c. his _____   e. her _____

   b. your _____   d. our _____   f. their _____

7. Now look at all of the words you marked. These words are called **possessive adjectives**. Put a wavy line under the word that comes after the possessive adjectives. (*Hint:* You should have nine.) What kind of word comes after possessive adjectives?

   possessive adjectives + _____

8. What questions do you have about this grammar?_____

   _____

   _____

   _____

   _____

Grammar Lesson

Adjectives

Adjectives are words that describe nouns or pronouns. Adjectives tell which (*this book, my book*), how many (*six books*), or what kind (*red roses*). Adjectives come in front of nouns (*a white ball*) or after *be* (*the room is white*).

Pronouns are words that take the place of nouns. (*Teresa is here.* → *She is here.*)

Possessive Adjectives

Subject Pronouns		Possessive Adjectives	Examples			
I	⟶	my	I	like	my	sandwich.
you	⟶	your	You	like	your	salad.
he	⟶	his	He	likes	his	soup.
she	⟶	her	She	likes	her	fries.
it	⟶	its	The cat	likes	its	food.
we	⟶	our	We	like	our	desserts.
they	⟶	their	They	like	their	food.

ONE-MINUTE LESSON

For an animal or a thing, we use the possessive adjective **its**. *A giraffe gets its name from an Arabic word.* For a pet, people usually use **his** or **her**, not *its*. *My dog's name is Brownie. His name comes from his color.* Pet owners do not use **its** to refer to their own animals.

Comparing Subject Pronouns and Possessive Adjectives

Subject Pronouns		Possessive Adjectives	
I	I play tennis.	my	This is my racket.
you	You are very good at singing.	your	What is your favorite song?
he	He is from Paris.	his	Marc is his name.
she	She drives her car to work.	her	Her car is dark gray.
it	It is a snake.	its	Its main color is brown.
we	We like our house a lot.	our	Our house is big and has a pool.
they	They run every morning.	their	Their day starts with a long run.

Rule 1. **Subject pronouns** are I, you, he, she, it, we, they. Subject pronouns usually occur before a verb.

Rule 2. **Possessive adjectives** are my, your, his, her, its, our, their. Possessive adjectives occur before a noun (*my car*) or an adjective + noun (*my new car*).

Rule 3. Possessive adjectives have no singular or plural. They are used with both singular and plural nouns (*my book, my books*).

BE CAREFUL!

Common Learner Errors	Explanation
1. Linda has a new car. ~~His~~ Her car has two doors.	His is for males; her is for females.
2. Do you know where ~~me~~ my book is?	Use a possessive adjective in front of a noun.
3. This is my book, and that is ~~your~~ your book.	A possessive adjective cannot work alone.

EXERCISE 1. Completing Phrases with Possessive Adjectives

Write the correct possessive adjectives on the lines.

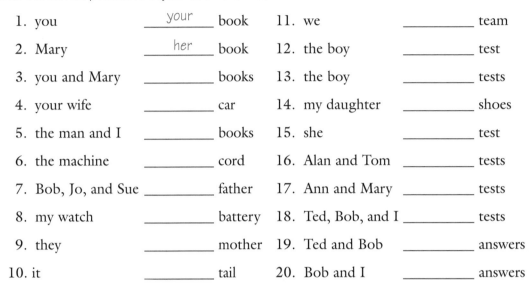

1. you   _____your_____ book   11. we   _____ team

2. Mary   _____her_____ book   12. the boy   _____ test

3. you and Mary   _____ books   13. the boy   _____ tests

4. your wife   _____ car   14. my daughter   _____ shoes

5. the man and I _____ books   15. she   _____ test

6. the machine   _____ cord   16. Alan and Tom   _____ tests

7. Bob, Jo, and Sue _____ father   17. Ann and Mary   _____ tests

8. my watch   _____ battery   18. Ted, Bob, and I   _____ tests

9. they   _____ mother   19. Ted and Bob   _____ answers

10. it   _____ tail   20. Bob and I   _____ answers

Do Online Exercise 2.1. My score: ____ /10. ____ % correct.

EXERCISE 2. Mini-Conversations

Circle the correct words in these eight mini-conversations.

1. A: Where is (you, your) car?

    B: I sold it, so this is (I, my) new car. Do you like it?

2. A: Is this John's watch?

    B: No, that isn't John's watch. (His, Her, Your, Their) watch is much bigger.

3. A: What is Mike's family's last name? Is (it, its, their, they) Brown or Bell?

    B: No, but you're right that (it, its) starts with B. (Its, His, Her, My) last name is Benson.

4. A: Can (you, your) tell me (you, your) phone number?

    B: Sure. (It's, Its) 555-9122. Call me later if you want.

5. A: Do (you, your) know Martha's brother?

    B: No, I don't know (her, his, their, your) brother, but I know (her, his, their, your) sister.

6. A: Amanda and Ashley, you have class now, right?

    B: No, it's only 9:20. (Our, We) class starts at 10. (Our, We) have forty more minutes.

7. A: Bob has a pet iguana.

    B: Are you kidding?

    A: No, (he, his, she, her) really has a pet iguana. (Its, It, Their) name is Red.

8. A: (You, Your) are such a good student. What did you get on yesterday's test?

    B: (You, Your, My, I) test score was 95.

ONE-MINUTE LESSON

What did you **get** *on the test?* means "What was your grade on the test?" When native speakers want to know about a grade on a test, they usually use the first question with the word **get**. Another possible question is *What did you* **make** *on the test?* You can answer with *I* **got** *95 on the test* or *I made 95 on the test.* Don't use the word **score**. It sounds too formal.

EXERCISE 3. Possessive Adjectives in a Dialogue

Write the correct possessive adjective on the lines. Use capital letters when needed.

Planning Food for a Party

Jose: We need a great idea for the food for the party. Who has a suggestion? Rick, what about you?

Rick: Sure, I have an idea. ❶ _____My_____ idea is to serve egg sandwiches.

Jose: I like ❷ _____ idea because eggs are pretty easy to cook. Does anyone else have a different idea?

Rick: Well, Susan has an interesting idea.

Jose: Really? Susan, what's ❸ _____ idea?

Susan: ❹ _____ idea is to serve cheeseburgers.

Jose: I love cheeseburgers, but that sounds like a lot of work. Someone has to cook the meat and then make the sandwiches. Does anyone else have an idea?

Susan: Yes, Ben told me about a great idea that he has.

Jose: Great, let's hear it. Hey, where is Ben?

Susan: I don't know. I'm surprised he isn't here.

Jose: Susan, since Ben isn't here, can you tell us ❺ _____ idea for the party food?

Susan: He wants all the guests to cook ❻ _____ favorite food and bring it to the party.

Jose: Oh, right. In the U.S., that's called a potluck dinner.

Rick: Hey, don't forget Martha and Lim. They have an idea for the party, too. ❼ _____ idea is to serve pizza.

Jose: I really like pizza. In fact, it's ❽ _____ favorite food. I like ❾ _____ idea, but we can't cook the pizzas here. We have to buy them from a restaurant.

Susan: I think I like Ben's idea the best. ❿ _____ suggestion of a potluck party is the best.

EXERCISE 4. Possessive Adjectives in Context

Underline the correct word in these sentences about zodiac signs.

Discussing Birthdays and Zodiac Signs

1. There are five people in (I, my) family.

2. (My, I) birthday is in September. I am a Virgo.

3. My mom's name is Janet. (She, Her) birthday is in July. She is a Cancer.

4. My dad is a Scorpio. (His, He) birthday is in October.

5. I have two brothers. They are twins. (Their, They) birthday is January 15th.

6. (They, Their) zodiac sign is Capricorn.

7. (I, My) family also has a dog. (We, Our) dog is just over two years old, but we don't know when (his, he) birthday is.

8. How about you? When is (your, you) birthday?

Do Online Exercise 2.2. My score: _____ /10. _____ % correct.

This, That, These, Those

	singular	plural
near the speaker	this	these
not near the speaker	that	those

Adjectives

This book is green.	That apple is fresh.
I don't know this word.	He watched that movie.
These books are green.	Those apples are fresh.
I don't know these words.	He watched those movies.

In these examples, this, that, these, and those are adjectives. They are in front of a noun.

Pronouns

This is a difficult book.	That looks delicious.
I can't read this.	Let's eat that.
These are difficult books.	Those look fresh.
I can't read these.	Let's eat those.

In these examples, this, that, these, and those are pronouns. They take the place of a noun.

 ## BE CAREFUL!

Common Learner Errors	Explanation
1. ~~This~~ These books are excellent.	Do not use this or that with plural examples.
2. ~~Those~~ That is my new car.	Do not use these or those with singular examples.

EXERCISE 5. Completing Phrases with Demonstrative Adjectives

Write *this, that, these,* or *those* on the lines.

Near the Speaker (=here): *this* or *these*

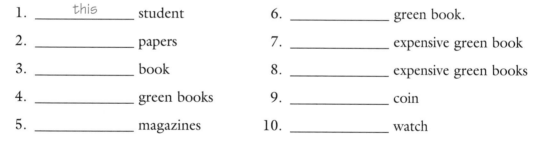

1. ____this____ student
2. _____ papers
3. _____ book
4. _____ green books
5. _____ magazines

6. _____ green book.
7. _____ expensive green book
8. _____ expensive green books
9. _____ coin
10. _____ watch

Not near the Speaker (=there): *that* or *those*

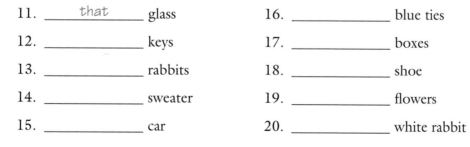

11. ____that____ glass
12. _____ keys
13. _____ rabbits
14. _____ sweater
15. _____ car

16. _____ blue ties
17. _____ boxes
18. _____ shoe
19. _____ flowers
20. _____ white rabbit

EXERCISE 6. Demonstrative Adjectives in Context

Write *this, that, these,* or *those* on the lines. Pay attention to capital letters.

1. (here) _____These_____ books are easy to read, and they have good vocabulary.

2. (here) Is _____ paper the best? I want to buy the best kind of paper.

3. (there) _____ postcards are very beautiful.

4. (here) In _____ class, we have two tests every week. They're never hard.

5. (there) _____ sweater is perfect for you. I think you should buy it.

6. (here) Peter likes _____ car the best. It's really nice.

7. (there) Are _____ stamps rare? They're really expensive.

8. (here) We have _____ kind of fruit in my country, too.

9. (there) _____ people are from Paris. They speak French.

10. (there) I think _____ questions are really difficult.

11. (here) _____ computer is easy to use.

12. (there) _____ nine books are not for you and me. They're for Jose.

EXERCISE 7. Demonstrative Words in Context

Write *this, that, these,* or *those* on the lines.

The Contents of the Box on Joe's Desk

Ann: Joe, what is _____that_____ on your desk?

Joe: What do you mean?

Ann: _____ box! What is in _____ box?

Joe: I brought _____ box from home.

Ann: Yes, but what is in _____ box?

(Joe puts his hand in the box. He takes out some coins and holds them up for Ann to see.)

Ann: What are _____?

Joe: _____ are coins. _____ coins are special. They are very old.

EXERCISE 8. Editing. Is it Correct?

If the sentence is correct, write a check mark (✔) on the line. If it is not correct, Write X on the line and circle the mistake. Then change the sentence to make it correct. Write the change above the sentence. (*Hint:* There are eight sentences. Two are correct, but six have mistakes.)

Kathy's Family

_____ 1. Kathy's family now lives in a new house. Its a large two-story building with a pool, a big back porch, and a garden.

_____ 2. The new house is much bigger than they're old house.

_____ 3. She loves being outdoors, and she enjoys taking care of the roses in his garden.

_____ 4. Her husband Leon does not like to work in the garden.

_____ 5. Leon likes to take care of the pool, and she cleans it once a week.

_____ 6. Kathy and his husband have two children.

_____ 7. The two boys spend most of their free time in their rooms playing video games.

_____ 8. Eric and her brother also enjoy swimming in the pool.

ONE-MINUTE LESSON

After the word **enjoy**, you have to use a noun: *I enjoy sports.* If you want to use an action word, you must add **–ing** to the verb: *Eric and his brother enjoy* **swimming** *in the pool.* Remember to use **VERB + -ing** after the word **enjoy**.

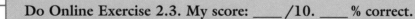

Do Online Exercise 2.3. My score: _____ /10. _____ % correct.

EXERCISE 9. Sentence Study for Critical Reading

Read the numbered sentences. Then read the three answer choices, and place a check mark in the yes or no boxes in front of each sentence to show if that answer is true based on the information in the original sentence. If there is not enough information to mark something as yes, then mark it as no. Remember that more than one true answer is possible.

1. This key is to my house, and those keys belong to Joshua.

    ☐ yes ☐ no   a. Joshua has more than one key.

    ☐ yes ☐ no   b. My key is in my office.

    ☐ yes ☐ no   c. Joshua has my key.

2. Karina is a doctor. Her sisters are teachers. All three live in this neighborhood.

    ☐ yes ☐ no   a. They live in the same house.

    ☐ yes ☐ no   b. They live in the same town.

    ☐ yes ☐ no   c. They live in the same state.

3. Laura and Amanda went to the mall yesterday, and Laura bought a blue dress. Amanda liked that dress, too. Both of the girls are glad that Laura bought it.

    ☐ yes ☐ no   a. Both girls bought a new dress at the mall.

    ☐ yes ☐ no   b. Laura bought something for Amanda.

    ☐ yes ☐ no   c. Laura's new dress is blue.

4. Kyle said, "This is an interesting book."

    ☐ yes ☐ no   a. The book is far from Kyle.

    ☐ yes ☐ no   b. Kyle is reading more than one book now.

    ☐ yes ☐ no   c. Kyle is talking about one book.

5. Wow, these are really colorful sweaters.

    ☐ yes ☐ no   a. There is only one sweater.

    ☐ yes ☐ no   b. The sweaters have one main color.

    ☐ yes ☐ no   c. The sweaters are very comfortable.

6. Those are beautiful fish in Sani's aquarium.

    ☐ yes ☐ no   a. There isn't just one fish.

    ☐ yes ☐ no   b. Sani has some goldfish.

    ☐ yes ☐ no   c. The aquarium is in the living room.

7. *Linda*: "My three brothers go to the university. My sister works at the bank."

   Mark: "Wow! And you have a great job as manager of this store."

   ☐ yes ☐ no a. His brothers are students.

   ☐ yes ☐ no b. Her sister does not work at the university.

   ☐ yes ☐ no c. Her brothers work at the university.

8. Sarah is a student at Miami Dade College. She attends school only in the morning. She has a grammar class at 8 AM, history class at 9 AM, and literature class at 10 AM. On Thursday, she works at the Grand Hotel from noon to 5 PM.

   ☐ yes ☐ no a. Her classes are in the morning.

   ☐ yes ☐ no b. She works every day.

   ☐ yes ☐ no c. Her history class is before her literature class.

EXERCISE 10. Speaking Practice: Which House Is Mine?

Step 1. Work with a partner. There are four streets with nine houses on each street, so there are 36 houses. Choose one house to be your house. Circle that house. Do NOT let your partner know which house is your house.

Step 2. Take turns asking yes-no questions to try to guess your partner's house. If the answer to a question is yes, then the questioner can continue asking. If the answer is no, the turn passes to the other student.

Step 3. The first partner to guess the right house is the winner. (You can't use the house numbers until the end!).

Example: A: Is your house on Mills Street?

B: No, my house isn't on Mills Street. (So it's Student B's turn to ask a question.)

B: Is your house on Pine Street?

A: Yes, my house is on Pine Street. (So B continues asking.)

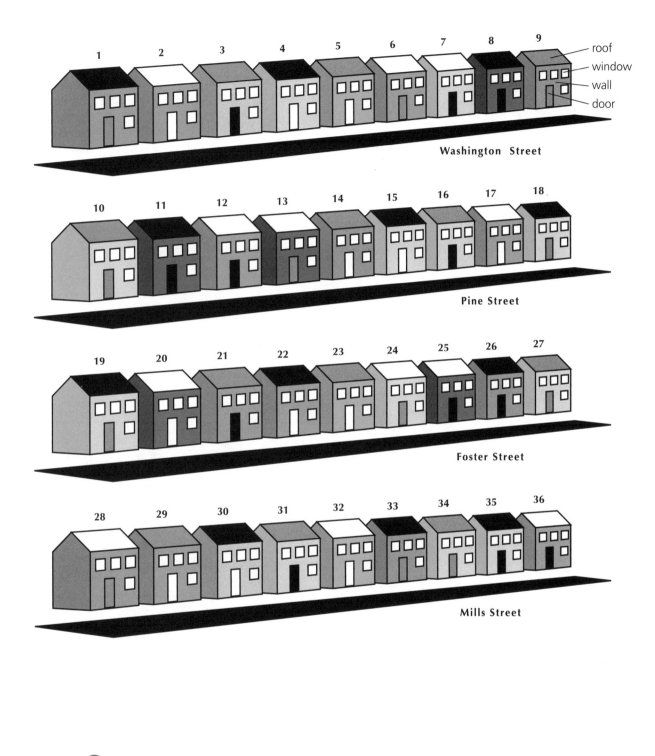

roof
window
wall
door

Washington Street

Pine Street

Foster Street

Mills Street

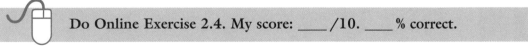

Do Online Exercise 2.4. My score: ____ /10. ____ % correct.

REVIEW   **EXERCISE 11. Review Test 1: Multiple Choice**

Circle the letter of the correct answer. Some are conversations.

1. I have a new job. _____ office is located on the third floor of a large building.

   a. His   b. My   c. Your   d. Her

2. Fabio Rodriguez is my new boss, and _____ job is to make sure that everyone does a lot of work and does it well.

   a. his   b. my   c. your   d. her

3. I share an office with a girl from Korea. Her name is Min. She is very intelligent, and I am impressed with _____ ability to solve problems fast.

   a. his   b. my   c. your   d. her

4. I now have many coworkers from different countries. _____ schedules are different, but we try to meet for lunch at noon.

   a. Your   b. Their   c. Our   d. Its

5. "Do you like the Beatles' music?"

   "No, I don't like _____ music. Do you?"

   a. their   B. they   C. its   D. it's

6. "Do you and your husband have a daughter named Trina? I think I know her."

   "Well, yes, we do. _____ daughter lives in Houston now."

   a. Her   b. Our   c. She   d. We

7. "Do you need a passport for your trip to China?"

   "Yes, we do. I have my passport right here, and Paul and Bob have _____ passports, too."

   a. his   b. your   c. our   d. their

8. "I'd like to cash this check, please."

   "OK, but I need to see _____ driver's license or some kind of ID."

   a. his   b. my   c. your   d. their

🕐 **ONE-MINUTE LESSON**

ID is a common way to say *identification*. Other short forms are UFO (unidentified flying objects), ASAP (as soon as possible), and ER (emergency room). In English, we usually read the letters (e.g., I-D or E-R) for these short forms. We don't pronounce them as words.

> REVIEW **EXERCISE 12. Review Test 2: Production and Evaluation**

Part 1.
Circle the correct words.

1. Melinda and Rick have a new car. What's your opinion of it? Do (you, your) like (her, his, its, their) car?

2. It is important for all of the passengers to have (his, her, their, your) passports now.

3. Do you know Mr. Piper's house? (Its, His, Her, Your, Their) house is gray and white.

4. Congratulations on your wonderful news! Show me (your, you) engagement ring.

5. I want to send this gift to (my, I) aunt, but (my, I) don't know (his, her, your) address.

6. (Our, We) class finishes at 9, so (our, we) can meet you around 9:30.

7. When do (we, our) have (we, our) next meeting?

8. Richard likes to listen to music. (He, His) favorite songs are from the 1980s.

9. Mrs. Gonzalez has a beautiful rose garden. (He, She) works in it every day, and that's why (he, she, his, her) roses are so beautiful.

10. Victor never makes good grades. (He, She, His, Her) grade so far is only a C or a D.

Part 2.
Read this short passage. Write the correct possessive adjective.

I am Rachel Hanks. This is a picture of ❶ _____ family. The woman on the left is ❷ _____ grandmother. ❸ _____ name is Rosa Hanks.

The man on the right is ❹ _____ uncle. ❺ _____ name is Ken. The woman near him is ❻ _____ wife. ❼ _____ name is Sarah.

Do you see the two kids in the lower right-hand corner of the photo? Those are my cousins. ❽ _____ names are Zane and Vicky. Can you see ❾ _____ cat? It's sitting on the floor. ❿ _____ name is Boots.

Of course there are many more people in my family, but they're camera shy!

EXERCISE 13. Reading Practice: A Conversation about Your Family

Read this short conversation between two friends. Then answer the six comprehension questions. The grammar from this unit is underlined for you.

Mrs. Perry: And here's a photo of <u>my</u> son Matt. Isn't he handsome? He has <u>my</u> hair, but <u>his</u> father's eyes.

Ms. Stone: He looks very nice. Is he <u>your</u> only child?

Mrs. Perry: Yes, he is. Matt has a lot of friends. They come to <u>our</u> house, or he visits <u>their</u> houses. He's a pretty popular guy.

Ms. Stone: I see. I guess he's very busy.

Mrs. Perry: Oh, yes. And he's also busy with <u>his</u> schoolwork. But he doesn't have to study all the time because he is so smart. He's especially good at math. I'm sure <u>his</u> math teacher is happy that he's in <u>her</u> class.

Ms. Stone: Uh, yes, I'm sure.

Mrs. Perry: And <u>his</u> coaches are happy, too! They say Matt's the best player on <u>their</u> teams. Did I tell you he plays both soccer and baseball?

Ms. Stone: I'm not surprised.

Mrs. Perry: Yes, <u>our</u> family is very proud of him. Say, I have a photo of Matt with <u>his</u> grandparents. Would you like to see it? <u>My</u> parents are wonderful people. They're really smart and talented. <u>My</u> father . . .

Ms. Stone: Oh, dear, look at the time! I have an appointment now, at . . . at the dentist's, so I really have to go. Bye!

1. How many sports does Matt play? _____

2. Does Matt study all the time? Explain your answer. _____

_____

3. Is Matt popular? Can you give two reasons for your answer?

_____

_____

4. How many photos are in this conversation? How many photos does Ms. Stone see?

_____

5. Can you describe Mrs. Perry?

_____

6. Do you think Ms. Stone is really going to the dentist's office now? Explain your answer.

_____

_____

EXERCISE 14. Vocabulary Practice: Word Knowledge

Circle the word or phrase that is most closely related to the word or phrase on the left. Use a dictionary to check the meaning of words you do not know.

Vocabulary	Answer Choices	
1. a nickname	Tommy for Thomas	Tommy for Tommy Smith
2. a dessert	a cake	a salad
3. a cover	the inside part of a book	the outside part of a book
4. to kid	to joke	to reply
5. in fact	a lie	the truth
6. twins	two babies	two meals
7. just over 25	26	52
8. male	boy or man	girl or woman
9. agree with	think differently	think the same
10. a mess	a customer	a problem
11. match	A + a	A + e
12. a scarf	for a baby	for a woman
13. clothes	photos, pictures	pants, shirts
14. every other	1A2B3C4D5E	12345ABCDE
15. a turtle	an animal	a vegetable
16. glad	happy	rich
17. a skirt	for a female	for a male
18. a couple	two people	thirteen people
19. a note	a short letter	a long letter
20. literature	for listening	for reading
21. a location	a place	a time
22. smart	daughter	intelligent
23. too	also	perhaps
24. ID	for a person	for a place
25. a passenger	a person	a place
26. congratulations	bad news	good news
27. an address	a person	a place
28. so far	around there	until now
29. handsome	smells good	looks good
30. popular	people don't like it	people like it
31. a coach	a person's parent	a team's leader
32. a porch	a part of a business	a part of a house

EXERCISE 15. Vocabulary Practice: Collocations

Fill in each blank with the answer on the right that most naturally completes the phrase on the left. If necessary, use a dictionary to check the meaning of words you do not know.

Phrase	Answer Choices	
1. _____ you to my family	introduce	meet
2. my favorite _____	sing	song
3. a _____ engine	bike	car
4. my _____ name	after	last
5. a _____ score	question	test
6. a great _____	idea	several
7. be good _____ math	at	by
8. _____ a suggestion	care	have
9. a _____ sweater	dark gray	gray dark
10. _____ about you?	What	Which
11. _____ minutes	more ten	ten more
12. serve _____	reasons	sandwiches
13. call me _____	late	later
14. a lot _____	of work	work
15. a potluck _____	dinner	restaurant
16. agree _____ someone	for	with
17. a _____ mess	big	large
18. a three-story _____	book	building
19. _____ care of	make	take
20. once _____ week	a	the
21. my free _____	place	time
22. _____ class	assist	attend
23. read a _____	college	note
24. a _____ of paper	glass	piece
25. _____ sure	get	make
26. _____ the garden	in	on
27. solve a _____	problem	schedule
28. _____ here	left	right
29. _____ a check	cash	change
30. _____ a meeting	have	put
31. a _____ license	congratulations	driver's
32. _____ popular	beautiful	pretty
33. lower right-hand _____	corner	floor
34. camera _____	coach	shy
35. proud _____ you	from	of

EXERCISE 16. Writing Practice: Introducing Your Family

Part 1. Editing Student Writing
Read this short paragraph about one student's family. Circle the 14 errors. Then write the line number where the error is located next to the type of error. (Some sentences may have more than one error.)

_____ a. no subject   _____ e. *have/be*

_____ b. *this, that, these, those*   _____ f. possessive adjective

_____ c. no verb   _____ g. no *a*

_____ d. singular-plural   _____ h. capital letter

	My Family
1	this short paragraph is about my family. My family has four peoples. In
2	addition to me, they are my mother, my father, my sister, and my brother.
3	My sister has 19 years old. She's hobby is basketball. Is really crazy about
4	basketball. my brother has 16 year old. He's hobby music. He's a very good
5	singer. We live in small house. Our house in Dallas, Texas. I think these city
6	is a great place to live. I love my family very much, and they love me.
7	We are very good family. Are very happy together.

Part 2. Original Student Writing
Now write a short paragraph (or some sentences) about your family. Use five words from the vocabulary on pages 55–56. Underline the five words. Use two new words from your dictionary. Circle the two dictionary words.

Unit 3

Simple Present Tense

Discover the Grammar

A reporter is interviewing someone with an unusual job. Read this interview, and then answer the five questions.

Line	
1	**Reporter**: My first guest today is Nate Williams. Nate, you have an unusual
2	job. What do you do for a living?
3	**Nate**: I'm a clown.
4	**Reporter**: A clown? That's really unusual. So what do you do every week?
5	**Nate**: Yes, you're right. My job is unusual. What do I do every week? Let's
6	see, I make people happy. If I do my job well, people laugh.
7	**Reporter**: Wow. I want your job. So, Nate, you don't work in an office.
8	**Nate**: No, I don't. I work in many places. I work at birthday parties. I tell
9	jokes, I paint children's faces, and I play games. I enjoy my work.
10	**Reporter**: Does your job have any negative points?
11	**Nate**: Well, yes, every job has problems. I can think of one problem.
12	It's my salary. A clown doesn't make a lot of money.
13	**Reporter**: OK, let me ask you a different question. Are you the first clown in
14	your family?

15	**Nate:**	No, I'm not. My cousin is also a clown. He works in the circus, so
16		he travels to a lot of different places. He doesn't work in one place.
17	**Reporter:**	Do you want a job in a circus?
18	**Nate:**	No, I don't. I don't like to work very far from home.
19	**Reporter:**	So you don't work with anyone else?
20	**Nate:**	No, I work alone. I don't want to work in a big circus. I'd rather
21		work alone.

1. Underline the eight examples of *don't* and *doesn't*. Can you explain when we use these two words?_____

    _____

2. Circle *works* and *travels* in Lines 15–16. Circle *work* (twice) in Line 8. Circle *have* in Line 1 and *has* twice in Line 11. When do we use these verbs with *-s*?

    _____

    _____

    _____

3. Explain the use of *No, I'm not* in Line 15 and *No, I don't* in Line 18. Can we use one for the other?

    _____

    _____

    _____

4. In *What do you do for a living* (Line 2), can you explain the two examples of *do*? Which one is the real verb (the most important verb)?

    _____

    _____

    _____

5. What questions do you have about this grammar?

    _____

    _____

    _____

Grammar Lesson

Simple Present Tense of Verbs: Affirmative

KEY 2

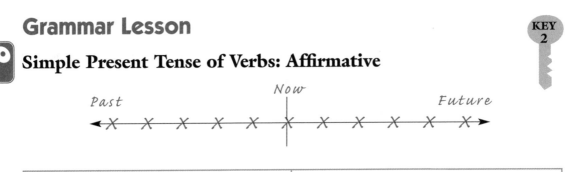

I, you, we, they + VERB	he, she, it + VERB + -s
I get up at 7:30 AM.	She gets up at 6:45 AM.
I eat a big breakfast.	She eats a light breakfast.
I walk to work.	She drives to work.
I work from 8 to 4.	She works from 7:45 to 2.
I come home at 4:30.	She comes home at 2:30.

<u>Rule 1</u>. In the simple present tense, a verb has two forms: VERB or VERB + -s.

<u>Rule 2</u>. VERB is used with *I, you, we,* and *they.*

<u>Rule 3</u>. VERB + -s used with *he, she,* and *it.*

<u>Rule 4</u>. Use simple present tense for actions that are always true or that happen always or sometimes. Common time expressions for simple present include *always, sometimes, never,* and *every _____ (every week).*

<u>Rule 5</u>. For verbs that end in **consonant + -y**, change the -y to -i and then add -es: *fly → flies* but *play → plays.*

<u>Rule 6</u>. For verbs that end in o, sh, ch, s, z, and x, add -es: *do → does.*

Other examples:

	work	eat	take	try	go	have
I	I work	I eat	I take	I try	I go	I have
you	you work	you eat	you take	you try	you go	you have
we	we work	we eat	we take	we try	we go	we have
they	they work	they eat	they take	they try	they go	they have
he	he works	he eats	he takes	he tries	he goes	he has
she	she works	she eats	she takes	she tries	she goes	she has
it	it works	it eats	it takes	it tries	it goes	it has

BE CAREFUL!

Common Learner Errors	Explanation
1. Laura ~~cook~~ **cooks** scrambled eggs for breakfast every day.	Remember to use **VERB** + s when the subject is **he, she,** or **it**.
2. Canada ~~have~~ **has** two official languages.	The -s form of **have** is *has*.
3. My baby sister ~~crys~~ **cries** when she is hungry.	If a verb ends in consonant + *-y*, remember to change -y to -i and add -es. Do not change y to i if the letter before y is a vowel (a, e, i, o, u): *s<u>a</u>y, says; enj<u>o</u>y, enjoys; b<u>u</u>y, buys.*
4. Zeke always ~~dos~~ **does** the dishes after dinner.	Remember to add -es after o, sh, ch, s, x, and z.
5. Collin and Laura ~~cooks~~ **cook** scrambled eggs for breakfast every day.	Use only **VERB** (no -s) when the subject is **I, you, we,** or **they**.
6. I ~~am walk~~ **walk** to school every day.	Do not use **be** with other verbs in simple present tense.

 ONE-MINUTE LESSON
The words **do** and **does** have different pronunciation. **Do** sounds like *you*, but **does** sounds like *fuzz*. This is different from the pair *go/goes* because the vowel in *go* is the same vowel in *goes*.

EXERCISE 1. Affirmative Simple Present Tense

Fill in the blanks with the correct forms of the verbs.

speak	watch	do	try
I _speak_	I _____	I _____	I _____
you _speak_	you _____	you _____	you _____
he _speaks_	he _____	he _____	he _____
she _speaks_	she _____	she _____	she _____
it _speaks_	it _____	it _____	it _____
we _speak_	we _____	we _____	we _____
they _speak_	they _____	they _____	they _____
Jo _speaks_	Jo _____	Jo _____	Jo _____
Jo and I _speak_	Jo and I _____	Jo and I _____	Jo and I _____
you and I _speak_	you and I _____	you and I _____	you and I _____

take	play	have	be
I _____	I _____	I _____	I _____
you _____	you _____	you _____	you _____
he _____	he _____	he _____	he _____
she _____	she _____	she _____	she _____
it _____	it _____	it _____	it _____
we _____	we _____	we _____	we _____
they _____	they _____	they _____	they _____
Jo _____	Jo _____	Jo _____	Jo _____
Jo and I _____	Jo and I _____	Jo and I _____	Jo and I _____
you and I _____	you and I _____	you and I _____	you and I _____

Do Online Exercise 3.1. My score: _____ /10. _____ % correct.

EXERCISE 2. Simple Present Tense in Context

Circle the correct form of each verb.

Everyday Activities

1. Mr. Smith (play, plays) golf every morning. He (play, plays) with Mr. Gonzalez. They (go, goes) to the golf course very early in the morning before the weather (get, gets) too hot. Both of them (enjoy, enjoys) this sport very much. Mr. Smith is good at golf, but Mr. Gonzalez is not. Mr. Gonzalez (like, likes) golf because it is good exercise.

2. I (do, does) my math homework every night before I (go, goes) to bed. I always (use, uses) a pencil. I (prefer, prefers) to use a pencil because sometimes I (make, makes) mistakes. My friend Brenda is the opposite. She rarely (make, makes) mistakes. She isn't afraid of making a mistake, so she (use, uses) a pen for her math homework.

3. Laura and Ellen (work, works) in the same office. Laura (work, works) in the morning, and Ellen (work, works) in the afternoon. Laura's day (begin, begins) at 8 AM, but Ellen's day (start, starts) at 1 PM. They (have, has) the same weekly schedule. They (work, works) from Monday to Friday.

4. Our class (begin, begins) at 8:30. The teacher (arrive, arrives) at 7:45, and the students (come, comes) to class between 8:20 and 8:30. The teacher (like, likes) the students to arrive on time. If a student (come, comes) late, our teacher (get, gets) angry.

5. Brian (work, works) at the bank. He (finish, finishes) work at 5:30. Then he (go, goes) home. He (love, loves) to listen to the news, so he (watch, watches) it on TV at 6:00. After that, he (eat, eats) dinner. Sometimes his friend Zack (come, comes) to his house. On Saturday afternoon, Brian and Zack usually (watch, watches) a college football game if there is one on TV.

EXERCISE 3. Simple Present Tense in Context

Fill in the blanks with the correct forms of the verbs.

Famous Cities

1. Vancouver _____is_____ (be) in British Colombia, Canada. Vancouver

    _____ (have) the second largest Chinatown in North America.

2. Approximately one million people _____ (live) in Abu Dhabi. Abu

    Dhabi _____ (be) the capital city of the United Arab Emirates. Many

    people _____ (call) the country the UAE instead of its full name.

3. The capital of Colombia _____ (be) Bogota. If you _____

    (want) to visit Bogota, we _____ (recommend) that you

    _____ (go) in January or February. It _____ (be) not a

    good idea to visit in October or November. In those two months, it

    _____ (rain) a lot, and sometimes the weather _____ (get)

    really bad in October. There _____ (be) many mountains around this

    beautiful city. The altitude of Bogota _____ (be) over 8,000 feet,

    which is about 2600 meters.

4. Each year many tourists _____ (visit) San Francisco. This city

    _____ (attract) a huge number of people because it _____

    (have) so many interesting places to see. Tourists _____ (want) to see

    the famous cable cars and the hills. In addition, San Francisco _____

    (have) the largest Chinatown in North America.

EXERCISE 4. Mini-Conversations

Circle the correct words in these eight mini-conversations.

1. A: Your food looks good.

   B: Yes, it's very good. I (like, likes) it a lot.

2. A: Can your brother sing well?

   B: Yes, he (sing, sings) really well.

3. A: What is Jill's phone number?

   B: I don't know. Let's ask Mark. I am sure that he (know, knows) it.

4. A: Your dad is in good shape.

   B: He (run, runs) three miles every day. Sometimes I (run, runs) with him.

5. A: Is Lin a student?

   B: Yes, he (study, studies) nursing at Weston College.

6. A: Are all of your cousins in this country?

   B: No, some (live, lives) in Mexico, and one (live, lives) in Peru.

7. A: Which is better for math class—a pen or a pencil?

   B: Most people (prefer, prefers) to use a pencil.

8. A: When I (travel, travels) to a different city, I almost always (rent, rents) a car.

   B: Really? I usually (do, does) the same thing.

ONE-MINUTE LESSON
Adverbs of frequency include **always, usually, often sometimes, rarely**, and **never**. These words usually come after *be* (*She is always on time*) but before other verbs (*She always arrives on time*).

EXERCISE 5. Speaking Practice: Verb Forms

Step 1. Choose five verbs from the list.

Step 2. Write your verbs on the top lines of the chart. Then write the correct forms for each verb for the subject in the columns.

Step 3. Work with a partner. Say your first verb. Your partner must then say all the correct forms of the verb. Then your partner says his or her first verb. You must then say all the correct forms of that verb. Take turns doing this.

arrive	begin	come	drink	eat	have
leave	like	live	practice	pronounce	sing
speak	teach	understand	work	read	practice
write	play	visit	want	learn	listen
repeat	talk	open	close	walk	run
do	send	take	think	make	call
be	go	use	type	wash	erase
catch	watch	know	get	need	forget

I					
you					
he					
she					
it					
we					
they					

Pronunciation of -s

You have seen that we add **-s** to verbs (for *he, she,* and *it*) and to nouns (for plural). This ending can be spelled with **-s** (*likes*), **-es** (*watches*), or **-ies** (*tries*). This ending can be pronounced three ways in English: /s/, /z/, /əz/. Many students are surprised to learn that the most common pronunciation for *-s* is /z/, not /s/ or /əz/.

-s or -es or -ies			
	Ending	**Verb**	**Noun**
1. Pronounce /z/ when the words ends in these voiced* sounds:	/b/	he grabs	3 cabs
	/d/	she needs	3 beds
	/g/	she logs in	3 bags
	/l/	he calls	3 balls
	/m/	it comes	3 dimes
	/ŋ/	it rings	3 songs
	/r/	she cares	3 cars
	/v/	he lives	3 knives
	all vowels	she goes	3 boys
2. Pronounce /s/ when the words ends in these voiceless* sounds:	/f/	he laughs	3 knives
	/k/	she speaks	3 ducks
	/p/	he keeps	3 cubs
	/t/	she writes	3 cats
3. Pronounce an extra syllable /əz/ when the words ends in these sounds:	/s/	he misses	3 classes
	/z/	she sneezes	3 noses
	/č/ (-ch)	he watches	3 watches
	/š/ (-sh)	she finishes	3 dishes
	/ǰ/ (-ge)	he changes	3 pages

Connecting Grammar and Vocabulary

English has thousands of verbs, but you need to learn the most frequent verbs. Learn this list of 12 common verbs used in conversation (in order of occurrence).

The Most Common Common Verbs in Conversation			
1. get	4. know	7. want	10. take
2. go	5. think	8. come	11. make
3. say	6. see	9. mean	12. give

Source: Biber, D., and Reppen, R. (2002). What does frequency have yo do with grammar teaching? *Studies in Second Language Acquisition 24*, 199–208.

*Voiced sounds have vibration in the vocal cords. Voiceless sounds have very little vibration in the vocal cords.

EXERCISE 6. Pronunciation of -s for 12 Common Verbs

Write the *he/she/it* form or the 12 most common conversation verbs in the column by the verb's correct final pronunciation.

/s/	/z/	/əz/
gets		

EXERCISE 7. Odd Man Out

Change the spelling of the verb to *he/she/it*. Circle the verb and the ending that has a different final sound. What is the sound of the different word? What is the sound of the other three verbs?

				Group Sound	Odd Sound
1. finish*es*	(do*es*)	watch*es*	kiss*es*	/əz/	/z/
2. eat	take	live	cough		
3. study	copy	go	create		
4. cook	drive	keep	think		
5. stay	learn	write	read		
6. find	lose	arrive	play		
7. want	know	say	mean		
8. catch	lose	wash	text		

ONE-MINUTE LESSON

The most common pronunciation for -s is /z/. Name the animals in the zoo and you'll immediately see that most of their plural names end in /z/: monkeys, tigers, lions, birds, etc. In addition, the possessive of most people's names end in /z/: Maria's, Chen's, Ricardo's, Jim's, Amanda's. (For more information, see page 67.)

   Do Online Exercise 3.2. My score: _____ /10. _____ % correct.

Simple Present Tense: Negative

Making a negative statement with verbs is easy. Study these two steps:		
Step 1	Check for a verb (not *be*).	Colombia and Brazil **have** kings. Colombia **has** a king.
Step 2	a. If the verb does not end in -s, put **do not** (OR **don't**) before the verb.	Colombia and Brazil **do** not **have** kings.
	b. If the verb ends in -s, remove the -s and put **does not** (OR **doesn't**) before the base (simple) verb. (The -s moves from the verb to the word **does**.)	Colombia **does** not **have** a king.

Other examples:

Statement		Negative
I have a car.	→	I do not have a bicycle.
We get off work at 6 PM.	→	We don't work after 6 PM.
Pierre speaks French.	→	He does not speak Spanish.
The class lasts for four months.	→	The class does not last for a year.

Rule 1. To make a negative statement with a verb, add **do not** OR **does not** before the base (simple) form of the verb.

Rule 2. It is also possible to use contractions for **do not** and **does not**: **don't**, **doesn't**.

 BE CAREFUL!

Common Learner Errors	Explanation
1. The U.S. ~~no~~ doesn't have 100 states.	Remember to use **don't** (do not) or **doesn't** (does not) with a verb (except *be*).
2. Nell and Vick ~~aren't~~ don't eat lunch together every day.	Do not use **am not**, **isn't**, or **aren't** with a verb. Use **don't** or **doesn't** only.
3. The coffee doesn't ~~smells~~ smell good to him.	If you have **does**, don't use -s with the verb. You need only one -s for he/she/it.

EXERCISE 8. Negative of Simple Present Tense

Fill in the blanks with the correct negative forms of the verbs. Follow the examples. Use the short forms *don't* and *doesn't*.

like	go	study	do
I _don't like_	I _____	I _____	I _____
you _don't like_	you _____	you _____	you _____
he _doesn't like_	he _____	he _____	he _____
she _doesn't like_	she _____	she _____	she _____
it _doesn't like_	it _____	it _____	it _____
we _don't like_	we _____	we _____	we _____
they _don't like_	they _____	they _____	they _____
Jo _doesn't like_	Jo _____	Jo _____	Jo _____

know	get	have	be
I _____	I _____	I _____	I _____
you _____	you _____	you _____	you _____
he _____	he _____	he _____	he _____
she _____	she _____	she _____	she _____
it _____	it _____	it _____	it _____
we _____	we _____	we _____	we _____
they _____	they _____	they _____	they _____
Jo _____	Jo _____	Jo _____	Jo _____
Jo and Sue _____	Jo and Sue _____	Jo and Sue _____	Jo and Sue _____

Do Online Exercise 3.3. My score: _____ /10. _____ % correct.

EXERCISE 9. Editing. Is It Correct?

If the sentence is correct, write a check mark (✓) on the line. If it is not correct, write X on the line and circle the mistake. Then change the sentence to make it correct. Write the change above the sentence. (*Hint:* There are eight sentences. Two are correct, but six have mistakes.)

Languages

_____ 1. Arabic speakers no write their language from left to right.

_____ 2. Instead, they write their language from right to left.

_____ 3. The Japanese language don't have the words *a* or *the*.

_____ 4. The German language have six ways to say *the: der, das, die, den, dem, des.*

_____ 5. To say 90, French speakers say *quatre-vingt-dix*, which means four-twenty-ten, because their language isn't have one word for this number.

_____ 6. It is difficult for Russians to use *a, an*, and *the* well in English because Russian no have articles.

_____ 7. Spanish is the main language in most South American countries, but people in Brazil don't speak Spanish.

_____ 8. In Nigeria, there have more than 200 languages.

ONE-MINUTE LESSON
Memorize the expressions **more than** and **less than**. After **more** or **than**, we use the preposition **than**. This is not the usual grammar pattern in many languages.

EXERCISE 10. Negative of Simple Present Tense in Context

Fill in each blank with the negative form of the verb in parentheses.

1. Cats usually like fish, but my cat is a little strange. My cat (like) _____ fish. Cats usually like milk too, but my cat (drink) _____ milk. Cats usually have a long tail, but my cat is different. My cat (have) _____ a long tail. It has a very, very short tail.

2. How many letters does the English alphabet have? Some students think the English alphabet has 24 letters. This (be) _____ correct. The English alphabet (have) _____ 24 letters. There are 26 letters in the English alphabet. Some languages have special marks on top of the letters. For example, Spanish has *é* and German has *ü*, but English (have) _____ any marks on alphabet letters.

3. Some of my friends use computers to do their homework. I have a computer, but I (do) _____ my homework on a computer. I (know) _____ how to type very well. I prefer to use a pencil when I do my homework.

4. Jody eats all her meals at a restaurant or at her friend's house. She likes to cook, but she never cooks at home. The reason for this is simple. Jody lives in a small apartment, and her apartment (have) _____ a stove, so Jody (eat) _____ at home.

5. Many students walk to school. They can do this because they (live) _____ far away. My house is very far from school, so I (walk) _____ to school every day.

6. Our homework is very short. It (have) _____ twenty questions. It has only six questions. It (be) _____ difficult. It (take) _____ me or anyone else a very long time to do this homework.

Do Online Exercise 3.4. My score: _____ /10. _____ % correct.

EXERCISE 11. Negative Sentences with Simple Present Tense

Write three negative sentences. *Use a different verb in each sentence.* Write true sentences about yourself, your family, your friends, your things (car, books, dictionary), or your classroom.

Example: I don't have a car.

1. _____
2. _____
3. _____

After you finish writing your sentences, read your sentences to a partner. Then your partner should read his or her sentences to you. Are there any surprises? Are there any interesting sentences?

EXERCISE 12. Speaking Practice: True or False?

Write four statements about yourself. Use present tense. Write three true statements and one false statement. Then work in small groups (of three to four people). Read your statements. Other students will guess which statement is false. (Do not use the verb *be* more than one time.)

1. _____
2. _____
3. _____
4. _____

Simple Present Tense: Making a Question

Making a question with a verb (not *be*) is easy. Study these four steps:		
Step 1	Check for a verb (not *be*).	Colombia and Brazil **have** kings. Colombia **has** a king.
Step 2	Put **do** or **does** at the beginning of the sentence.	**do** Colombia and Brazil **have** kings. **does** Colombia **has** a king.
Step 3	Make sure the verb is in the base (simple) form.	**do** Colombia and Brazil **have** kings. **does** Colombia **have** a king.
Step 4	Use a capital letter for the first word of the question, and change the period (.) to a question mark (?).	**Do** Colombia and Brazil have kings? **Does** Colombia have a king?

Other examples:

Statement		Question
I talk fast.	→	Do I talk fast?
You like black coffee.	→	Do you like black coffee?
We have two classes together	→	Do we have two classes together?
They live on Green Street.	→	Do they live on Green Street?
He takes a bus to work.	→	Does he take a bus to work?
She has a new car.	→	Does she have a new car?
It rains a lot in summer.	→	Does it rain a lot in summer?

Rule 1. To make a question with a verb (not *be*), add **do** OR **does** before subject.

Rule 2. Be sure to use only the base (simple) form of the verb.

 BE CAREFUL!

Common Learner Errors	Explanation
1. ~~Are~~ Do you speak English?	Do not use *be* (am, is, are) with other verbs in simple present tense.
2. Does your car ~~has~~ have a good radio?	Do not put -s on the verb in *yes-no* questions. Use only the base (simple) form of the verb. For he/she/it, you need only one -s in the question. If you have **does**, the verb doesn't have -s.
3. ~~Do~~ Does China export wheat?	Remember to use **does** with he, she, and it. Use **do** with other subjects.

EXERCISE 14. Mini-Conversations

Circle the correct words in these eight mini-conversations. *Hint:* If you need help, find the main verb first.

1. A: (Do, Does, Is, Are) you understand this lesson?

   B: Yes, I do. I think (it does, does, it's, is) an easy lesson.

2. A: (Do, Does, Is, Are) I snore?

   B: Yes, you (snore, snores) really loudly!

3. A: (Do, Does, Is, Are) you drive a red car?

   B: Yes, I (drive, drives) a red sports car.

4. A: (Do, Does, Is, Are) that toy use four batteries?

   B: Yes, it (do, does, uses). (Do, Does, Is, Are) you have four batteries?

   A: No, I don't.

   B: You (have, has) to buy some then.

   A: (Do, Does, Is, Are) you know a place where I can buy batteries?

   B: Yes, go to Wilson's. They (sell, sells) batteries there.

5. A: (Do, Does, Is, Are) September have 31 days?

   B: No, it (isn't, doesn't) have 31 days. It (have, has, does) only 30.

6. A: (Do, Does, Is, Are) you understand the difference between *do* and *does*?

   B: I think so. *Does* (is, are) for *he, she* and *it*. *Do* (is, are) for *I, we, you,* and *they.*

7. A: (Do, Does, Is, Are) there many Spanish-speaking students in your class?

   B: Yes, there (do, does, is, are) a lot.

8. A: (Do, Does, Is, Are) you ready to leave?

   B: Yes, we (do, does, is, are). Let's go!

ONE-MINUTE LESSON
What does **let's** mean? We use **let's** + **VERB** to suggest an activity. For example, you could tell some friends, *Let's order a pizza* or *Let's take a taxi to the airport.*

EXERCISE 14. Yes-No Questions with Simple Present Tense

Write the correct words to complete these questions using the verbs in parentheses.

1. (have) _____*Does*_____ Matt _____*have*_____ a dark blue car?

2. (go) _____ this bus _____ to Miami?

3. (rain) _____ it _____ a lot in this area in the summer?

4. (study) _____ she _____ English every night?

5. (want) _____ Mary and Jack _____ more coffee now?

6. (read) _____ you _____ anything before you go to sleep?

7. (take) _____ you _____ a shower at night or in the morning?

8. (drive) _____ people in Mexico _____ on the right or on the left side of the road?

9. (cook) _____ Paul usually _____ his own food?

10. (speak) _____ Paul and John _____ French fluently?

11. (have) _____ you and John _____ a class together?

12. (play) _____ you _____ volleyball very well?

 ONE-MINUTE LESSON
We use the word **play** with sports (*I play baseball*), musical instruments (*I play the piano*), and games (*I play chess*).

Do Online Exercise 3.5. My score: _____ /10. _____ % correct.

Simple Present Tense: Questions with Full and Short Answers

Answering a question with a short answer is not difficult. Study these four steps:

Step 1	Listen for a question that begins with **do** or **does**.	Do Colombia and Brazil have kings?
Step 2	Decide if the answer is yes or no.	No
Step 3	Use a pronoun for the noun subject.	No, **they**
Step 4	Repeat the form of **Do** or **Does** that is in the question. Add **not** for negative. (The negatives **do not** and **does not** can also be contractions: **don't, doesn't**.)	No, they **do not.**

Other examples:

Questions	Full Answers	Short Answers
Do you speak Chinese?	Yes, I speak Chinese. No, I do not speak Chinese.	Yes, I do. No, I do not.
Does *dozen* mean "twelve"?	Yes, *dozen* mean "twelve."	Yes, it does.
Does *dozen* mean "ten"?	No, *dozen* doesn't mean "ten."	No, it doesn't.

Rule 1. To answer a yes-no question with a short affirmative answer, use **does** or **do**.

Rule 2. To answer a yes-no question with a short negative answer, use **does not, doesn't, do not,** or **don't** in your answer.

 ## BE CAREFUL!

Common Learner Errors	Explanation
1. Do Bolivia and Switzerland have beaches? No, they ~~are~~ do not.	Do not use am/is/are as a short answer for do/does questions.
2. Does Canada have states? No, it ~~hasn't~~ doesn't.	Be careful with the verb **have** in short answers.

EXERCISE 15. Practice with Simple Present Tense

You are a travel agent. Josie calls you for information about a cruise for her and her husband. Use the information from the advertisement and write yes/no answers to her questions.

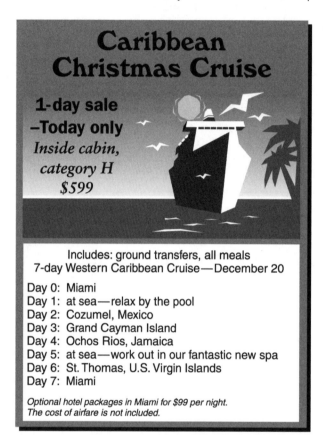

Caribbean Christmas Cruise

1-day sale
—Today only
Inside cabin, category H $599

Includes: ground transfers, all meals
7-day Western Caribbean Cruise—December 20

Day 0: Miami
Day 1: at sea—relax by the pool
Day 2: Cozumel, Mexico
Day 3: Grand Cayman Island
Day 4: Ochos Rios, Jamaica
Day 5: at sea—work out in our fantastic new spa
Day 6: St. Thomas, U.S. Virgin Islands
Day 7: Miami

*Optional hotel packages in Miami for $99 per night.
The cost of airfare is not included.*

Agent: Hello. This is Unique Travel. How may I help you?

Josie: I need some information about the Caribbean cruise in your ad.

Agent: How can I help you?

Josie: I have a few questions.

Agent: Ok, what is your first question?

Josie: Does the ship have a pool?

Agent: _____

Josie: Does the ship stop in Ocho Rios?

Agent: _____

Josie: I see the price is $599. Are all meals included in this price?

Agent: _____

Josie: Does the price include the airfare?

Agent: _____

Josie: Do we return to Miami on December 27th?

Agent: _____

Josie: Does the ship stop in Puerto Rico?

Agent: _____

Josie: Do we get a free hotel stay in Miami?

Agent: _____

Josie: Do I need to pay for it today?

Agent: _____

Josie: OK. I am going to come by your office later today.

EXERCISE 16. Giving Short Answers

Write the two possible short answers for each question.

1. Do most people in that country speak English?

   _____ (OR _____)

2. Does it snow in your country?

   _____ (OR _____)

3. Does your brother play hockey?

   _____ (OR _____)

4. Do you and Ben have math class together?

   _____ (OR _____)

5. Does that word mean "twelve"?

   _____ (OR _____)

6. Do I have your book?

   _____ (OR _____)

7. Does the teacher ride a bike to school?

   _____ (OR _____)

8. Does an orange have a lot of Vitamin C?

   _____ (OR _____)

Do Online Exercise 3.6. My score: _____ /10. _____ % correct.

EXERCISE 17. Sentence Study for Critical Reading

Read the numbered sentences. Then read the three answer choices and place a check mark in the yes or no boxes in front of each sentence to show if that answer is true based on the information in the original sentence. If there is not enough information to mark something as yes, then mark it as no. Remember that more than one true answer is possible.

1. My uncle Pat is my mother's brother. He lives in Detroit, but we live in Denver. He comes to our house about twice a year.

   ☐ yes ☐ no   a. I have a brother. His name is Pat.

   ☐ yes ☐ no   b. Pat lives in Denver. We visit his house two times each year.

   ☐ yes ☐ no   c. I have an uncle. His name is Pat.

2. Most people in Switzerland speak German and French.

   ☐ yes ☐ no   a. They speak two languages

   ☐ yes ☐ no   b. They speak German and French equally well.

   ☐ yes ☐ no   c. Switzerland has more people than Germany and France.

3. I don't usually get up early on the weekend.

   ☐ yes ☐ no   a. I don't usually wake up early on Saturdays.

   ☐ yes ☐ no   b. I usually play tennis early on Sunday mornings.

   ☐ yes ☐ no   c. I usually sleep late on Sundays.

4. Ben has milk for breakfast every day.

   ☐ yes ☐ no   a. Ben drinks milk every day.

   ☐ yes ☐ no   b. Ben doesn't drink milk on the weekends.

   ☐ yes ☐ no   c. Ben almost never drinks milk.

5. Karen and I don't watch television because we don't have a television.

   ☐ yes ☐ no   a. I do not have a television.

   ☐ yes ☐ no   b. Karen does not have a television.

   ☐ yes ☐ no   c. I have a television, but I never watch it.

6. Your brother has a great job. He is assistant manager at First National Bank. He works at the branch on Jefferson Street near the high school.

   ☐ yes ☐ no   a. He works at a bank on Jefferson Street.

   ☐ yes ☐ no   b. He doesn't have a checking account at the bank.

   ☐ yes ☐ no   c. His brother works at the high school on Jefferson Street.

7. This radio takes six type AA batteries. This is strange because many radios of this size take only two type AA batteries.

   ☐ yes ☐ no a. One possibility for this radio is four type A batteries.

   ☐ yes ☐ no b. This radio needs six batteries.

   ☐ yes ☐ no c. This is a usual radio.

8. Paella is a Spanish dish. It consists of rice that is cooked with many kinds of seafood. One interesting thing about this dish is that the shrimp are still in their whole shells.

   ☐ yes ☐ no a. Paella has rice in it.

   ☐ yes ☐ no b. Paella includes seafood.

   ☐ yes ☐ no c. Paella is a Spanish dish.

ONE-MINUTE LESSON
Many words have two or more meanings. **Branch** can be a part of a tree, an office, or a business: *My office is downtown, but we have another branch by the airport.*

EXERCISE 18. Speaking Pratice: Interviewing a Classmate

Write five original questions using *do* or *does*. Then ask someone your questions. Write the answers. Don't write questions that are very easy. Learn new information about your classmate. For example, don't ask, "Do you study English?" because you know the answer.

Example: <u>Do you cook your own food?</u>

<u>No, I don't. I am not a good cook.</u>

1. Q: _____

   A: _____

2. Q: _____

   A: _____

3. Q: _____

   A: _____

4. Q: _____

   A: _____

5. Q: _____

   A: _____

REVIEW

EXERCISE 19. Review Test 1: Multiple Choice

Circle the letter of the correct answer. Some are conversations.

1. "_____ *elephant* mean a kind of animal?"

   "Yes, that's correct. It's a huge gray animal."

       a. Does   b. Is   c. Do   d. Are

2. His last name _____ a dozen letters. It has only nine letters.

       a. don't has   b. doesn't has   c. doesn't have   d. don't have

3. "Do you and your brother work at the same bank?"

   "No, we don't. I work at Nations Bank, and my brother _____ at First Bank."

       a. work   b. works   c. don't work   d. doesn't work

4. "Are you and Joshua students?"

   "Yes, we _____. We both take classes at Evergreen Community College."

       a. students   b. do   c. he and I   d. are

5. "_____ the movie have a happy ending?"

   "I don't want to tell you that. It's a surprise!"

       a. Does   b. Is   c. Do   d. Are

6. "_____ a garage?"

   "Yes, and it's a very big garage."

       a. Is your new house has   c. Is your new house have

       b. Does your new house has   d. Does your new house have

7. "Do you like to eat eggplant?"

   "Eggplant? What _____?"

       a. means eggplant   c. does eggplant mean

       b. eggplant means   d. does eggplant means

8. "Does Joseph _____ help with his project?"

   "No, he doesn't. He says he can finish his project by himself."

       a. needs   b. is   c. want   d. has

REVIEW **EXERCISE 20. Review Test 2: Production and Evaluation**

Part 1.

Fill in the blanks with a negative word from the word list.

word list	isn't	aren't	don't	doesn't

I don't like winter. Summer is my favorite season. I **❶** _____ like winter

for four reasons. First, the weather in winter **❷** _____ very nice. Second,

the trees **❸** _____ have leaves, and the grass **❹** _____ green. Finally,

the days **❺** _____ very long.

Susan is my best friend. She is different from me. She and I **❻** _____

have the same opinion about the seasons. She really likes winter a lot. She loves

cold weather. She really **❼** _____ like warm weather. Her favorite sport is

skiing, so she **❽** _____ happy in June or July.

Susan **❾** _____ like spring, and I have the same opinion. I

❿ _____ like spring. In the spring, it rains a lot. Sometimes the sun

⓫ _____ shine for two or three days. The plants need the rain, but it

⓬ _____ good for us.

Part 2.

Read this short passage. There are five mistakes with negatives. Circle the mistakes, and write the
correction above each mistake.

Some of the classes at my school are very large, but my class does not very

large. There are only 12 students in my class. The students do not from the same

country. They are from three countries. Seven of the students are from Japan,

three are from Mexico, and two are from Egypt. The students do not speak the

same language. Their languages no are the same. Some of the students speak

Spanish, some speak Japanese, and some speak Arabic. The students from Mexico

are not speak Arabic, and the students from Japan does not speak Spanish.

EXERCISE 21. Reading Practice: Advice Letters

Read this letter asking for help and the reply letter with advice (on page 87). Then answer the eight comprehension questions on page 88. The grammar from this unit is underlined for you.

Dear Dr. Helper,

I am 19 years old, and I <u>have</u> a problem. I <u>don't know</u> what to do. I <u>don't like</u> my job. My boss <u>doesn't like</u> me, and my work is difficult. Every day I <u>feel</u> sad and angry. My coworkers <u>don't help</u> me because they <u>don't understand</u> me or my problems, so I <u>don't talk</u> to them very often. I'm a good worker, but I'm not happy. I <u>eat</u> lunch alone. I <u>get</u> to work late, and I <u>leave</u> early. I <u>take</u> many days off, but I still <u>feel</u> bad.

I <u>need</u> my job. I <u>need</u> the money! My job <u>does not interest</u> me. My job <u>does not excite</u> me. What can I do?

Sincerely,

Wrong Job

Dear Wrong Job,

I <u>don't think</u> you are a good worker. A good worker <u>doesn't</u> get to the office late and <u>doesn't</u> <u>go</u> home early. A good worker <u>talks</u> to her coworkers. And a good worker <u>doesn't take</u> off many days!

You <u>need</u> the money. I <u>understand</u> that, but you <u>have</u> a choice. Look for a new job! Think about what you like. <u>Do</u> you <u>like</u> to work outside? <u>Do</u> you <u>enjoy</u> working with animals? <u>Do</u> you <u>like</u> children? <u>Do</u> you <u>have</u> any special skills? <u>Do</u> you <u>have</u> a university degree? <u>Do</u> you <u>speak</u> a second language? A good worker <u>uses</u> her skills. Use your friends and family, too! <u>Does</u> your father <u>know</u> about any good jobs? <u>Do</u> your old high school teachers <u>have</u> any ideas for you? <u>Does</u> your best friend <u>work</u> somewhere nice? If so, ask that friend for help.

Stop complaining, change your attitude, and look for a new job. Please write to me again. I <u>care</u> about your problem a lot.

Best wishes,
Dr. Helper

ONE-MINUTE LESSON
We sometimes use a noun after the verb **stop**. *At a red light, we stop our cars.* If you have an action after the verb **stop**, we use **VERB + -ing**: *I hope you stop* **complaining.**

1. In one sentence, what is the letter writer's problem?

   _____

   _____

2. How many people does Wrong Job usually eat lunch with?

   _____

   _____

3. Does Wrong Job ever miss work?

   _____

   _____

4. Does Dr. Helper agree with Wrong Job's opinion? Explain.

   _____

   _____

5. Why does Dr. Helper ask if Wrong Job likes working with animals?

   _____

   _____

6. What does Dr. Helper mean by saying, "Stop complaining"?

   _____

   _____

7. Do you think Wrong Job is male or female? Why?

   _____

   _____

8. Do you agree with Dr. Helper's advice? Why or why not? Would you suggest anything else?

   _____

   _____

   _____

EXERCISE 22. Vocabulary Practice: Word Knowledge

Circle the word or phrase that is most closely related to the word or phrase on the left. Use a dictionary to check the meaning of words you do not know.

Vocabulary	Answer Choices	
1. your job	your work	your face
2. alone	one person	many people
3. a mistake	an error	a schedule
4. opposite	up—high	up—down
5. a tourist	a visitor	a worker
6. rising	34, 35, 36, 37, 38	38, 37, 36, 35, 34
7. both	A and B	A, B, and C
8. a meal	food	letters
9. approximately 100	98	173
10. a surprise	you expect it	you don't expect it
11. snore	shopping	sleeping
12. unusual	similar	strange
13. a hill	like a small mountain	like a small river
14. snow	in the summer	in the winter
15. full	always	complete
16. optional	you choose	you listen
17. rarely	almost correct	almost never
18. work out	exercise	vitamin
19. erase	with a key	with a pencil
20. a beach	an apple	an ocean
21. on top of	a hat on your head	a watch on your arm
22. large	big	small
23. get up	call up	wake up
24. recommend	suggest	understand
25. scramble	mix	select
26. a ship	in the air	in the water
27. free	no cost	no office
28. twice	one time	two times
29. assistant	a person who attends	a person who helps
30. whole	half	all
31. gray	a color	a garage
32. an eggplant	a special place	a vegetable
33. complain	if you are happy	if you are unhappy

EXERCISE 23. Vocabulary Practice: Collocations

Fill in each blank with the answer on the right that most naturally completes the phrase on the left. If necessary, use a dictionary to check the meaning of words you do not know.

Phrase	Answer Choices	
1. every _____	person	people
2. scrambled _____	eggs	rules
3. I'd _____	anyone	rather
4. _____ the dishes	do	make
5. _____ a mistake	do	make
6. What do you do for a _____?	living	working
7. a light _____	breakfast	circus
8. _____ January	in	on
9. make _____	money	travel
10. _____ talking	make	stop
11. _____ TV	in	on
12. _____ angry	get	take
13. listen _____	at	to
14. a phone _____	number	place
15. be in _____ shape	good	well
16. too _____ chairs	many	much
17. _____ a game	play	run
18. instead _____	of	on
19. _____ six months	for	with
20. _____ a test	put	take
21. let's _____	do	did
22. _____ a question	ask	sell
23. get off _____	travel	work
24. _____ our area	in	on
25. _____ a joke	say	tell
26. _____ bus	by	for
27. too _____ caffeine	many	much
28. _____ from here	far	near
29. _____ coffee	black	step
30. _____ Green Street	in	on
31. _____ a bus	go	take
32. _____ a bike	put	ride
33. on _____	December	December 27th
34. a checking _____	account	seafood
35. consist _____	in	of

EXERCISE 24. Writing Practice: The Daily Activities of a Worker

Part 1. Editing Student Writing

Read these sentences about the daily activities of a worker. Circle the 17 errors. Then write the number of the sentence with the error next to the type of error. (Some sentences may have more than one error.)

_____ a. no subject   _____ d. possessive adjectives

_____ b. –s for verb   _____ e. negative

_____ c. no verb   _____ f. capital letter

A Bank Teller
1. Pamela Taylor a teller at Youngstown Bank.
2. Arrives at work at 7 AM every day, but she no work on Saturday or sunday.
3. First, she make coffee for everyone in his office.
4. Making coffee is no part of his job.
5. She makes coffee because likes to drink coffee to begin his day.
6. The bank open at 8 AM.
7. Then helps the bank's customers.
8. for example, if a customer wants to cash a check, she makes sure that the customer sign his or her name on the back of the check.
9. Pamela answer customers' questions.
10. Pamela finish work at 4 PM., and then she home.

Part 2. Original Student Writing

Now write some sentences about the daily activities of a profession. You may choose any profession.

Unit 4

Descriptive Adjectives

Discover the Grammar

Read the information about the photo, and then answer the five questions.

Line	
1	There are three young girls in this photo. They are very cute. The middle
2	girl and the third girl are sisters. In fact, they are twins. The first girl is their
3	cousin. The twins' names are Mandi and Melissa. Mandi is in the middle, and
4	Melissa is on the right. Mandi has straight black hair, and Melissa has straight
5	black hair, too. Mandi is wearing a light scarf, but Melissa is wearing a dark
6	scarf. Their cousin's name is In-Su. In-Su is not wearing a scarf. In-Su has
7	long black hair. The twins are wearing striped shirts. Their shirts have short
8	sleeves. In-Su is wearing a sleeveless shirt. Her shirt is not striped. In this
9	photo, In-Su is pointing at a little dog that is near them. The weather today is
10	great, but it is a very hot day. These three little girls are having a really good
11	time in the park today.

1. Which of these twelve descriptive adjectives are in this story?

    cute   *great*   *hot*   *sunny*   *green*   *curly*

    striped   *short*   *long*   *young*   *old*   *pretty*

2. There are many examples of descriptive adjectives that are in front of a noun. Find three examples. Write the adjective, the noun, and line number.

    <u>adjective</u>   <u>noun</u>

    a. _____ + _____ Line _____

    b. _____ + _____ Line _____

    c. _____ + _____ Line _____

3. Find three adjectives that are after the verb *be*. Write the form of *be*, the adjective, and the line number.

    <u>be</u>   <u>adjective</u>

    a. _____ + _____ Line ____

    b. _____ + _____ Line ____

    c. _____ + _____ Line ____

4. Look at these two examples of *little* from the story.

    a. In-Su is pointing at a *little* dog that is near them. (Line 9)

    b. These three *little* girls are having a really good time in the park today. (Line 10)

    In English, a noun usually adds -*s* if it is plural. What about adjectives? Is there any difference for adjectives for singular and plural?

    _____

    _____

5. What questions do you have about descriptive adjectives? _____

    _____

    _____

    _____

Grammar Lesson

Descriptive Adjectives

subject + *be* + adjective	adjective + noun
The Nile is long.	The Nile is a long river.
The Nile and the Amazon are long.	The Nile and the Amazon are long rivers.
Math is difficult.	Math is a difficult subject.
Math and science are difficult.	Math and science are difficult subjects.

Rule 1. **Descriptive adjectives** describe people or things: *a young boy; a young giraffe*.

Rule 2. A descriptive adjective tells how a person or a thing
- looks (*a red ball, a beautiful flower*),
- sounds (*a quiet person, a barking dog*),
- tastes (*a sweet cookie, a sour drink*),
- smells (*your stinky socks, fresh bread*), or
- feels (*a baby's soft skin, an itchy sweater*).

Rule 3. Descriptive adjectives can appear after *be* (*Today is* hot) or before a noun (*It is a* hot *day*).

Rule 4. Adjectives do not change for singular and plural: *a blue car; ten blue cars*

Rule 5. It is possible to put one, two, or more descriptive adjectives before a noun: *a long, difficult French test*. However, spoken English usually has zero or only one descriptive adjective before a noun: *a test* OR *a long test*. Written English may have two or more descriptive adjectives before a noun, but it is not so common. It is very rare in spoken English.

ONE-MINUTE LESSON
Adjectives are powerful words. Every time you learn a new adjective, try to use it in a short phrase or sentence. For example, the adjective *smelly* means something has a bad smell. Remember the phrase *smelly socks* or the sentence *his apartment was smelly*.

BE CAREFUL!

Common Learner Errors	Explanation
1. This ~~book interesting~~ interesting book has no photos.	Descriptive adjectives go before nouns.
2. India and China are two ~~bigs~~ big countries in Asia.	Adjectives do not add -s for plural.
3. It was a ~~long, difficult, important~~ long exam.	It is usual for a noun to have either no or just one descriptive adjective. It is possible to have two descriptive adjectives (usually in written English), but a combination of three or four descriptive adjectives is very rare.

Connecting Grammar and Vocabulary

English has thousands of adjectives, but you need to learn the most frequent adjectives. Learn this vocabulary.

20 Most Frequent Adjectives in English	
1. a good person	11. the right answer
2. my new car	12. a big classroom
3. the first reason	13. a high score
4. the last sandwich	14. a different way
5. a long trip	15. a small drink
6. a great time	16. a large t-shirt
7. a little puppy	17. the next day
8. your own room	18. an early meeting
9. my other sister	19. a young man
10. an old house	20. an important job

<u>Source</u>: World of Words, Catherine Soanes, accessed at: <u>www.oxforddictionaries.com</u>.

Common Adjectives in Phrases

a big problem	← →	a little girl
a large drink	← →	a small t-shirt
a short man	← →	a tall woman
a short meeting	← →	a long movie
a hot day	← →	a cold room
a good movie	← →	a bad idea
an old building	← →	a new car
an old woman	← →	a young person
a pretty picture	← →	an ugly snake
a fat cat	← →	a thin slice
a fat person	← →	a skinny person
a happy face	← →	a sad person
a full schedule	← →	an empty glass
a dark room	← →	a light color
a funny story	← →	a serious movie
an interesting story	← →	a boring book
a cheap ticket	← →	an expensive car
a high shelf	← →	a low place
a deep valley	← →	a shallow river
a healthy life	← →	a sick person
a rich woman	← →	a poor man
a tiny insect	← →	a huge house
a soft pillow	← →	a hard bed
an easy test	← →	a difficult question
a clean room	← →	a dirty kitchen
a safe place	← →	a dangerous situation
the same answer	← →	a different reason
an early class	← →	a late meeting
a sharp knife	← →	a dull knife
a strong animal	← →	a weak person
the top shelf	← →	the bottom shelf
antique furniture	← →	modern furniture
a public school	← →	a private school

my favorite food	a great idea	a beautiful dress
a busy day	a friendly person	a hungry baby
a free moment	a tired worker	a thirsty boy

the previous president   the current president   the future president

freezing   cold   cool   OK   warm   hot   boiling

miniscule   tiny   small   regular   big   huge   gigantic

bald   thinning hair   straight hair   wavy hair   curly hair

EXERCISE 1. *Be* and Descriptive Adjectives

Write a sentence with *is* or *are* plus one of the adjectives from the word list. Sometimes more than one answer is possible.

word list	interesting	tired	sour	cold	deep	hot
	~~expensive~~	round	huge	rich	old	sweet

1. A ticket to Rio de Janeiro ___is expensive_____.

2. The Atlantic Ocean _____.

3. Coins _____.

4. Whales and elephants _____.

5. A coin from 1879_____.

6. The weather in winter _____.

7. A summer afternoon _____.

8. People with a million dollars _____.

9. Lemon juice _____.

10. A sugar cookie _____.

11. Good movies _____.

12. At the end of every work day, our teacher _____.

Do Online Exercise 4.1. My score: _____ /10. _____ % correct.

EXERCISE 2. Describing Your Family Members

Write eight true sentences about your family members by using *is, isn't, are, aren't,* and an adjective from pages 95 and 96.

Example: My father is friendly.

1. _____

2. _____

3. _____

4. _____

5. _____

6. _____

7. _____

8. _____

EXERCISE 3. Adjective and Noun Examples in Context

Circle the adjective or noun that best completes the word combination. Then write a short example sentence using your new phrase.

1. a (big, skinny) problem *We have a big problem with our car.*

2. my (favorite, strong) holiday _____

3. a little (boy, day) _____

4. a (large, serious) movie _____

5. a (funny, low) book _____

6. a soft (shelf, towel) _____

7. a (shallow, small) drink _____

8. an (easy, empty) classroom _____

9. a deep (bed, lake) _____

10. a light (color, ticket) _____

11. a (happy, striped) blouse _____

12. a pretty (color, life) _____

13. a sharp (fork, knife) _____

14. a cute (baby, bone) _____

15. short (parks, sleeves) _____

EXERCISE 4. Increasing Adjectives in Your Vocabulary

Study the two examples for these 12 categories of adjectives. For each category, fill in two more examples of adjectives that are important for you when you want to explain something in English. Use your dictionary for help.

Color		Age		Shape	
red	_____	old	_____	round	_____
green	_____	new	_____	flat	_____

Size		Personality		Smell	
big	_____	happy	_____	stinky	_____
huge	_____	friendly	_____	fresh	_____

Time		Sound		Touch	
current	_____	noisy	_____	smooth	_____
monthly	_____	quiet	_____	sticky	_____

Taste		Nationality/Origin*		Material	
sweet	_____	American	_____	wooden	_____
juicy	_____	Turkish	_____	plastic	_____

ONE-MINUTE LESSON
Common endings for nationalities are -*an* (Mexican), -*ian* (Canadian), -*ese* (Japanese), and -*ish* (Swedish). Some of these nationality words are difficult, so check a dictionary or the Internet.

EXERCISE 5. Using *is/are* in Context

Fill in the box with *is* or *are*. Then fill in the blanks with the color adjective.

Colors

1. In the U.S., paper money | is | _____green_____ .

2. In a deck of cards, there | | four kinds of cards: heart, diamond, spade, and club. If your card | | a heart or a diamond, then you have a _____ card. However, if you have a spade or a club card, your card | | _____ .

3. A rose | | a very special flower. A rose can be many colors. Common colors for a rose | | _____, _____, and _____ .

4. Rice comes in two main colors. The most common rice | | _____ rice. However, some people prefer to eat _____ rice because they think it's better for your health.

5. The most common color for all people's eyes | | _____ . Two other possible colors | | _____ and _____ .

6. Peppermint | | a kind of candy. Peppermint | | usually _____ and _____ .

7. Wood, chocolate, and peanut butter | | different shades of _____ .

8. If toast | | _____, this means that you burned it and can't eat it.

9. The flags of Russia, Thailand, France, Norway, Chile, the U.S., and Czech Republic | | _____, _____, and _____ .

10. The Spanish flag | | _____ and _____ .

Do Online Exercise 4.2. My score: _____ /10. _____ % correct.

EXERCISE 6. Editing. Is It Correct?

If the sentence is correct, write a check mark (✔) on the line. If it is not correct, write X on the line and circle the mistake. Then change the sentence to make it correct. Write the change above the sentence. (*Hint:* There are eight sentences. Two are correct, but six have mistakes.)

My Favorite Singer

_____ 1. The last name of my favorite singer is Rippoll, but everyone knows her by her first name Shakira.

_____ 2. Shakira is a Colombia singer.

_____ 3. She is a singer famous who has a beautiful voice. In addition, she is an excellent dancer.

_____ 4. She sings in several languages. For example, she knows Spanish and the language English very well.

_____ 5. I like her song "Whenever, Wherever." Is very beautiful this song.

_____ 6. Shakira's first album was "Magia," which means "magic" in English.

_____ 7. She is a very popular all over the world.

_____ 8. Shakira donates a lot of money to help poors children in Colombia.

EXERCISE 7. Mini-Conversations

Circle the correct words in these eight mini-conversations.

1. A: What (am, is, are) the current population of Australia?

   B: Australia (am, is, are) (a really big country, a country really big), but the population (am, is, are) not so large. It (am, is, are) only 22,000,000.

2. A: Which painting do you like?

   B: Well, I like this one, but that one over there with all the flowers (am, is, are) beautiful. I'd like to buy (a very colorful painting, a painting very colorful).

3. A: Who (am, is, are) (your best friend, your friend best)?

   B: I have many really good friends, but my best friend (am, is, are) Kevin.

4. A: Do you have (cell phone service good, good cell phone service)?

   B: Yes, we like our service because our (monthly plan, plan monthly) is cheap.

5. A: What (am, is, are) hurricanes? I (am, is, are) from Colombia, and we don't have any hurricanes there.

   B: Well, a hurricane (am, is, are) (a storm tropical, a tropical storm) with very strong winds and (very heavy rain, rain very heavy).

6. A: How (am, is, are) (your apartment new, your new apartment)?

   B: It (am, is, are) great. Both two bedrooms (am, is, are) really nice.

7. A: We are going to fly to Japan on a 747. A 747 is (a huge jet, a jet huge).

   B: Yes, that (am, is, are) right. It can hold more than 400 passengers.

8. A: (Am, Is, Are) you good at math?

   B: Yes, I (am, is, are). I like math a lot. (Is easy math, Math is easy) for me.

ONE-MINUTE LESSON

Some adjectives are usually followed by a certain preposition. You have to learn these combinations. Some common examples are *good + at, interested + in, afraid + of, sorry + about, famous + for, married + to.*

EXERCISE 8. Speaking Practice: Describing with Adjectives

See page 105 for directions.

Step 1. Work with a partner. Each student should pick one of the women in the chart. Remember the name. Do not let your partner know who you have chosen. Your job is to guess the name of the person your partner picked.

Step 2. Take turns asking yes-no questions using descriptive adjectives (like *curly, striped, long*). If the answer is yes, the questioner keeps asking questions. If the answer is no, the partner can ask questions. The first person to guess the partner's person is the winner.

<u>Examples</u>: "Is she wearing a black shirt?" or "Is her hair blond?"

Common Endings for Descriptive Adjectives

-y	angry	dirty	funny	hungry	noisy	scary	sunny
	busy	easy	greedy	juicy	oily	shiny	thirsty
	cloudy	empty	happy	lazy	rainy	skinny	tiny
	crazy	fancy	healthy	lucky	ready	sleepy	ugly
	curly	filthy	heavy	messy	salty	spicy	windy
-ful	beautiful	careful	colorful	grateful	harmful	thankful	useful
-ous	curious	delicious	famous	jealous		nervous	previous
	dangerous	fabulous	hilarious	mysterious		numerous	
-al	additional	central	international	national		usual	
	casual	final	logical	several		unusual	
-ing	amazing	beginning	exciting	interesting		relaxing	
	annoying	boring	hard-working	outgoing		surprising	
-ed	amazed	bored	excited	interested		prepared	surprised
	annoyed	divorced	fried	married		cared	tired
-er	bigger	crazier	earlier	madder		smaller	thicker
	brighter	darker	heavier	nicer		stronger	weaker
	busier	deeper	lighter	shorter		taller	

<u>Rule 1.</u> Many descriptive adjectives have no special ending: *good, last, next, small.*

<u>Rule 2.</u> It is very difficult to know the correct ending to make an adjective. To change the noun *color* into an adjective, do you add **-ful** (*colorful*) or **-ous** (*colorous*) or **-y** (*colory*)? (Only *colorful* is possible.) There is no way to predict the ending. Therefore, these endings are useful to recognize adjectives, but it is difficult to use them to create adjectives correctly.

<u>Rule 3.</u> There are two ways to compare adjectives: **-er** and **more**. We use **-er** for adjectives with one-syllable (*tall → taller, cheap → cheaper*) and two-syllable adjectives that end in **-y** (*crazy → crazier, happy → happier*). We use **more** for other adjectives of two or more syllables (*common → more common, interesting → more interesting*).

EXERCISE 9. Descriptive Adjectives in Context

Fill in the blank with the correct adjectives from the box. Two of the words are not used.

word list	scared	big	grateful	international	famous	smaller
	married	oily	fried	hilarious	funny	shiny
	annoyed	tired	beautiful	dangerous	earlier	windy

1. I don't like food that is _____ or _____.

2. I don't like to fly on airplanes. When I am on any flight, I am really _____.

3. Yes, I am _____. My husband's name is Jim.

4. Today is not a good day to play tennis because it's too_____.

5. He is a really _____ person. I love his jokes. They are always
   _____.

6. After working in the yard all day, we are really _____.

7. Fireworks are _____, but they are also _____.

8. We can take the 5 o'clock bus, but if you want to take an _____
   bus, there is a departure at 3:30.

9. If you are on an _____ trip, you always need your passport.

10. Who do you think is the most _____ athlete in your country?

11. I am very _____ to you for all of your time and help.

12. This shirt is size 16. It's too _____. I need a _____
    shirt.

ONE-MINUTE LESSON

The word **too** has two different meanings: (1) *also* (*I want some coffee,* **too**), (2) *very much* (*that coffee is* **too** *hot to drink now*). In Number 2, **too** has a negative meaning. It means that something is not possible. If you ask someone if he wants to go to the store with you and he answers, *I'm* **too** *tired*, the answer is no. It is not common to use **too** with positive adjectives. We say *it's* **too** *expensive*, not *it's* **too** *cheap*.

Do Online Exercise 4.3. My score: _____ /10. _____ % correct.

EXERCISE 10. Noticing Descriptive Adjectives in Context

Read this TV weather report for Boston. Underline the descriptive adjectives in each sentence. The number in parentheses indicates the number of descriptive adjectives in that sentence.

The Weather in Boston on December 20th

1. Good morning, Boston! This afternoon the weather will be sunny. (1)

2. Today will be cooler than yesterday. (1)

3. The high temperature today will be in the mid 50s. (2)

4. In general, we can expect light but steady winds will be from the west 5 to 10 mph. (2)

5. We may have some strong gusts in the early hours of this afternoon. (2)

6. Tonight will be cloudy with a low temperature in the upper 30s. (3)

7. For tomorrow, you can expect a welcome change from our current cold weather. (3)

8. The sky will clear completely, and we can expect lots of sunshine and mild temperatures for tomorrow and the entire weekend. (2)

ONE-MINUTE LESSON
In informal language, we can use **lots** instead of **a lot**. You might hear a friend say, *There are* **lots** *of new movies at the theater.* You should not use **lots** in formal or academic language.

Do Online Exercise 4.4. My score: _____ /10. _____ % correct.

EXERCISE 11. Speaking Practice: Talking about the Weather

Part 1.

Work with a partner to choose a city that you have never visited. Find a current weather report in a newspaper or on the Internet like the one below for that city, and bring it to class. Talk about any new vocabulary that you find, especially descriptive adjectives. How many new descriptive adjectives can you find?

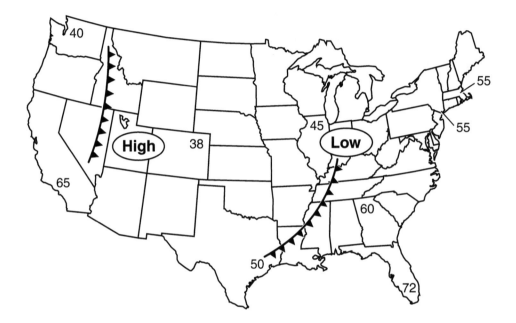

Part 2.

Now work with a partner or in small groups. Take turns telling about the weather in your city. Can other students understand your oral report?

EXERCISE 12. Sentence Study for Critical Reading

Read the numbered sentences. Then read the three answer choices, and place a check mark in the yes or no boxes in front of each sentence to show if that answer is true based on the information in the original sentence. If there is not enough information to mark something as yes, then mark it as no. Remember that more than one true answer is possible.

1. To me, this movie is interesting, but that movie is more interesting.

    ☐ yes ☐ no   a. There are two movies.

    ☐ yes ☐ no   b. One of the movies is very bad.

    ☐ yes ☐ no   c. The speaker prefers the first movie.

2. The black wool sweater is more expensive than the white cotton sweatshirt, but that is not surprising because wool costs more than cotton.

    ☐ yes ☐ no   a. The sweatshirt is white.

    ☐ yes ☐ no   b. There are two kinds of sweaters.

    ☐ yes ☐ no   c. The sweatshirt is made of cotton.

3. Several of the Colombian students in my class are from Bogota.

    ☐ yes ☐ no   a. More than one student is from Colombia.

    ☐ yes ☐ no   b. More than one student is from Bogota.

    ☐ yes ☐ no   c. Most of the students in my class are from Colombia.

4. Carla is an excellent student. She's good at math, science, and English.

    ☐ yes ☐ no   a. Her best class is math.

    ☐ yes ☐ no   b. Her best class is science.

    ☐ yes ☐ no   c. Her best class is English.

5. The Spanish flag is yellow and red, the Argentinean flag is blue and white, and the Korean flag is white, red, blue, and black.

    ☐ yes ☐ no   a. The Spanish flag has two colors that the other two flags do not have.

    ☐ yes ☐ no   b. There is one common color in all three countries' flags.

    ☐ yes ☐ no   c. The Korean flag and the Argentinean flag have two colors in common: blue and white.

6. Two delicious rice dishes are jambalaya and fried rice. Jambalaya is a very spicy dish of rice, seafood, and meat from Louisiana. Fried rice is a mixture of rice, meat, and vegetables that is fried very quickly. Fried rice is popular in Malaysia, Indonesia, Thailand, and China.

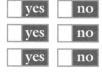 a. Both dishes contain rice.

[ ] yes [ ] no   b. Both dishes contain meat.

[ ] yes [ ] no   c. Both dishes are spicy.

7. The house at 338 Landon Street is for sale. It is a big house with two stories. The house is white, and the roof is gray. It has four large bedrooms, two bathrooms, a spacious living room, and a nice kitchen with modern appliances.

[ ] yes [ ] no   a. The living room is the same size as the kitchen.

[ ] yes [ ] no   b. The first bathroom is the same size as the second bathroom.

[ ] yes [ ] no   c. This is a white house with a black roof.

8. Argentina is bigger than Mexico. Saudi Arabia is bigger than Mexico. Argentina is bigger than Saudi Arabia. Australia is bigger than Argentina. Mexico is bigger than Peru.

[ ] yes [ ] no   a. Saudi Arabia is bigger than Peru.

[ ] yes [ ] no   b. Mexico is bigger than Argentina.

[ ] yes [ ] no   c. Australia is bigger than any of the other five countries.

 ONE-MINUTE LESSON

For comparisons, we use the preposition **than**. We say, *Mexico is bigger* **than** *Panama* or *I have more books* **than** *you*. Be sure to use **than**, not another word. Common mistakes include **that** or **from**. Only **than** is correct for comparisons.

REVIEW **EXERCISE 13. Review Test 1: Multiple Choice**

Circle the letter of the correct answer. Some are conversations.

1. She has three _____, and all of them are 100% wool."

   a. beautiful sweaters   c. sweaters beautiful

   b. beautifuls sweaters   d. sweaters beautifuls

2. My hobby is collecting old stamps. I especially like _____ stamps from Bhutan.

   a. coloring   c. colorful

   b. colorous   d. colory

3. The _____ belong to me.

   a. blue card   c. blue cards
   b. cards blues   d. cards blue

4. Mrs. Walton is an excellent manager. She is very _____.

   a. hard-working   c. hard work

   b. hard worker   d. work hard

5. "Where are the boys?"

   "In front of the TV in the living room. Their _____ is on now."

   a. favorite program TV   c. program TV favorite

   b. favorite TV program   d. program favorite TV

6. "Do you think grammar class is easy?"

   "No, it isn't. In my opinion, grammar _____."

   a. the most difficult class   c. is the most difficult class

   b. the class most difficult   d. is the class most difficult

7. If something is hilarious, it means that it is very _____.

   a. usual   c. lazy

   b. funny   d. outgoing

8. The adjective *spicy* is used for

   a. special things   c. weather

   b. special people   d. food

EXERCISE 14. Review Test 2: Production and Evaluation

Part 1.
Read this short passage. Put the words in parentheses in the correct order, and then fill in the blanks.

In general, there are ❶ _____ (*kinds of people two*).

Some people are ❷ _____ (*and quiet shy very*). They do

not like to be around ❸ _____ (*people many*). They usually

have only ❹ _____ (*a close friends number of small*).

These people are called introverts. ❺ _____ (*people other*) like

to talk. They enjoy meeting ❻ _____ (*new people*). They like

to socialize. ❼ _____ (*are they outgoing*). They

usually have ❽ _____ (*large a number*) of friends and

acquaintances. These people are called extroverts. What kind of person are you?

Do you think you are an introvert or an extrovert?

Part 2.
Read the short passage. There are six mistakes. Circle the mistakes, and write the correction above each mistake.

The language French is widely spoken in
Africa. Twenty Africans countries use French as
their language official. Some important French-
speaking countries in Africa are Ivory Coast,
Madagascar, Mali, Senegal, and Zaire. These
Africans nations were French or Belgian colonies,
but they became independents nations in the early
1960s. A large part of the population in the
northern countries African of Morocco, Algeria,
and Tunisia also speaks French.

EXERCISE 15. Reading Practice: International Weather Reports

Read the information about the weather in these three world cities. Then fill in the chart, and answer the six comprehension questions on page 114. The grammar from this chapter is underlined for you.

Cairo, Egypt

December 20

Today's weather will be <u>clear</u> and very <u>nice</u>, which is <u>normal</u> for this time of the year. The <u>high</u> temperature today will be 68, and the <u>low</u> temperature tonight will be 53. The weather tomorrow will be <u>similar</u>, but we will see a few clouds in the <u>morning</u> sky. Tomorrow's temperatures will be 1 to 2 degrees lower. There is no chance of rain. We don't expect any rain until possibly <u>next</u> week. This is <u>great</u> weather for the locals and the tourists!

Singapore

December 20

It's the <u>rainy</u> season, so our weather today will be <u>cloudy</u> and <u>wet</u> with a very <u>high</u> chance of a thunderstorm or two. Some thunderstorms may be <u>severe</u>, so please be <u>prepared</u>. The high today will be 84, and our low will be ten degrees less. The chance of rain is 70%. We expect 1 to 2 inches of rain. Most of the rain will leave our area right around sunset. Tomorrow will be a repeat of today with <u>cloudy</u> skies in the morning and <u>wet</u> weather from noon on.

Vancouver, Canada

December 20

The weather today will be a mix of clouds and sun until <u>mid</u> morning. By noon, the sky will be <u>cloudy</u>, and we will have a 40% chance of snow. After the <u>cold</u> front passes, we can expect mostly <u>sunny</u> weather, but it may be a bit <u>windy</u> at times. Expect <u>cold</u> temperatures. The <u>high</u> temperature today will be around 35, and our <u>low</u> tonight will be 30. However, we predict <u>beautiful</u> weather for the weekend. We'll have <u>sunny</u> skies, so get <u>ready</u> for your <u>favorite</u> <u>outdoor</u> activities.

City	High Temperature	Low Temperature	Rain or Snow?	Tomorrow's Forecast?
Cairo				
Singapore				
Vancouver				

1. Which city will have very cold weather today?

   _____

2. If you want to play tennis today, which city is the best place?

   _____

3. Which two cities can expect the same weather tomorrow as they do today?

   _____

4. Will it rain tomorrow morning in Singapore? In Cairo? In Vancouver? How do you know?

   _____

   _____

   _____

5. Which two statements are true?
   a. The high temperature in Cairo today will be warmer than the high temperature in Singapore.
   b. The high temperature in Vancouver today will be warmer than the high temperature in Cairo.
   c. The low temperature in Singapore today will be warmer than the high temperature in Cairo.
   d. The low temperature in Cairo today will be warmer than the high temperature in Vancouver.

6. Different people like different kinds of places and different kinds of weather. If you could visit one of these three cities today, which one would you like to visit and why?

   _____

   _____

   _____

   _____

   _____

EXERCISE 16. Vocabulary Practice: Word Knowledge

Circle the word or phrase that is most closely related to the word or phrase on the left. Use a dictionary to check the meaning of words you do not know.

Vocabulary	Answer Choices	
1. a giraffe	an animal	a bicycle
2. stinky	a bad smell	a good smell
3. middle	a d p b c f w	a d w c f p b
4. a joke	angry	funny
5. sour	a flower	a lemon
6. shallow	not deep	not weak
7. a pillow	in the bedroom	in the kitchen
8. an insect	usually huge	usually tiny
9. bald	no color	no hair
10. to point	with your hair	with your hand
11. rude	not polite	not poor
12. itchy	a good feeling	a bad feeling
13. bigger	27	72
14. an occupation	a doctor	a number
15. height	dark/light	short/tall
16. a subject	in a school	in a whale
17. coins	food	money
18. boiling	hot water	cold weather
19. dirty	not clean	not different
20. an exam	a park	a test
21. twins	one	two
22. quiet	no taste	no sound
23. empty	not full	not serious
24. I'd like to be there now	I am not there now	I am there now
25. a roof	on top of a house	on top of a shelf
26. donate	take	give
27. main	most careful	most important
28. monthly	every month	at the end of the month
29. fireworks	colorful	annoyed
30. scared	afraid	always
31. mild	not high, not low	not big, not small
32. skinny	not fat	not soft
33. two stories	two floors	two sizes
34. appliances	in a car	in a kitchen

EXERCISE 17. Vocabulary Practice: Collocations

Fill in each blank with the answer on the right that most naturally completes the phrase on the left. If necessary, use a dictionary to check the meaning of words you do not know.

Phrase	Answer Choices	
1. my favorite _____	holiday	shelf
2. an outgoing _____	sweater	person
3. _____ hair	cousin	straight
4. a dark _____	color	sandwich
5. is wearing a _____	roof	shirt
6. a striped _____	shirt	whale
7. _____ sleeves	short	tall
8. _____ a good time	have	make
9. a sweet _____	cookie	sock
10. fresh _____	bread	furniture
11. a huge _____	morning	problem
12. a combination _____ words	by	of
13. a boring _____	movie	pencil
14. _____ same answer	a	the
15. a safe _____	place	tree
16. a _____ school	curly	public
17. have a free _____	airplane	moment
18. a _____ idea	great	round
19. wavy _____	cousins	hair
20. the current _____	mountain	weather
21. a _____ afternoon	juicy	summer
22. a _____ ring	hilarious	shiny
23. a _____ cookie	grateful	sugar
24. at the end _____ a day	for	of
25. a deck of _____	cards	parts
26. a wool _____	flag	sweater
27. a fancy _____	baby	restaurant
28. bigger _____	from	than
29. a _____ person	hard-working	spicy
30. over _____	piece of art	there
31. good _____ something	at	to
32. in _____ ,	addition	several
33. a piece of _____	art	homework

EXERCISE 18. Writing Practice: Your Opinion about a Current Topic

Part 1. Editing Student Writing

Read these sentences about one student's opinion about a current topic. Circle the 15 errors. Then write the number of the sentence with the error next to the type of error. (Some sentences may have more than one error.)

_____ a. no subject   _____ d. word order

_____ b. *am/is/are* (wrong form)   _____ e. adjective ending

_____ c. no verb   _____ f. capital letter

Texting and Driving
1. Texting is useful, but texting when you drive are a huge problem.
2. I think this a very bad idea.
3. for drivers, this is very danger.
4. Can have a accident terrible.
5. Every year there is hundreds of horribles accidents because people text when they drive.
6. maybe we need a law special to stop texting and driving.
7. In my opinion, this foolish combination of texting and driving really bad.
8. smart drivers know they might kill another being human.
9. Texting is popular. However, is a problem serious in our country today.

Part 2. Original Student Writing

Now write some sentences about a current topic or idea that you support or disagree with.

Unit 5

Past Tense of *Be*

 Discover the Grammar

Read this conversation between an adult and a teenager. Then answer the five questions.

Line	
1	**Family friend**: Hello, Chris, do you remember me? I was your neighbor.
2	**Chris**: Of course I remember you. Hello, Mrs. Eagleton.
3	**Family friend**: So. . . . you're 11 years old now, right?
4	**Chris**: No, I was 11 three years ago. I'm 14 now.
5	**Family friend**: 14! Oh, my! So you're in middle school now.
6	**Chris**: Actually, I was in middle school last year. Now I'm in high
7	school. I'm in 9th grade.
8	**Family friend**: Oh, of course. And do you still play soccer? Your team is the
9	Wildcats, right?
10	**Chris**: Oh, no, I'm not on that team now.
11	**Family friend**: Really? But they're champions!
12	**Chris**: Well, they were champions three years ago. They were
13	champions when I was in middle school. They're not
14	champions now. But I'm on the basketball team at school
15	this year.

16	**Family friend**: Basketball? That's a change!
17	**Chris**: Yes, well, I was pretty short, but I'm tall now.
18	**Family friend**: Yes, I can see that. You are much taller than the last time I
19	saw you.
20	**Chris**: Well, it has been very good to see you. I need to go do my
21	homework now. Good-bye, Mrs. Eagleton.
22	**Family friend**: Bye, Chris. I'll see you . . . in a few more years, I guess!

1. Are these things true about Chris now, in the past, or both? Put a check mark (✔) in the correct column.

	now	past	**both now and past**
a. 11 years old			
b. in high school			
c. on the soccer team			
d. on the basketball team			
e. short			

2. Underline the five examples of *was* and *were*. Can you explain when we use these two words? (Why not *am, is, are?*)

_____

_____

3. Write N if the verb shows what is true now. Write P if the verb shows what was true in the past.

   a. *am* _____   b. *are* _____   c. *was* _____   d. *is* _____   e. *were* _____

4. Look at these sentences from Line 4: *I was 11 three years ago. I'm 14 now.* What is the meaning of *ago?* What is the pattern for *ago?*

_____

_____

5. What questions do you have about *was/were* or *am/is/are?*

_____

_____

_____

Grammar Lesson

Simple Past Tense of *Be*: Affirmative

KEY
3

Singular	Plural
I was in the park yesterday.	Maria and I were in the park yesterday. We were in the park.
You were my first friend here.	You and Mike were my first friends here. You were my first friends here.
Miguel was at work last night. He was there from 5 PM to 11 PM.	Miguel and Marcos were at work last night. They were there from 5 PM until 11 PM.
Pam was a good swimmer in middle school. She was very fast.	Pam and Hank were good swimmers in middle school. They were very fast.
Gasoline was cheap in 1999. It was cheap in 1999.	Gasoline and food were cheap in 1999. They were cheap in 1999.

Rule 1. In the simple past tense, be has two forms: was, were.

Rule 2. We use was with *I, he, she, it*; were with *you, we, they*.

Rule 3. It is necessary to include a subject (noun or pronoun) with was and were.

Rule 4. If there is an adjective after was or were, the correct word order is subject + *was/were* + adjective.

Rule 5. Common time expressions for simple past tense include yesterday, last _____ (last week, last month), and _____ ago (two years ago).

⚠ BE CAREFUL!

Common Learner Errors	Explanation
1. Carlos ~~is~~ was in Mexico last month.	Do not use am, is, or are in past tense sentences.
2. I ~~born~~ was born in 1991.	Remember to use was or were.
3. Thomas Edison invented the light bulb. ~~Was~~ He was a very clever person.	Use a subject with am, is, and are.
4. My parents ~~was~~ were in Korea last summer.	Use was for I, he, she, and it: use were for you, we, and they.
5. Today's weather was not good. ~~Was humid the air~~ The air was humid.	If there is an adjective after was or were, the correct word order is subject + *was/were* + adjective.

EXERCISE 1. Affirmative *was/were*

Fill in the blanks with the correct forms of *be: was* or *were*.

1. you _____
2. Mary _____
3. you and Mary _____
4. your husband _____
5. the man and I _____
6. that computer _____
7. Lim, Fong, and Bo _____
8. my sister _____
9. my sisters _____
10. Flight 227 _____

11. we _____
12. yesterday's newspaper _____
13. the book _____
14. the chapter _____
15. the chapters _____
16. the chapters in this book _____
17. Ann and Mary _____
18. Ted, Bob, and I _____
19. Ted and Bob _____
20. the people _____

Do Online Exercise 5.1. My score: _____ /10. _____ % correct.

EXERCISE 2. Affirmative *Be* in Context

Read these sentences, and then fill in the blanks with *is, are, was,* or *were.*

The World in 1900 and the World Now

1. Today the population of Japan _____ approximately 130,000,000. However, the population of Japan _____ about 44,000,000 in 1900.

2. Finland _____ a country in northern Europe. In 1900, Finland _____ part of Russia.

3. In 1900, Ireland _____ a part of the United Kingdom. Today Ireland _____ an independent nation.

4. In 1900, there _____ 45 states in the U.S. Today there _____ 50 states.

5. The capital of Brazil today _____ Brasilia. However, the capital of this South American country in 1900 _____ Rio de Janeiro.

6. Today there _____ two Koreas: North Korea and South Korea. In 1900, however, there _____ only one Korea.

EXERCISE 3. Affirmative *was/were* in Context

Fill in the first blank with *was or were*, and fill in the second blank with true information to complete the sentence.

1. When I was a child, my favorite food _____ _____.

2. My first pet _____ a _____. Its name _____

    _____.

3. When I was in school, my two best subjects _____ _____ and

    _____ .

4. When I was in school, my worst subject _____ _____.

5. My breakfast this morning _____ _____.

6. The weather last Saturday _____ _____.

7. My great-grandfather's name _____ _____.

8. The name of the last movie that I saw _____ _____.

9. The titles of the last two books that I read _____ _____ and

    _____.

10. The last time that I interviewed for a job _____ _____.

    (*Hint:* Fill in the second blank with a time expression.)

11. In my opinion, the three most important inventions of the last one hundred years

    _____ _____, _____, and _____.

12. In my opinion, a very important person in the history of my country _____

    _____.

Do Online Exercise 5.2. My score: _____ /10. _____ % correct.

EXERCISE 4. Editing. Is It Correct?

If the sentence is correct, write a check mark (✔) on the line. If it is not correct, write X on the line and circle the mistake. Then change the sentence to make it correct. Write the change above the sentence. (*Hint:* There are eight sentences. Two are correct, but six have mistakes.)

Two Famous U.S. Presidents

_____ 1. Who was George Washington and Abraham Lincoln? Do you know?

_____ 2. Washington is the first president of the United States.

_____ 3. Abraham Lincoln is the sixteenth president.

_____ 4. Lincoln was president during the Civil War.

_____ 5. Washington is born in 1732.

_____ 6. Lincoln were born in 1809.

_____ 7. Lincoln is born ten years after Washington died.

_____ 8. Washington died in 1799.

George Washington

Abraham Lincoln

- born February 22, 1732
- died December 14, 1799
- 1st U.S. President

- born February 12, 1809
- died April 15, 1865
- 16th U.S. President

EXERCISE 5. Pair Speaking: Talking about the Past

Step 1. Work with a partner. Decide who is Student A and who is Student B. Work only in that box.

Step 2. Number the boxes from 1 to 8 in any order. Do not number them in order.

Step 3. Fill in the blanks with *was* or *were* to make correct sentences. Check your answers with another student who did the same part (A or B) as you.

Step 4. Now work with a partner with a different letter. Student B will close his or her book. Student A will read out all eight items in numerical order. Student B must complete Student A's items correctly. Say the word *blank* for the line. For example, Student A will say, "You blank here" and Student B must say, "You are here." If this is correct, Student A says, "That's correct." If this is not correct, Student A says, "That isn't correct. Try again" and repeats the item. When all of the items are finished, Student B will read out his or her eight items, and Student A will answer.

Student A

☐. You _____ here last week.   ☐. He _____ lucky in 2009.

☐. My last vacation _____ expensive.   ☐. Rachel _____ here ten minutes ago.

☐. The giraffes at the zoo _____ very tall. ☐. My old apartment _____ too small.

☐. Yesterday _____ my birthday.   ☐. Karen and I _____ good friends.

Student B

☐. Joe and Pam _____ late.   ☐. The teacher _____ sick yesterday.

☐. Fabio and Paolo _____ at work last   ☐. We _____ in Brazil last year.
night.

☐. The boys _____ in class yesterday.   ☐. My first car _____ silver.

☐. I _____ really hungry this morning.   ☐. The weather last week _____ hot.

 **Simple Past Tense of *Be*: Negative**

Making a negative statement with verb *be* is easy. Study these two steps:		
Step 1	Check for verb *be*.	Yesterday's exam was very difficult.
Step 2	Put *not* after *be*.	Yesterday's exam was not very difficult.
Contractions are possible: was not → wasn't were not → weren't		

Other examples:

Statement	Question
I was sick yesterday. →	I was not sick yesterday.
→	I wasn't sick yesterday.
You were on the phone for an hour. →	You were not on the phone for an hour.
→	You weren't on the phone for an hour.
My ticket was more than $1,000. →	My ticket was not more than $1,000.
→	My ticket wasn't more than $1,000.

<u>Rule 1</u>. We use the word **not** to make a negative sentence with the verb be: was not, were not.

<u>Rule 2</u>. It is possible to use contractions for was not and were not: wasn't, weren't.

⚠ BE CAREFUL!

Common Learner Errors	Explanation
1. The dessert ~~no was~~ was not too sweet.	Do not use no was or no were.
2. I ~~don't was~~ wasn't here yesterday.	Do not use don't, doesn't, or didn't with was and were.
3. California, Texas, and ~~Alaska not~~ Alaska were not U.S. states in 1800.	Remember to include was or were.

EXERCISE 6. Negative *was/were:* Information Game

How much world information do you know? Write T for true by the five true statements and F for false by the five false statements. For the false statements, make the verb negative, and then explain the true information on the line below the false sentence.

Example: Columbus ~~was~~ wasn't born in 1400.

He was born in 1451.

_____   1. The 2010 Winter Olympic Games were in Tokyo.

_____

_____   2. Alexander Graham Bell was the inventor of the first telephone.

_____

_____   3. Barack Obama was born in 1971.

_____

_____   4. The first person to walk on the moon was Russian.

_____

_____   5. William Shakespeare was born in 1564.

_____

_____   6. Mozart was from Austria.

_____

_____   7. In the first United States, there were 13 states.

_____

_____   8. Corazon Aquino was the first woman president of Vietnam.

_____

_____   9. The Wright brothers were from the U.S.

_____

_____   10. The 1896 Olympic Games were in Paris.

_____

Do Online Exercise 5.3. My score: _____ /10. _____ % correct.

Simple Past Tense of *Be*: Making a Question

Making a past question with verb *be* is easy. Study these three steps:		
Step 1	Check for verb be.	Yesterday's exam was very difficult.
Step 2	Move be to the front of the sentence.	was yesterday's exam very difficult.
Step 3	Use a capital letter for the first word of the question, and change the period (.) to a question mark (?).	Was yesterday's exam very difficult?

Other examples:

Statement		Question
I was right.	→	Was I in your chair?
You were tired after the game.	→	Were you tired after the game?
We were in France in 2008.	→	Were we in France in 2008?

<u>Rule 1.</u> To make a question with was or were, begin the question with was or were.

<u>Rule 2.</u> In a question, the word after was or were is a noun or pronoun (the subject).

BE CAREFUL!

Common Learner Errors	Explanation
1. ~~Did you were~~ Were you born in 1980?	Do not begin was/were questions with do, does, or did.
2. ~~You were~~ Were you with your friends yesterday?	In writing, do not forget to begin was/were questions with was or were. NOTE: In speaking, it is common to use statement word order in a question.
3. ~~Was very expensive the book?~~ Was the book very expensive?	If there is an adjective with was or were, the correct word order is was/were + subject + adjective + ?

EXERCISE 7. *Was/Were* in Email

Read this email message from Ana to her brother Pablo. Fill in the blanks with the correct form of the verb *be*. Sometimes you will have to use a negative form.

Date: Mon. 3 May 2010 12:09:45 -0400 (EDT)
From: anafrommexico@intl.com
To: pablo1555@housethenet.com
Subject: We miss you!!!

Pablo,

Where ❶ _____ you last night? I tried and tried to call you, but you

❷ _____ home. Please write me back soon so that I know you that

❸ _____ OK now. Hey, here ❹ _____ some news from

home. Mama ❺ _____ sick last week. She was so sick that I took her to

the doctor's office. We ❻ _____ at his office for 4 hours. She's OK now,

but I think she misses you very much. You live so far away, and she loves you so much.

Please call her soon, OK?

So, how ❼ _____ you your big math test last week? How

❽ _____ your French test before that? I really hope your grades on

those tests ❾ _____ so bad. Hey, when ❿ _____ your

last visit home? You need to come home. You need to see your family. Pablo, we miss

you a lot. Write me back soon, and remember to call Mama.

I love you,

Ana

ONE-MINUTE LESSON
For commands, we use the simple base form of the verb: **Write** *me back soon or* **Remember** *to call Mom.* If you want to be more polite, use the word **please**: **Please** *write me back soon.* If you want to be more formal, you can use **would you please**: **Would you please** *remember to call Mom?*

Do Online Exercise 5.4. My score: _____ /10. _____ % correct.

Simple Past Tense of *Be*: Questions with Full and Short Answers

Answering a *be* question with a short answer is easy. Study these four steps:		
Step 1	Listen for a question that begins with was or were.	Was yesterday's exam very difficult?
Step 2	Decide if the answer is yes or no.	No
Step 3	Use a pronoun for the noun subject.	No, it
Step 4	Repeat the form of be that is in the question. (Add not for negative.)	No, it was not.

Other examples:

Questions	Full Answers	Short Answers
Were you sleepy last night?	Yes, I was sleepy last night. No, I was not sleepy last night.	Yes, I was. No, I was not.
Were the apple pies hot?	Yes, the apple pies were hot. No, the apple pies were not hot.	Yes, they were. No, they weren't.

<u>Rule 1.</u> In short answers with be, use the correct form of be (was, were) for the subject.

<u>Rule 2.</u> In an affirmative short answer, do not use a contraction.

BE CAREFUL!

Common Learner Errors	Explanation
1. Was Ning home last night? No, he ~~did not~~ was not.	Do not use do/does/did as a short answer for was/were questions.

    Do Online Exercise 5.5. My score: _____ /10. _____ % correct.

EXERCISE 8. Mini-Conversations

Circle the correct words in these eight mini-conversations.

1. A: (Was, Were) you a good student in high school?

   B: Well, this may surprise you, but yes, I (was, were) always good in school.

2. A: How old (was, were) your husband when you met him?

   B: Mark (was, were) 22, and I (was, were) a year older. Why do you ask?

3. A: You visited three countries on your trip last summer, right?

   B: Yes, I went to New Zealand, Australia, and Singapore. All three (was, were) very interesting, but New Zealand (was, were) the most beautiful.

4. A: How much (was, were) those pencils?

   B: The pencils (was, were) on sale. They (was, were) twenty-five cents a piece, but a box of ten (was, were) only two dollars.

5. A: Hey, here is a photo of our old house. This is where my brothers and I (was, were) born and grew up.

   B: Wow, you (wasn't, weren't) born in a hospital?

6. A: What (was, were) the low temperature last night?

   B: I am not sure, but I think it (was, were) about 15 degrees.

7. A: The country of Yugoslavia does not exist any longer. Do you know where it (was, were)?

   B: Yes, I do. We studied this in our geography class. Yugoslavia (was, were) in southeastern Europe between Greece and Austria. Slovenia, Croatia, and Serbia are independent countries today, but these nations (was, were) part of Yugoslavia in the last century.

8. A: How (was, were) your interview last Friday? Did everything go well?

   B: I think it (was, were) pretty good. The manager telephoned me to ask for a second interview next week, so that's a good sign, right?

ONE-MINUTE LESSON

The word **so** has different meanings: (1) very (*It is so cold in this room*), (2) result (*I need cash,* **so** *I need to find an ATM*), (3) reason (*Our teacher marks our mistakes* **so** *we can improve our English*), and (4) yes (*I think* **so**). Punctuation: When **so** means result, we use a comma (as in example Number 8B).

EXERCISE 9. Speaking Practice: Guessing Past Information

Interview a student in your class. Choose any four of the eight questions. Write the questions on the lines before you do the interview. Make a prediction about how many yes answers your partner will give to your questions.

Questions
Were you a good student in elementary school?
When you were a child, was your favorite food a vegetable?
Were you born in a hospital?
Was the TV on last night when you went to sleep?
Was your first pet a dog?
In school, were you good at math?
Was your cell phone bill last month more than $100?

Student's name: _____   Prediction YES _____   NO _____

Question 1: _____

Answer: Your prediction: _____   His/Her real answer _____

Question 2: _____

Answer: Your prediction: _____   His/Her real answer _____

Question 3: _____

Answer: Your prediction: _____   His/Her real answer _____

Question 4: _____

Answer: Your prediction: _____   His/Her real answer _____

More practice: Now do this exercise again with another student. Use some of the same questions or make your own original questions. Practice using *was* and *were*.

EXERCISE 10. Sentence Study for Critical Reading

Read the numbered sentences. Then read the three answer choices and place a check mark in the yes or no boxes in front of each sentence to show if that answer is true based on the information in the original sentence. If there is not enough information to mark something as yes, then mark it as no. Remember that more than one true answer is possible.

1. What a wonderful dinner my mom cooked! The steaks and the cake were delicious, and the broccoli salad was excellent.

   ☐ yes ☐ no   a. There was broccoli in the salad.

   ☐ yes ☐ no   b. My parents cooked the dinner.

   ☐ yes ☐ no   c. The cake was not very good.

2. *Keith:* "How was your picnic on Sunday?"
   Elena: "We had a good time. Diana and a few other friends went with me."
   Keith: "The weather was really good on Sunday."
   Elena: "Yes, it was perfect for an afternoon picnic."

   ☐ yes ☐ no   a. The picnic was on Saturday.

   ☐ yes ☐ no   b. Only three people were at the picnic.

   ☐ yes ☐ no   c. The weather on Sunday afternoon was great.

3. My job begins at 9 AM Monday through Friday. Yesterday all of the office workers were on time except for Nathan.

   ☐ yes ☐ no   a. Nathan arrived after 9 AM.

   ☐ yes ☐ no   b. The other workers arrived at the office before Nathan.

   ☐ yes ☐ no   c. I don't go to the office on Saturday.

4. The last time I went to see a movie was about two months ago.

   ☐ yes ☐ no   a. I saw a movie about two months ago.

   ☐ yes ☐ no   b. The movie was two hours long.

   ☐ yes ☐ no   c. This sentence is talking about the past.

5. My friends weren't happy with their test scores

   ☐ yes ☐ no   a. Their grades were good.

   ☐ yes ☐ no   b. They didn't receive grades.

   ☐ yes ☐ no   c. They don't want to make the same grades on the next test.

6. Unfortunately, my car wasn't in the garage during the heavy rainstorm.

   ☐ yes ☐ no   a. Now my car is wet.

   ☐ yes ☐ no   b. Now my car is very hot.

   ☐ yes ☐ no   c. Now my car is not working well.

7. Leslie was the winner of the bowling tournament last Saturday. In fact, her score was a record for the tournament.

   ☐ yes ☐ no   a. Leslie was happy about this.

   ☐ yes ☐ no   b. Leslie was angry about this.

   ☐ yes ☐ no   c. Leslie was sick after this happened.

8. *Bob:*   "How was your flight? Did you have a good seat?"

   Jim: "My seat was 21A. It was a window seat, so I was able to see everything."

   Lynn: "My seat was 21C. I was sitting next to the aisle."

   ☐ yes ☐ no   a. Jim and Bob were on the same plane.

   ☐ yes ☐ no   b. Lynn and Bob were on the same plane.

   ☐ yes ☐ no   c. Bob, Jim, and Lynn were on the same plane.

ONE-MINUTE LESSON

on vs **in** for transportation: In general, we use **on** for all transportation: **on** *a plane*, **on** *a bus*, **on** *a ship*, **on** *a motorcycle*, **on** *a bike*. The exception is for cars and trucks: **in** *my car*, **in** *a truck*. (You can also use **by** + transportation without *a, an, my*, etc.: **by** *plane*, **by** *car*.)

Do Online Exercise 5.6. My score: _____ /10. _____ % correct.

EXERCISE 11. Speaking Practice: Identifying a Famous Person

Step 1. Work with a partner. Each student chooses one famous person who is no longer alive. Be sure to choose someone that you are sure that your partner knows about.

Step 2. Take turns asking yes-no questions about the person. Your job is to guess the name of your partner's mystery famous person. Use *was* and *were* when possible. If the answer is yes, the questioner continues asking questions. If the answer is no, the partner can ask questions. The first person to guess the famous person is the winner.

Examples: "Was your person a man?" or "Was your person a politician?"

Write your famous person's name here: _____

Here are some useful questions:

- Was your person a man? a woman?

- Was your person a politician? a singer? an actor? an inventor? an educator? an athlete?

- Was your person over the age of 50 (40, 60) when he or she died?

- Was your person from Latin America? Asia? the United States? Canada? etc.

- Was your person killed?

- Was your person famous for an event? a product? a song? an invention?

- Was your person tall? short?

- Was your person alive in 1800? 1900? 2000?

ONE-MINUTE LESSON
in, at, on for time: Use **in** with years (**in** *2015*). We also use **in** for months (**in** *June*) and seasons (**in** *summer*). We use **at** with clock time (**at** *2:30*) and **on** with days (**on** *Monday*). For information about **at/on/in** for *time*, see pages 268–70 in Unit 10.

REVIEW   **EXERCISE 12. Review Test 1: Multiple Choice**

Circle the letter of the correct answer. Some are conversations.

1. "Was the movie good?"

   "_____ I enjoyed it very much."

      a. No, was not good.   c. No, it wasn't.

      b. Yes, it was.   d. Yes, I was.

2. The name on all of the books _____ Mary D. Smith.

      a. was   c. were

      b. it was   d. they were

3. "I'm so tired today."

   "_____ tired yesterday, too?"

      a. Was I   c. Am I

      b. Were you   d. Are you

4. "Was Raihan in math class yesterday?"

   "I'm not sure, but I think she _____ there."

      a. is   c. are

      b. was   d. were

5. "_____ at Linda's house fun?"

   "Yes, it was. We had a good time there."

      a. The party was   c. Was the party

      b. The people were   d. Were the people

6. "Was the bus trip very long?"

   "Yes, it was. _____"

      a. The driver was extremely tired.   c. I wasn't tired.

      b. The driver wasn't extremely tired. d. The driver and I weren't tired.

7. "How was the beach yesterday?"

   "Wonderful. It wasn't very hot, and the water _____ very clear. It was great."

      a. are   c. were

      b. is   d. was

8. "Were all the answers on your test correct?"

   "No, _____. Number 7 was wrong."

      a. they were not   c. they are were

      b. it isn't   d. it wasn't

REVIEW > **EXERCISE 13. Review Test 2: Production and Evaluation**

Part 1.

Read this short passage. Fill in the blanks with a form of *was* or *were*.

Joe and I went to see a movie last night. We both liked the movie a lot. Joe

❶ _____ really happy because our tickets ❷ _____ not

expensive! A ticket at that theater is usually $9 for one person, but last night a

ticket ❸ _____ only $3. The movie ❹ _____ very good. The

main character died at the end of this movie, so the ending ❺ _____

sad. We both agreed that it ❻ _____ a very powerful movie. At the

end of the movie, Joe and I ❼ _____ glad we went to see that movie.

Part 2.

Read this short passage. There are five mistakes. Circle the mistakes, and write the correction
above each mistake.

When I was a little boy, my best pet was a cat. My cat's name is Sammy.

Sammy was a beautiful cat. His face was white, and his ears are black. His body is

black and white. Sammy liked to play outside. He is a really good pet. I have a

picture of Sammy in my photo album. This picture is taken many years ago. In

fact, I believe it was in 1988.

EXERCISE 14. Reading Practice: A Family Tree

Read the information about this family. Then fill in the Currier family tree and answer the eight comprehension questions. The grammar from this unit is underlined for you.

- Edward and Florence Currier had two children. Their names <u>were</u> Richard and Dorothy.
- Richard and Shirley Currier had two sons. Their sons' names are Michael and David. Michael <u>was</u> born in 1958, and David <u>was</u> born in 1961.
- David Currier's uncle's name <u>was</u> Charles Decker.
- David Currier's parents' names <u>were</u> Shirley and Richard.
- Kathleen Decker's grandmother <u>was</u> born in 1907.
- Kathleen Decker's aunt's name <u>was</u> Shirley Smith Currier.
- Edward and Florence Currier's daughter <u>was</u> born in 1930.

The Currier Family Tree

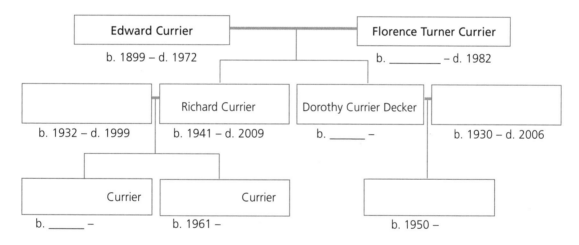

Comprehension Questions

1. Which two people <u>were</u> born in the same year? _____

2. Who <u>was</u> born first, Richard Currier or Charles Decker? _____

3. Based on the information in this family tree, who <u>was</u> an only child? _____

4. Who <u>was</u> not living in 2000? _____

5. How old <u>was</u> Richard when his niece Kathleen <u>was</u> born? _____

EXERCISE 15. Vocabulary Practice: Word Knowledge

Circle the word or phrase that is most closely related to the word or phrase on the left. Use a dictionary to check the meaning of words you do not know.

Vocabulary	Answer Choices	
1. a niece	female	male
2. invent	create	forget
3. I guess	I'm not sure	I'm sure
4. humid	dry	wet
5. the capital	the main city	the main language
6. population	peace	people
7. soon	in a long time	in a short time
8. a pet	an animal	a sport
9. worst	very bad	very good
10. a subject	at home	at school
11. title	age	name
12. a president	a fact	a person
13. broccoli	an animal	a vegetable
14. silver	a color	a food
15. crowded	a few people	many people
16. a meal	something you drive	something you eat
17. I miss you	I don't want to see you	I want to see you
18. a nation	a chapter	a country
19. be on sale	cheap	second
20. a grade	in the morning	on a test
21. a score	in the morning	on a test
22. the aisle	between	under
23. bowling	an animal	a sport
24. a politician	a country	a person
25. murder	born	die
26. a product	a person	a thing
27. enjoy	like	take
28. clear	easy to play	easy to see
29. a character	a fact	a person
30. a champion	a person who loses	a person who wins
31. your uncle	your father's brother	your mother's sister
32. a picnic	inside	outside

EXERCISE 16. Vocabulary Practice: Collocations

Fill in each blank with the answer on the right that most naturally completes the phrase on the left. If necessary, use a dictionary to check the meaning of words you do not know.

Phrase	Answer Choices	
1. it's been a long _____	prediction	time
2. really _____	age	old
3. six years _____	ago	team
4. from 7 AM _____ noon	before	until
5. my great-_____	friend	grandmother
6. in my _____	opinion	Friday
7. on your last _____	class	trip
8. a good _____	sign	under
9. _____ exist any longer	does	doesn't
10. a quiet _____	baby	salad
11. we _____ a good time	did	had
12. _____ the football team	in	on
13. to be _____ work	at	in
14. a very important _____	complete	person
15. during the _____	mix	war
16. _____ born	does	was
17. _____ grade	nine	ninth
18. pretty _____	good	year
19. _____ five minutes from now	after	in
20. _____ 2009	in	on
21. too _____	friend	small
22. more _____ $1,000	of	than
23. were there _____ two hours	at	for
24. _____ about something	happy	tired
25. in _____,	fact	parent

EXERCISE 17. Writing Practice: A Past Trip

Part 1. Editing Student Writing.

Read these sentences about one student's family vacation. Circle the 15 errors. Then write the number of the sentence with the error next to the type of error. (Some sentences may have more than one error.)

_____ a. no subject   _____ d. no verb

_____ b. *was/were* (wrong form)   _____ e. negative

_____ c. word order   _____ f. verb tense

My Last Family Vacation
1. In 2008, my family took our summer vacation in New York City. We are there for five days.
2. We stayed at a big hotel in Manhattan. Was wonderful.
3. My parents saw two Broadway shows. Their favorite show "The Lion King."
4. We visited the Empire State Building and the United Nations Building. Were amazing these two famous places.
5. We was in New York City in July.
6. Everyone knows the weather in New York in July is not so good. Sometimes is very hot and humid.
7. In the summer of 2008, we was lucky because our weather no was bad.
8. On this trip, the temperature every day is around 80.
9. July was usually a very wet month, but there was no any rain when we were in New York.
10. When we in Chinatown, we ate at a restaurant with food traditional.
11. The food were incredible. In particular, I will always remember the taste wonderful of "Chili Fish."

Part 2. Original Student Writing

Now write a short paragraph (or some sentences) about a past trip. Use five words from the vocabulary on pages 138–39. Underline the five words. Use 2 new words from your dictionary. Circle around the two dictionary words. Tell where you were, when you were there, why you were there. Tell the places where you were. Describe what you saw and did on your trip.

Unit 6

Past Tense of Regular and Irregular Verbs

 ## Discover the Grammar

Read this vacation postcard, and then answer the six questions.

Line	
1	Dear Jorge,
2	Hello from sunny Florida! My brother and I came by
3	plane. After our long flight here, we checked into our
4	hotel, talked for a little while, and went to bed. This
5	morning we sat on the beach. We got there really early,
6	and we watched the sunrise and just listened to the
7	ocean. I brought my guitar and played it for a while.
8	It sounded very beautiful. My brother tried to teach me
9	to surf. I didn't understand his instructions. He
10	explained it all to me again, and I practiced all day.
11	I didn't surf well today, but I had a great time!
12	Your friend, Yuka
13	P.S. Did you feed my cat? Did you check my mail?

Jorge Santander
2517 La Siena Way
Los Angeles, CA 70741

1. Circle the nine past tense verbs that end in *-ed*. These are called regular past tense verbs. Write the line each one appears on, the past form, and the base form.

Line	past tense	base form	Line	past tense	base form
____	_____	(_____)	____	_____	(_____)
____	_____	(_____)	____	_____	(_____)
____	_____	(_____)	____	_____	(_____)
____	_____	(_____)	____	_____	(_____)
____	_____	(_____)			

2. Underline the six different past tense verbs that do not end in *-ed*. These verbs are called irregular verbs. Write the line each one appears on, the past form, and the base form.

Line	past tense	base form	Line	past tense	base form
____	_____	(_____)	____	_____	(_____)
____	_____	(_____)	____	_____	(_____)
____	_____	(_____)	____	_____	(_____)

3. Two of the past tense verbs are negative. What do you think the affirmative forms for these two verbs are?

negative past tense	affirmative past tense
Line 9: I <u>didn't understand</u> his instructions.	I _____ his instructions.
Line 11: I <u>didn't surf</u> well today.	I _____ well today.

4. Study the two past tense questions from Line 13. What do you think the formula or pattern is for making a question for simple past tense?_____

    _____

5. What questions do you have about this grammar?

    _____

    _____

    _____

    _____

Grammar Lesson

Simple Past Tense of Regular Verbs: Affirmative

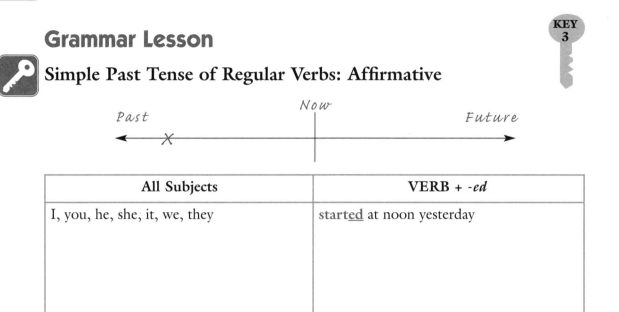

All Subjects	VERB + -*ed*
I, you, he, she, it, we, they	start<u>ed</u> at noon yesterday

Rule 1. In the simple past tense, a regular verb has one form: VERB + -ed.

Rule 2. Use simple past tense for actions that happened in the past and are completely finished. Common time expressions for simple past tense include *yesterday, last _____ (last week), _____ ago (two weeks ago)*.

Spelling Rule 3. For verbs that end in **consonant + -y**, change the -y to -i and then add -ed: *try → tried* and *worry → worried*. However, for verbs that end in **vowel + -y**, just add -ed: *stay → stayed* and *enjoy → enjoyed*.

Spelling Rule 4. For one-syllable verbs that end in **consonant + vowel + consonant**, double the final consonant: *stop → stopped* and *plan → planned*. However, do not double final letters for verbs that end in *-w* (*snowed*), *-x* (*taxed*), or *-y* (*played*).

Spelling Rule 5. For two-syllable verbs that end in consonant + vowel + consonant with stress on the second syllable, double the final consonant: *ocCUR → occurred* and *perMIT → permitted*. However, if the stress is on the first syllable, just add -ed: *HAPpen → happened* and *LISten → listened*.

Other examples:

	want	need	add	subtract	play	pass
I, you, he, she, it, we, they	I wanted	you needed	he added	she subtracted	we played	they passed

BE CAREFUL!

Common Learner Errors	Explanation
1. My great-grandparents ~~live~~ **lived** in Chicago.	Remember to use simple past tense. Don't use **VERB** or **VERB** + -s for a past action.
2. Carlos ~~was worked~~ **worked** in Miami last month.	Do not use **was** or **were** with simple past tense of regular verbs.
3. Thomas Edison was a very clever man. ~~Invented~~ **He invented** the light bulb.	Use a subject with a simple past verb.
4. My baby sister ~~cryed~~ **cried** a lot last night.	Don't forget to change y to i and add -ed.
5. According to the radio report, two masked men ~~robed~~ **robbed** the bank about an hour ago.	If a verb ends in **consonant-vowel-consonant (C-V-C)**, don't forget to double the consonant before adding -ed.

EXERCISE 1. Comparing Simple Present and Simple Past

Write the forms of *work* in present and past tenses.

Present

1. I ___work___ every day.
2. You _____ at night.
3. He _____ all of the time.
4. She _____ every day.
5. It _____ most of the time.
6. We _____ every afternoon.
7. They _____ here every day.

Past

8. I ___worked___ yesterday.
9. You _____ last night.
10. He _____ an hour ago.
11. She _____ last week.
12. It just _____ a few minutes ago.
13. We _____ in the summer of 2008.
14. They _____ here yesterday.

15. List the time expressions used with Numbers 1 through 7. These are time expressions that we can use with simple present tense: _____

_____

16. List the time expressions used with Numbers 8 through 14. These are time expressions that we can use with simple past tense: _____

_____

EXERCISE 2. Affirmative Simple Past Tense

Write the past tense forms of the verbs.

1. I want   _____I wanted_____   11. she listens   _____

2. they attend   _____   12. I wait   _____

3. you repeat   _____   13. he learns   _____

4. we talk   _____   14. they explain   _____

5. we need   _____   15. she uses   _____

6. it repeats   _____   16. you like   _____

7. I count   _____   17. she adds   _____

8. they type   _____   18. I shop   _____

9. I watch   _____   19. we study   _____

10. you shout   _____   20. he answers   _____

Do Online Exercise 6.1. My score: _____ /10. _____ % correct.

EXERCISE 3. Simple Past Tense in Context

Use the 14 verbs in the word list to complete these sentences. Spell the past tense forms correctly. You will use some verbs more than once.

word list	add	chop	cover	decide	fry	reduce	serve
	allow	cook	cry	enjoy	pour	turn	use

Cooking Vegetable Soup for Dinner

1. The weather yesterday was cold, so I _____ to make vegetable soup.

2. First, I _____ up two cup of onions into tiny pieces.

3. Of course I _____ because the onions were strong.

4. I _____ the onions in some oil.

5. I _____ in some chicken meat.

6. I _____ the meat and onions for about 10 minutes.

7. Then I _____ four cups of assorted vegetables.

8. I _____ a big potato, four carrots, a piece of broccoli, and some green peas because these are my favorites.

9. I _____ these vegetables to the pan with the meat and onions.

10. I _____ this mixture to cook for another fifteen minutes.

11. Then I _____ in 6 cups of water.

12. Finally, I _____ the heat and _____ the pot with a heavy lid.

13. Thirty minutes later, I _____ off the heat and _____ the soup to my family for dinner.

14. Everyone could smell the soup in the house, and we were hungry. We really _____ this delicious dish.

Pronunciation of -ed

You have seen that we add -ed to verbs for simple past tense. This ending can be spelled with -ed (liked) or -ied (tried). This ending can be pronounced three ways in English: /d/, /t/, /əd/. Many students are surprised to learn that the most common pronunciation for -ed is /d/, not /əd/ or /t/.

-ed or -ied		
1. Pronounce /d/ when the words ends in these voiced* sounds:	/b/	he grabbed
	/g/	she logged in
	/ǰ/(-ge)	he changed
	/l/	he called
	/m/	it seemed
	/ŋ/	it belonged
	/r/	she cared
	/v/	he lived
	/z/	she sneezed
	all vowels	she played
2. Pronounce /t/ when the words ends in these voiceless* sounds:	/č/ (-ch)	he watched
	/f/	he laughed (gh = /f/)
	/k/	we baked
	/p/	she helped
	/s/	he missed
	/š/ (-sh)	she finished
3. Pronounce an extra syllable /əd/ when the words ends in these sounds:	/d/	he needed
	/t/	she wanted

IMPORTANT: Remember that the last **sound** is important, **not** the last **letter**.
1: live: The last letter is e, but the last sound is v.   lived: the -ed sounds like /d/.
2: laugh: The last letter is h, but the last sound is f. laughed: the -ed sounds like /t/.

*Voiced sounds have vibration in the vocal cords. Voiceless sounds have very little vibration in the vocal cords.

ONE-MINUTE LESSON
If you have problems hearing the final /t/ or /d/ of a verb ending in **-ed**, then practice saying the verb in a phrase where the next word begins with a vowel sound. For /t/, try *She washed all the cups.* Say this 10 times, and you should hear the word **tall**. For /d/, try *He closed all the windows.* Say this 10 times, and you should hear the word **doll**.

Connecting Grammar and Vocabulary

Most verbs in English form the past tense by adding -*ed*, so there are thousands of regular past tense verbs. You do not need to learn so many verbs, but you should focus on the most frequent of these verbs. Study these two lists carefully.

The Most Common Regular Past Tense Verbs in General English*

Here are examples of ten common verbs from general English (in frequency order):
1. Everyone **looked** at the crying baby.
2. The teacher **seemed** very tired at the end of class.
3. They all **wanted** a piece of chocolate cake.
4. She **asked** me about the homework.
5. He is sure that he **turned** off the light.
6. I **showed** my driver's license to the police officer.
7. The moon **looked** so beautiful last night.
8. We **called** our friend to help us.
9. I **used** your cell phone to call my office.
10. My grandmother **died** in 2007.

*spoken and written English, compiled from the British National Corpus

The Most Common Regular Past Tense Verbs in Academic English**

Here are examples of ten common verbs from academic English (in alphabetical order):
1. People **assumed** Henry's story was true.
2. The teacher **created** two copies of the exam.
3. In that story, humans **established** a city on the moon in 2000.
4. They **estimated** the value of the coin to be over one million dollars
5. Saudi Arabia **exported** over $350 billion of oil products in 2008.
6. The police **identified** the person who robbed the bank.
7. My dad's last health test **indicated** that he had high blood pressure.
8. The accident **involved** a car and a truck.
9. Several problems **occurred** when the inventors tested their new product.
10. Prior to 2005, the city **required** pet owners to walk their dogs on a leash.

**Source: Academic Word List (Coxhead, 2000), Regular Verbs in Sublist 1

EXERCISE 4. Pronunciation of -ed in 20 Common Verbs

Write the simple past tense form of the 20 common verbs on page 149 in the column by the verb's correct final pronunciation. The first one from both boxes has been done for you.

/d/	/t/	/əd/
assumed	looked	

EXERCISE 5. Odd Man Out for -ed Pronunciation

Write the correct simple past tense spelling of each verb, and then circle the verb and ending that has a different final sound. What is the sound of the different verb? What is the sound of the other three verbs?

				Group Sound	Odd Sound
1. walked	visited	added	stated	/əd/	/t/
2. want	listen	attend	repeat		
3. cook	cash	erase	clean		
4. repeat	answer	attend	create		
5. iron	use	need	pull		
6. cough	shave	remember	belong		
7. rain	fold	enjoy	study		
8. like	shop	rent	pass		
9. smile	snow	sign	wash		
10. brush	chop	reach	raise		

EXERCISE 6. Practicing -ed Pronunciation in Context

Say the past tense of each verb. There are five verbs with /t/, six verbs with /d/, and four verbs with /əd/.

Step 1. Circle the sound of the letters -ed.

Step 2. Then use these words to complete the sentences.

a.	robbed	/t/ /d/ /əd/	h.	passed	/t/ /d/ /əd/
b.	waited	/t/ /d/ /əd/	i.	ironed	/t/ /d/ /əd/
c.	needed	/t/ /d/ /əd/	j.	signed	/t/ /d/ /əd/
d.	erased	/t/ /d/ /əd/	k.	cooked	/t/ /d/ /əd/
e.	washed	/t/ /d/ /əd/	l.	carried	/t/ /d/ /əd/
f.	failed	/t/ /d/ /əd/	m.	helped	/t/ /d/ /əd/
g.	sneezed	/t/ /d/ /əd/	n.	folded	/t/ /d/ /əd/

1. John's answer was wrong, so he _____ it.

2. A man with a mask _____ the bank yesterday.

3. Barbara _____, and Jill said "Bless you."

4. I _____ my name at the bottom of the check.

5. Robert _____ steak and potatoes for dinner last night.

6. The clothes were dirty, so I _____ them. When they were dry, I

   _____ the pants and I _____ the towels, socks,

   and underwear.

7. The books were very heavy, so I only _____ half of them.

8. The math homework was difficult, so Susan _____ me with it.

9. I walked to the store because I _____ some bread.

10. John _____ the grammar test. His score was only 45.

11. Tim _____ the reading test. His score was 93.

12. Yesterday we _____ for the bus for one hour!

EXERCISE 7. Speaking Practice: Correct Pronunciation of -ed

-ed Pronunciation	Verbs
/d/	assume, belong, call, clean, die, enjoy, fail, identify, involve, iron, occur, pull, rain, raise, remember, require, rob, seem, shave, show, sign, smile, sneeze, snow, stay, study, use
/t/	ask, brush, cash, chop, cook, cough, erase, establish, help, like, look, pass, reach, shop, walk, wash
/əd/	add, attend, count, create, estimate, export, fold, indicate, need, rent, repeat, state, subtract, taste, visit, wait, want

Step 1. In the boxes, write any 12 verbs from the list. Use verbs from all three groups.

Step 2. Work with a partner. Say your first verb. Your partner must say the past tense with the correct ending. Take turns doing this.

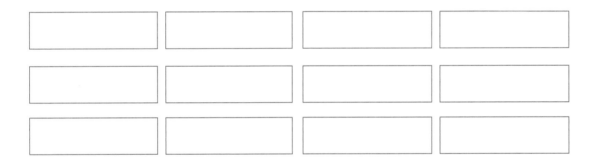

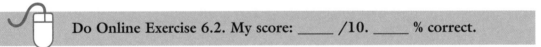

Do Online Exercise 6.2. My score: _____ /10. _____ % correct.

EXERCISE 8. Mini-Conversations

Circle the correct words in these eight mini-conversations.

1. A: How was your dinner last night?

   B: Yes, it was great. I (like, liked) it a lot.

2. A: Can your mother speak Russian?

   B: Yes, she (speak, speaks) it well. She (study, studies, studied) in Moscow.

3. A: What happened downtown?

   B: I don't know much, but someone (rob, robs, robbed) the bank.

4. A: Does your mom work at Boston Bank?

   B: No, she doesn't, but she (work, works, worked) there in 2007.

5. A: Was Lin a student at Clearview College?

   B: Yes, he (study, studies, studied) there from 2005 to 2009.

6. A: Is your car OK now?

   B: Yes, it is. It (need, needs, needed) a new battery.

7. A: How was your trip to Seattle?

   B: It was great. We (stay, stays, stayed) at an amazing hotel downtown.

8. A: When you (work, works, worked) in Korea in 2008, where did you live?

   B: We (rent, rents, rented) an apartment in Seoul.

Simple Past Tense of Irregular Verbs: Affirmative

In past tense, more than 99% of all English verbs are regular: attended, died, hoped, liked, worked.

Irregular past tense verbs do not use -ed. Instead, they change in many different ways. See Appendix 3 for irregular verbs.

Only about 175 English verbs are irregular in simple past tense. However, these verbs are extremely common when talking about the past. In fact, some experts* say that approximately 57% of English speaking and writing about past events uses a very small number of these irregular verbs.

*Source: Grabowski, E., and Mindt, D. (1995). A corpus-based learning list of irregular verbs in English *ICAME Journal, No. 19*, 5–22.

Rule 1. In the simple past tense, an irregular verb has one form, but it is difficult to predict the form. You have to memorize the correct form.

Rule 2. For irregular verbs, do not use -ed.

Rule 3. Use simple past tense for actions that happened in the past and are completely finished. Common time expressions for simple past tense include **yesterday**, last _____ (last week), _____ ago (two weeks ago).

ONE-MINUTE LESSON

To talk about the past, we use the word **ago**, but we put the time *before* **ago**: *I called you two hours* **ago**. A common error is to use the word **before**: *before two hours*. Only **ago** is correct in this example. (The opposite of **ago** is **in**: *I will call you* **in** *two hours*.)

BE CAREFUL!

Common Learner Errors	Explanation
1. My sister ~~goed~~ went to England last year. Remember to use an irregular verb.	Don't add -ed to an irregular verb.
2. Carlos ~~was took~~ took a trip to Miami last month.	Do not use was or were with simple past tense of irregular verbs.
3. I got a bad grade on my math test. ~~Made~~ I made too many simple mistakes.	Use a subject with a simple past irregular verb.

 Connecting Grammar and Vocabulary

Many students make the mistake of studying long lists of irregular verbs, usually from big dictionairies on the Internet. In Level 1, do not waste your time learning irregular verbs like *forsake → forsook* or *slay → slew*. Learn this list of 33 common irregular past tense verbs. (A longer list of 60 verbs, which includes these 33, can be found in Appendix 3.)

33 Frequently Used Irregular Past Tense Verbs					
Present	Past	Present	Past	Present	Past
1. begin	began	12. go	went	23. send	sent
2. bring	brought	13. have	had	24. sleep	slept
3. buy	bought	14. hear	heard	25. speak	spoke
4. choose	chose	15. leave	left	26. spend	spent
5. come	came	16. lose	lost	27. stand	stood
6. do	did	17. make	made	28. take	took
7. drink	drank	18. put	put	29. tell	told
8. eat	ate	19. read	read	30. think	thought
9. forget	forgot	20. say	said	31. understand	understood
10. get	got	21. see	saw	32. wake	woke
11. give	gave	22. sell	sold	33. write	wrote

EXERCISE 9. Irregular Past Forms of Verbs

Write the past tense of the verbs on the lines.

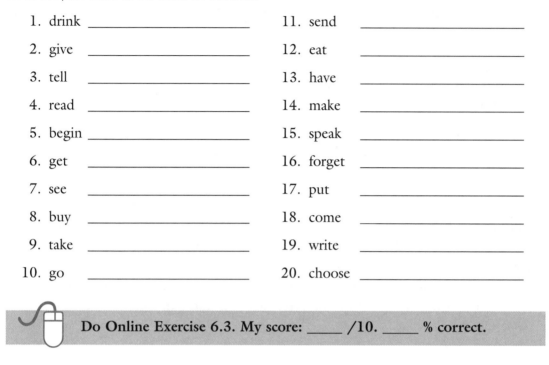

1. drink _____

2. give _____

3. tell _____

4. read _____

5. begin _____

6. get _____

7. see _____

8. buy _____

9. take _____

10. go _____

11. send _____

12. eat _____

13. have _____

14. make _____

15. speak _____

16. forget _____

17. put _____

18. come _____

19. write _____

20. choose _____

Do Online Exercise 6.3. My score: _____ /10. _____ % correct.

EXERCISE 10. Your Own Irregular Verb Test

Make a test for a classmate. What are 10 of the most difficult verbs for you? Write the present tense of ten verbs on the left lines. Then give your book to a classmate. The classmate should write the correct past tense. Check your partner's answers.

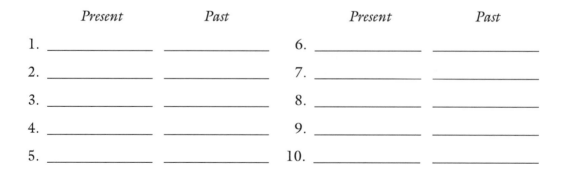

	Present	Past		Present	Past
1.			6.		
2.			7.		
3.			8.		
4.			9.		
5.			10.		

EXERCISE 11. Irregular Past Tense in Context

Use the verbs in each word list to complete the sentences in that paragraph. Be sure to spell the past tense forms correctly. Some words are used more than once.

word list	begin	choose	do	hear	get	take	wake

Yesterday

Yesterday was Friday, and I ❶ _____ what I do every weekday. I

❷ _____ my alarm clock ring, so I ❸ _____ up and

❹ _____ my day. First, I ❺ _____ a shower Then, I

❻ _____ dressed. The weather was cold, so I ❼ _____ a

long-sleeved shirt and a sweater.

word list	bring	drink	eat	have	make	read	put

I wasn't very hungry, so I ❽ _____ a simple breakfast. I

❾ _____ in the newspaper and ❿ _____ it during

breakfast. For breakfast yesterday, I ⓫ _____ two pieces of whole

wheat toast. I ⓬ _____ some jam and butter on my toast. I

⓭ _____ a cup of coffee with some cream and sugar. I also

⓮ _____ a small cup of fresh fruit for breakfast.

word list	give	go	say	see	spend	think

At 9 o'clock, I ⑮ _____ to a special meeting with my boss. My boss, who is usually very quiet, ⑯ _____ in a very angry voice, "We have a problem. Last month we ⑰ _____ too much money on telephone calls!" My boss ⑱ _____ me a copy of the company telephone bill. I ⑲ _____ the huge amount on the bill. I ⑳ _____ it was really expensive.

word list	send	speak	tell	understand	write

At that moment, I ㉑ _____ why our boss was so angry. She and I ㉒ _____ about this problem and how to solve it. I ㉓ _____ an email about the meeting, and then I ㉔ _____ this email to the 20 people who work in my department. I ㉕ _____ them that the boss was angry because our telephone bill was so high.

word list	forget	leave	sleep

I worked all afternoon, and then I ㉖ _____ the office at 5 PM. That night I ㉗ _____ all about my long day at work. I didn't wake up early on Saturday. In fact, I ㉘ _____ until almost noon. I guess I was really tired.

Do Online Exercise 6.4. My score: _____ /10. _____ % correct.

🔑 Simple Past Tense: Negative

Making a negative statement with regular and irregular verbs is easy. Study these two steps:		
Step 1	Check for a verb (not **be**).	The girl **wanted** the keys, so she **took** them.
Step 2	Put **did not** (OR **didn't**) before the base (simple) verb. (In regular verbs, the -ed moves from the verb to the word **did**.)	The girl **didn't want** the keys, so she **didn't take** them.

Other examples:

Statement		Negative
I called up John.	→	I did **not** call up Sue.
We got off work at 6 PM.	→	We didn't get off work at 5 PM.
Pierre put on his watch.	→	Pierre did **not** put on his ring.
The class lasted for four months.	→	The class didn't last for a year.

<u>Rule 1.</u> To make a negative statement with a verb, add **did not** before the base (simple) form of the verb.

<u>Rule 2.</u> In informal English, it is possible to use contractions for **did not**: **didn't**.

 ## BE CAREFUL!

Common Learner Errors	Explanation
1. Your cousin ~~no went~~ didn't go to the bank.	Remember to use **did not** (**didn't**) with the base form of the verb.
2. Nell and Vick ~~weren't~~ didn't like the food at the party very much.	Do not use **was not** (**wasn't**) or **were not** (**weren't**) with VERB. Use **did not** (**didn't**) only.
3. The meeting didn't ~~started~~ start on time.	If you have the helping verb **did**, don't use -ed with the verb. You need only one -ed or past time marker.

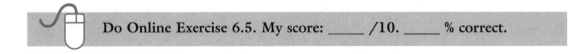

EXERCISE 12. Editing. Is It Correct?

If the sentence is correct, write a check mark (✔) on the line. If it is not correct, write X on the line and circle the mistake. Then change the sentence to make it correct. Write the change above the sentence. (*Hint:* There are eight sentences. Two are correct, but six have mistakes.)

Early Postage Stamps

_____ 1. The United Kingdom introduce the first stamp on May 1, 1840.

_____ 2. With this first stamp, the sender has to pay for the stamp.

_____ 3. Before this, the person who received the letter paid. In other words, the sender did not pay.

_____ 4. The first stamp not have the name of the United Kingdom on it because there was not any reason to have the country's name on it then.

_____ 5. Even today, stamps from the U.K. did not have the name of the country on them.

_____ 6. In fact, the U.K. is the only country that do not put its name on its stamps.

_____ 7. The U.S. begin using stamps in 1847.

_____ 8. In 1883, a stamp for a letter in the U.S. cost two cents, and this price did not change until 1933.

Do Online Exercise 6.5. My score: _____ /10. _____ % correct.

EXERCISE 13. Pair Speaking: How Well Do You Know Me?

Write six negative sentences in the past about anything about yourself. Make three of the sentences true and three of the sentences false. Use a different verb in each sentence. Circle T if your sentence is true and F if it is False. Then read your sentence to see if your partner can guess if your sentence is true or false. Take turns guessing. Who can guess more correct answers?

Example: (T) F   *My brother didn't call me last week.* _____

1. T F _____

2. T F _____

3. T F _____

4. T F _____

5. T F _____

6. T F _____

(*After you finish:* Are there any surprises? Are there any interesting facts?)

Simple Past Tense: Making a Question

Making a question with a past tense verb (not *be*) is easy. Study these four steps:		
Step 1	Check for a verb (not *be*).	You **wanted** a cheese sandwich. You **ate** a sandwich for lunch.
Step 2	Put **did** at the beginning of the sentence.	**did** you **wanted** a cheese sandwich. **did** you **ate** a sandwich for lunch.
Step 3	Make sure the verb is in the base (simple) form.	**did** you **want** a cheese sandwich. **did** you **eat** a sandwich for lunch.
Step 4	Use a capital letter for the first word, and then change the period (.) to a question mark (?).	**Did** you **want** a cheese sandwich? **Did** you **eat** a sandwich for lunch?

Other examples:

Statement		Question
I arrived after you.	→	Did I arrive after you?
You ran four miles every day last week.	→	Did you run four miles every day last week?
He worked in Mexico one year.	→	Did he work in Mexico one year?
She knew all of the answers.	→	Did she know all of the answers?
It snowed last month.	→	Did it snow last month?
You and I had the same idea.	→	Did you and I have the same idea?

Rule 1. To make a question with a past tense verb (not be), add **did** before the subject.

Rule 2. Be sure to use only the base (simple) form of the verb.

BE CAREFUL!

Common Learner Errors	Explanation
1. ~~Were~~ Did you watch the news last night?	Do not use be (was, were) with other verbs in simple past tense.
2. Did your car ~~needed~~ need a new radio?	Do not use -ed or the irregular past form of the verb in yes-no questions. Use only the base (simple) form of the verb. **Did** is past, and you only need a past tense form in one place in the verb.

EXERCISE 14. Questions about Someone's Vacation

The Lee family took a vacation last year. Use the information to ask them questions about their vacation.

1. stay at a nice hotel   *Did you stay at a nice hotel?* _____

2. visit a museum   _____

3. fly there   _____

4. have a good time   _____

5. eat good food   _____

6. take many photos   _____

7. spend much money   _____

8. send any postcards   _____

Do Online Exercise 6.6. My score: _____ /10. _____ % correct.

Simple Past Tense: Questions with Full and Short Answers

Answering a past question with a short answer is easy. Study these four steps:		
Step 1	Listen for a question.	**Did** your dinner at that restaurant cost more than $50?
Step 2	Decide if the answer is yes or no.	**No**
Step 3	Use a pronoun for the noun subject.	No, it
Step 4	Repeat **did.** Add **not** for negative. (The negative **did not** can also be a contraction: **didn't.**)	No, it **did not.**

Other examples:

Questions	Full Answers	Short Answers
Did you study Chinese in high school?	Yes, I studied Chinese in high school. No, I did not study Chinese in high school.	Yes, I did. No, I did not.
Did Edison invent the light bulb?	Yes, Edison invented the light bulb.	Yes, he did.
Did Edison invent the radio?	No, Edison didn't invent the radio.	No, he didn't.

<u>Rule 1.</u> To answer a yes-no question with a short affirmative answer, use **did.**

<u>Rule 2.</u> To answer a yes-no question with a short negative answer, use **did not** or **didn't** in your answer.

⚠ BE CAREFUL!

Common Learner Errors	Explanation
1. Did you watch TV last night? No, I ~~was~~ did not.	Do not use was/were as a short answer for **did** questions.
2. Did you have a good time? Yes, I ~~have~~ did.	Be careful with the verb **have** in short answers.

EXERCISE 15. Speaking Practice: The Shopping Bag Game

Step 1. Work with a partner. Each partner chooses one of the 16 shopping bags.

Step 2. Take turns asking yes-no questions to find out which bag is your partner's bag. If Student B's answer is yes, Student A continues asking questions. If the answer is no, then Student B asks questions. The first student to guess the price of his or her partner's shopping bag is the winner. Use "Did you buy _____?" and "Yes, I did" or "No, I didn't" in your conversations.

$61
gray socks
a cotton sweater
a medium T-shirt
a black belt

$66
gray socks
a cotton sweater
a medium T-shirt
a brown belt

$63
gray socks
a cotton sweater
a large T-shirt
a black belt

$68
gray socks
a cotton sweater
a large T-shirt
a brown belt

$81
gray socks
a wool sweater
a medium T-shirt
a black belt

$86
gray socks
a wool sweater
a medium T-shirt
a brown belt

$83
gray socks
a wool sweater
a large T-shirt
a black belt

$88
gray socks
a wool sweater
a large T-shirt
a brown belt

$60
green socks
a cotton sweater
a medium T-shirt
a black belt

$65
green socks
a cotton sweater
a medium T-shirt
a brown belt

$62
green socks
a cotton sweater
a large T-shirt
a black belt

$67
green socks
a cotton sweater
a large T-shirt
a brown belt

$80
green socks
a wool sweater
a medium T-shirt
a black belt

$85
green socks
a wool sweater
a medium T-shirt
a brown belt

$82
green socks
a wool sweater
a large T-shirt
a black belt

$87
green socks
a wool sweater
a large T-shirt
a brown belt

EXERCISE 16. Sentence Study for Critical Reading

Read the numbered sentences. Then read the three answer choices and place a check mark in the yes or no boxes in front of each sentence to show if that answer is true based on the information in the original sentence. If there is not enough information to mark something as yes, then mark it as no. Remember that more than one true answer is possible.

1. Kwan's English isn't so good, but he spoke to many people at the party. He didn't understand everything they said, but he didn't ask anyone to repeat.

    ☐ yes ☐ no   a. Kwan didn't speak to many people at the party.

    ☐ yes ☐ no   b. Because his English is not so good, Kwan had to ask people to repeat a lot.

    ☐ yes ☐ no   c. People asked Kwan to repeat his statements a lot.

2. Don asked Nina for help with his homework because it was difficult, but she didn't understand it either.

    ☐ yes ☐ no   a. Don understood his homework.

    ☐ yes ☐ no   b. Nina didn't understand Don's homework.

    ☐ yes ☐ no   c. Nina didn't ask Don for help.

3. Nancy didn't like the purple shirts, so she chose the red shirts instead. The purple shirts were really cheap, but she bought two red shirts.

    ☐ yes ☐ no   a. Nancy didn't buy any red shirts.

    ☐ yes ☐ no   b. The red shirts cost more than the purple shirts.

    ☐ yes ☐ no   c. Nancy didn't like the purple shirts.

4. Houston, Texas, became a city on June 5, 1837. Houston's population grew rapidly in the 1970s, and today Houston is one of the largest cities in the United States.

    ☐ yes ☐ no   a. Houston became a city more than one hundred years ago.

    ☐ yes ☐ no   b. The population of Houston grew a lot in the 1960s.

    ☐ yes ☐ no   c. Houston is the largest city in the United States today.

5. Louise didn't feel well yesterday, so she visited the doctor. The doctor gave her some medicine.

    ☐ yes ☐ no   a. Louise didn't see the doctor.

    ☐ yes ☐ no   b. The doctor says that Louise is not sick.

    ☐ yes ☐ no   c. The medicine made Louise feel sick.

6. My weekend was very busy. I wrote a ten-page paper for my English class, and I studied for a history test and a math test.

- [ ] yes [ ] no   a. I studied for my math test before I studied for my history test.
- [ ] yes [ ] no   b. My English paper was ten pages long.
- [ ] yes [ ] no   c. I studied for a history test.

7. Maria made some delicious vegetable soup for lunch for her family. For their dinner, she cooked spaghetti with chicken.

- [ ] yes [ ] no   a. Maria's family ate spaghetti with chicken for dinner.
- [ ] yes [ ] no   b. Maria's lunch took more time than her dinner.
- [ ] yes [ ] no   c. Her family enjoyed the spaghetti more than the soup.

8. Fred flew to Los Angeles and spent a week with his sister. They drove around the city and saw many interesting sights.

- [ ] yes [ ] no   a. Fred and his sister live in Los Angles.
- [ ] yes [ ] no   b. Fred went to Los Angeles to visit his sister there.
- [ ] yes [ ] no   c. Fred's visit was for seven days.

ONE-MINUTE LESSON
We use 's to express possession: *Maria's family, Fred's visit.*

REVIEW ▶ **EXERCISE 17. Review Test 1: Multiple Choice**

Circle the letter of the correct answer. Some are conversations.

1. "What's wrong? What's the problem?"

   "The test _____ really difficult. My score was only 53 out of 100."

       a. did   b. didn't   c. was   d. wasn't

2. How did Bertha go to her parents' house yesterday? _____ there, or did she drive her car?

       a. Does she walk   b. Did she walk   c. Does she walks   d. Did she walked

3. The police officer _____ that car because the driver was speeding.

       a. stopped   b. stopping   c. stoped   d. stops

4. Ming had a headache, so she _____ an aspirin and rested.

       a. took   b. takes   c. was took   d. was take

5. Paolo listened to English movies to improve his English. He also _____ to learn new vocabulary.

       a. tryed   b. was tryed   c. tried   d. was tried

6. "Tom, the dinner tonight was excellent. Thanks so much!!"

   "Yes, Tom, it was great. You always _____ so well."

   "Thank you both for the nice words. Please come again."

       a. cook   b. cooked   c. were you cook   d. did you cook

7. Anthony finished work at 6 PM, but he _____ home until almost 8 because there was so much traffic on the highway.

       a. didn't got   b. not got   c. didn't get   d. doesn't got

8. "Did you watch the football game that was on TV last night?"

   "No, I _____. I was really busy last night."

       a. don't   b. didn't   c. wasn't   d. watched

🕐 **ONE-MINUTE LESSON**

We use **on** with television. We say *The game was* **on** *TV last night* and *The best news program is* **on** *Channel 7.*

EXERCISE 18.   Review Test 2: Production and Evaluation

Part 1.
Read this short passage. Fill in the blanks with a form of the verb in parentheses.

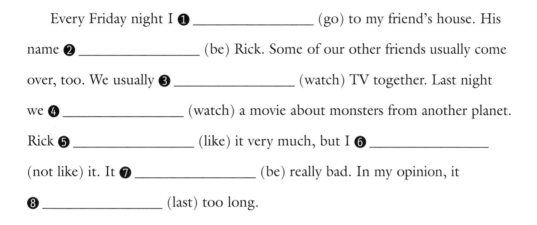

Every Friday night I ❶ _____ (go) to my friend's house. His

name ❷ _____ (be) Rick. Some of our other friends usually come

over, too. We usually ❸ _____ (watch) TV together. Last night

we ❹ _____ (watch) a movie about monsters from another planet.

Rick ❺ _____ (like) it very much, but I ❻ _____

(not like) it. It ❼ _____ (be) really bad. In my opinion, it

❽ _____ (last) too long.

Part 2.
Read this short passage. There are five mistakes. Circle the mistakes, and write the correction
above each mistake.

Do you remember your first flight? My first flight were great. In January

2009, I fly with my family from Miami to New York. We get up very early that

day. In fact, we were woke up at 4 AM because our flight departed at 8 AM.

Of course I was a little nervous and a little afraid, but this did not bothered

me. I enjoyed my first flight a lot, and I'm glad that my family traveled with

me that day.

EXERCISE 19. Reading Practice: An Advice Letter

Read the information in this letter a student wrote to Mr. Advice. In her letter, the student asks for help with a problem. After you read the letter, read Mr. Advice's answer. After reading both letters, answer the five comprehension questions on page 171. The grammar from this unit is underlined for you.

Dear Mr. Advice,

I need your help! I am a college student with a very difficult roommate. Let me tell you my problem. Two weeks ago, my roommate <u>began</u> guitar lessons. Unfortunately, she practices every night, and her practice place is our room! Last night <u>was</u> really bad. She <u>played</u> the guitar for four hours. <u>Did she think</u> about me? No, she <u>didn't</u>. <u>Did she play</u> she quietly? No, she <u>didn't</u>. She <u>didn't think</u> about me at all! I <u>went</u> to the store and <u>bought</u> some ear plugs, but that didn't help. Finally, I <u>spoke</u> to her about our problem. <u>Did she care</u>? No, <u>she didn't care</u> about my problem. She <u>told</u> me to put a pillow over my head! What can I do now?

Sincerely,

Sleepless in Toronto

Dear Sleepless in Toronto,

I'm so sorry to hear about your situation. It seems to me that you <u>gave</u> your roommate many chances to change, but she <u>didn't change</u> anything. You <u>told</u> her that her music is a problem. You <u>asked</u> her to play more quietly, but she <u>didn't do</u> that. I think you should tell her that she cannot live with you any longer. Then you need to find another roommate. You <u>tried</u> your best. It's time to change things.

Sincerely,

Mr. Advice

Comprehension Questions

1. In one sentence, what is the letter writer's problem? _____

   _____

2. When did the roommate start guitar lessons? _____

   _____

3. How long did the roommate play the guitar last night? _____

   _____

4. What did Sleepless in Toronto buy? _____

   _____

5. What did the roommate recommend to help Sleepless sleep? _____

   _____

ONE-MINUTE LESSON
We use the word **college** if we attend a university, college, or community college. You can hear someone say *After high school, I went to* **college***. I attended the University of Ohio for four years.*

EXERCISE 20. Vocabulary Practice: Word Knowledge

Circle the word or phrase that is most closely related to the word or phrase on the left. Use a dictionary to check the meaning of words you do not know.

Vocabulary	Answer Choices	
1. occur	find	happen
2. it belongs to me	it's mine	it's not mine
3. shave	cook	cut
4. clever	happy	intelligent
5. fail	a bad grade on the test	a good grade on the test
6. reduce	$10 \rightarrow 9 \rightarrow 8 \rightarrow 7$	$7 \rightarrow 8 \rightarrow 9 \rightarrow 10$
7. depart	arrive (at a place)	leave (a place)
8. log in	start (on a computer)	start (on a trip)
9. get (to a place)	arrive	select
10. toast	bread	fruit
11. peas	an animal	a vegetable
12. add	$3 + 2 = 5$	$3 - 2 = 1$
13. export	from a country	from a person
14. an ocean	air	water
15. chop	cut	find
16. solve	an answer for a problem	a question for a teacher
17. state	say something	take something
18. sneeze	with your ears	with your nose
19. snow	in the summer	in the winter
20. sunrise	AM	PM
21. invent	make something new	take something old
22. bought	past of *bring*	past of *buy*
23. shout	speak softly	speak loudly
24. establish	make	use
25. a weekday	Monday	Sunday

EXERCISE 21. Vocabulary Practice: Collocations

Fill in each blank with the answer on the right that most naturally completes the phrase on the left. If necessary, use a dictionary to check the meaning of words you do not know.

Phrase	Answer Choices	
1. attend a _____	bank	meeting
2. an alarm _____	clock	driver
3. _____ a great time	do	have
4. I got 88 _____ my test	in	on
5. spend a _____	week	word
6. all of _____	time	the time
7. a wool _____	student	sweater
8. turn _____ the lamp	for	off
9. pour _____	coffee	fruit
10. check into the _____	hotel	restaurant
11. erase a _____	book	mistake
12. according _____	for	to
13. _____ your hair	brush	fold
14. _____ a lesson	practice	take
15. stay at a _____	hotel	problem
16. a driver's _____	cake	license
17. a _____ on a pot	let	lid
18. feed a _____	book	cat
19. in _____ words	other	some
20. _____-grandparents	great	heart
21. _____ my mail	call	check
22. tiny _____	information	pieces
23. a battery for a _____	car	table
24. a long-sleeved _____	building	shirt
25. they robbed a _____	bank	check

ONE-MINUTE LESSON

rob vs **steal**: The meanings of these words are connected, but we use them differently. We **rob** a place (*they* **robbed** *the bank*) or a person (*they* **robbed** *me of $500*), and we **steal** a thing (*they* **stole** *$500*).

EXERCISE 22. Writing Practice: A Past Problem

Part 1. Editing Student Writing

Read these sentences about one student's past problem. Circle the 15 errors. Then write the number of the sentence with the error next to the type of error. (Some sentences may have more than one error.)

_____ a. irregular past tense   _____ d. no subject

_____ b. word order   _____ e. possessive adjectives

_____ c. verb tense   _____ f. negative

A Translation Problem
1. In July 2009, I flied to San Jose, Costa Rica, to study Spanish, but this trip had a beginning very interesting.
2. I started by looking on the Internet for schools, and I finally founded a good school in Costa Rica.
3. I wanted to write an email to the school, but didn't knew any Spanish.
4. For this important reason, I writed my email in English.
5. Then I asked my friend Sandra for help because speaks both English and Spanish really well.
6. In my email, I asked for more information about the program Spanish, the teachers, and the costs.
7. Then Sandra translated my email from my English to his Spanish.
8. Then I sended the email to the school language.
9. Unfortunately for me, the school's answer was in Spanish, so I have to ask Sandra to translate this second email for me.
10. When Sandra read the school's letter, she laughs.
11. At that moment, I don't knew why Sandra laughed, so she explained the situation to me.
12. Here is exactly what the letter said, "Thank you for your email. Our school is excellent, but we didn't have any class for you because your Spanish is already excellent."

Part 2. Original Student Writing

Now write a short paragraph (or some sentences) about a past problem. Use five words from the vocabulary on pages 172–73. Underline the five words. Use two new words from your dictionary. Circle the two dictionary words. Tell what the problem was, where it happened, when it happened, why it happened, or how you solved the problem.

ONE-MINUTE LESSON

We use **quotation marks** in English to mark someone's direct words: *Lisa said, "I want to eat at that new restaurant."*

Unit 7

Wh– Questions (*who, what, when, where, why, which, how many/much, how long*)

Discover the Grammar

Read this conversation between a travel agent and a customer, and then answer the four questions.

Line		
1	**Customer:**	I'd like to plan a special vacation. Do you have any ideas?
2	**Travel agent:**	Certainly. I can help you with that. Where do you want to go?
3	**Customer:**	Well, I like warm weather. What do you recommend?
4	**Travel agent:**	I recommend a vacation in the Bahamas or Las Vegas. Which is
5		better for you?
6	**Customer:**	I think Las Vegas is nice, but I would rather be on a beach in
7		the Bahamas.
8	**Travel agent:**	Ok, I recommend several days on a sunny beach with palm
9		trees.
10	**Customer:**	That sounds perfect. Do you know a good place?
11	**Travel agent:**	When do you want to go? How long do you want to stay there?

12	**Customer:**	I can go in the third week of May. Yes, I can leave on May 17th.
13		I have about ten days of vacation then.
14	**Travel agent:**	OK, I have a good price for a cruise to the Bahamas.
15	**Customer:**	The Bahamas? That sounds wonderful. But a cruise… That
16		sounds very expensive. How much does a cruise cost?
17	**Travel agent:**	Well, there are different cruises. This cruise for $800 is for five
18		days. And then we also have a luxury cruise for $1,200.
19	**Customer:**	Hmmm. How many days is the second cruise for?
20	**Travel agent:**	Eight days. Here you go. Take this information, and call me or
21		email me after you think about it. OK?
22	**Customer:**	Thanks, I will. Oh, uh, who should I ask for?
23	**Travel agent:**	Oh, sorry. I'm Marsha Moore. Here's my card.

1. What is the difference between these two groups of questions from the conversation?

Questions from Lessons 1–6	Questions in Lesson 7
• *Do you have any ideas?*	• *Where do you want to go?*
• *Is your birthday in June?*	• *What do you recommend?*
• *Were you late yesterday?*	• *How many days is the second cruise for?*

_____

_____

_____

2. Underline these question words in the conversation and write the line number where they are located.

___ how long	___ how many	___ how much	___ what
___ when	___ where	___ which	___ who

3. Write the question word that you think goes with each meaning and examples. Use the question words from Number 2 on page 177.

_____ a. a person (*Marsha Moore*)

_____ b. a date (*May 17th*)

_____ c. a price (*$1,200*)

_____ d. a thing (*a cruise*)

_____ e. the amount of time (*for five days*)

_____ f. a place (*Las Vegas*)

_____ g. one choice from a group of choices (*a vacation in the Bahamas*)

_____ h. a number (*eight*)

4. What questions do you have about this grammar?

_____

_____

_____

 ONE-MINUTE LESSON

The verb **sound** is frequently followed by an adjective: *That* **sounds** *perfect. That* **sounds** *wonderful.*

Grammar Lesson

Question Words

Question Word(s)	Examples of Questions	Short Answers	Meanings
What	*What is that?*	a book	things
	What did you eat for breakfast?	scrambled eggs	
When	*When were you born?*	January 10, 1994	time
	When did you go to Texas?	last summer	
Where	*Where are the books?*	on my desk	places
	Where do you keep your keys?	in the top drawer	
Why	*Why are you so white?*	because I feel sick	reasons
	Why do you shop at that store?	because it's cheap	
Who	*Who are your best friends?*	Naj and Elena	people
	Who took my pencil?	Marcos	
Which	*I can go there in May or June. Which is better?*	May	a choice of a thing or a person from several possibilities
	Which boy in this photo is your nephew?	the tall boy in the back	
How many	*How many letters are there in your alphabet?*	26	the number of things or people (It is for things or people that we can count, such as *books, students,* or *dishes.*)
	How many days does March have?	31	
How much	*Excuse me. How much does that sweater cost?*	$60	price (It is also for things that we cannot count, such as *sugar* or *homework.*)
	How much homework do you have?	two exercises	
How long	*How long do Canadians go to school?*	12 years	length of time (It is also for the length of things, such as *a river* or *a race.*)
	How long is the Mississippi River?	2,300 miles	
What time	*What time does your class end?*	11:50	clock time
	What time did your flight arrive?	around midnight	
How old	*How old are you?*	27	age
	How old is the Eiffel Tower?	about 125	

! BE CAREFUL!

Common Learner Errors	Explanation
1. ~~Which~~ What is your name?	Be careful with **what** and **which**. Use **which** only when there is a list or set of choices.
2. ~~How much money~~ How much is that car?	To ask a price, use **how much**. Do not use *how much money* for a price.
3. ~~How long time~~ How long did you live in Mexico?	Use **how long** to ask the length of time, not *how long time*.
4. How old ~~do you have~~ are you?	With **how old**, use to be, never *to have*.
5. ~~What age~~ How old are you?	Use **how old** for age.

EXERCISE 1. Information Questions in Context

Circle the correct question words in this conversation between two students.

Talking about Classes

Kyoko: Susana, ❶ (where, how many, how much) classes do you have?

Susana: I have a total of five classes.

Kyoko: Really? ❷ (What, Where, Which) are they?

Susana: I have English, science, math, writing, and speech.

Kyoko: ❸ (When, Which, Why) is your favorite?

Susana: I think I like my science class the best.

Kyoko: Science? That's my worst class. ❹ (When, Which, Why) do you like science so much?

Susana: I don't know. I just think it's a really interesting class. I like the subject, and I like the teacher.

Kyoko: ❺ (When, Which, Who) is your teacher for that class?

Susana: It's Dr. Wang. She's excellent. She knows the material so well, and she is a great teacher, too.

Kyoko: ❻ (How many, When, Where) do you have that class?

Susana: On Mondays and Wednesdays.

Kyoko: ❼ (How long, How many, How much) does it last?

Susana: The class lasts for 75 minutes. In that class, the time seems to fly. The only thing I don't like is that the class is so big.

Kyoko: Really? ❽ (How many, Where, Which) people are in your science class?

Susana: I don't know exactly, but my guess is about 150.

Kyoko: Wow, you're right. That is a huge class.

EXERCISE 2. Mini-Conversations

Circle the correct words in these eight mini-conversations.

1. A: (Where, Which, How many, When) is your big math test?
   B: It's on Tuesday.

2. A: I would like to buy you a t-shirt. (How much, How many, How long, What) is your favorite color?
   B: It's dark green.

3. A: (Why, Where, Who, When) washed the dishes?
   B: Teresa.

4. A: (What, Where, Why, When) did you go to the store?
   B: Because we were out of bread and milk.

5. A: (How much, How old, How many, How long) is your grandfather?
   B: I'm not exactly sure, but I think he's in his 80s.

6. A: (Who, Why, How many, How old) are your best friends?
   B: Rachel and Gwen.

7. A: Paulo, (what, where, when, how much) did you eat for lunch today?
   B: Beans and rice with a small piece of meat and some salad.

8. A: (Who, When, Which, How many) of those cars is yours?
   B: It's the small black car on the left.

    Do Online Exercise 7.1. My score: _____ /10. _____ % correct.

Grammar Lesson

Question Word Order with *Be*

	(wh- word)	*be*	subject	rest of sentence	short answer
yes-no		*Is*	*John*	*in Room 114 now ?*	Yes, he is.
wh-	*Where*	*is*	*John*	*now?*	In Room 114.

Step 1	Check for verb **be.**	John **is** in Room 114 now.
Step 2	For a yes-no question with verb *be*, you move the *be* verb (*am, is, are, was, were*) before the subject.	John **is** in room 114 now. → **is** John in room 114 now.
Step 3	For a **wh-** question, you then change the information (*in Room 114*) to the correct question word (*where*).	is John in room 114 now. → is John **where** now.
Step 4	Move the question word to the front of the question.	**where** is John now.
Step 5	Use a capital letter for the first word of the question, and add a question mark (?) at the end.	Where is John now?

<u>Rule 1.</u> Information questions begin with a question word.

<u>Rule 2.</u> With questions with **be**, you must put **be** before the subject.

BE CAREFUL!

Common Learner Errors	Explanation
1. Where ~~Mustafa is~~ **is** Mustafa?	Move **be** before the subject.
2. Where ~~is~~ **are** Cameroon and Morocco?	Be careful with singular and plural forms of **be**.
3. Who ~~is~~ **was** the first queen of England?	Be careful with present and past tense forms of **be**.

EXERCISE 3. Interviewing Someone

Write the correct information question word and the verb *be*.

Interviewing a Student from Brazil

Questions	Answers
1. ___What___ ___is___ your first name?	Marilia
2. _____ _____ your last name?	Santos
3. _____ _____ you from?	Brazil
4. _____ _____ you born?	in Rio de Janeiro
5. _____ _____ your hometown?	Manaus
6. _____ _____ Manaus?	in the state of Amazonas
7. _____ states _____ there in Brazil?	There are 26 states in Brazil.
8. _____ _____ the capital of Brazil?	Brasilia
9. _____ _____ you?	I'm 32.
10. _____ _____ your birthday?	October 7th
11. _____ _____ your hobbies?	running and eating international food
12. _____ _____ your favorite runner?	Usain Bolt He's great!
13. _____ _____ Bolt from?	Jamaica
14. _____ _____ your favorite food?	feijoada
15. _____ _____ feijoada?	a Brazilian dish with beans and meat
16. _____ _____ you in this class?	to improve my pronunciation
17. _____ _____ your plans after this class?	to get a job at an international bank and buy my own house

Do Online Exercise 7.2. My score: _____ /10. _____ % correct.

Question Word Order with Simple Present and Simple Past

	(wh- word)	do/does/did	subject	rest of sentence	short answer
yes-no		Does	Amir	go shopping on Monday?	Yes, he does.
wh-	When	does	Amir	go shopping ?	On Monday.

Step 1	Check for a verb (not be).	Amir goes shopping on Monday.
Step 2	For a yes-no question with simple present tense and simple past tense, you use do, does, or did before the subject and the simple form of the verb.	does Amir go shopping on Monday.
Step 3	For a wh- question, you then change the information (on Monday) to the correct question word (when).	does Amir go shopping when.
Step 4	Move the question word to the front of the question.	when does Amir go shopping.
Step 5	Use a capital letter for the first word of the question, and add a question mark (?) at the end.	When does Amir go shopping?

Rule 1. Information questions begin with a question word.

Rule 2. For simple present and simple past tense of verbs (not be), use do, does, or did before the subject.

BE CAREFUL!

Common Learner Errors	Explanation
1. Why ~~Mr. Iijima went~~ did Mr. Iijima go to the bank?	Remember to use do, does, or did before the subject.
2. How many letters ~~do~~ does the English alphabet have?	Be careful with singular and plural forms of the verbs.
3. Where ~~do~~ did Muhamad live in 2007?	Be careful with the present and past tense forms.
4. Where does she ~~works~~ work?	Use the base form of the verb with does.
5. When did you ~~lived~~ live in Korea?	Use the base form of the verb with did.

EXERCISE 4. Interviewing Two People

Write the correct information question word and add then *do, does,* or *did* for these questions you are asking an older married couple.

Interviewing a Married Couple

Questions	The Couple's Answers
1. _____ _____ you get married?	We got married in 1955.
2. _____ _____ you first meet?	in Boston
3. _____ _____ you know each other before you got married?	about a year
4. _____ _____ you live now?	in a small town near Boston
5. _____ children _____ you have?	We have one son.
6. _____ _____ he live?	He lives in California with his family.
7. _____ _____ he move to California?	to take a banking job
8. _____ children _____ he have?	He and his wife have two kids.
9. _____ times each year _____ you visit them?	twice a year
10. _____ place do you prefer—Boston or California?	Boston

EXERCISE 5. Writing *what* Questions

Write a yes-no question, and give a short answer. Then write a *wh-* question using *what,* and give a short answer.

1. Rui writes <u>newspaper ads</u> at work.

   (yes-no) Does Rui write newspaper ads at work?

   Yes, she does.

   (what) What does she write at work?

   Newspaper ads.

2. The largest country in South America is <u>Brazil</u>.

   (yes-no) _____

   _____

   (what) _____

   _____

3. Paul reads <u>mystery stories</u> on the weekend.

   (yes-no) _____

   _____

   (what) _____

   _____

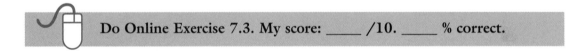

Do Online Exercise 7.3. My score: _____ **/10.** _____ **% correct.**

EXERCISE 6. Writing *when* Questions

Write a yes-no question, and give a short answer. Then write a *wh-* question using *when,* and give a short answer.

1. Victor began the work <u>at 10 AM.</u>

   (yes-no) _____

   _____

   (when) _____

   _____

2. The girls watch a scary movie <u>every Friday night</u>.

   (yes-no) _____

   _____

   (when) _____

   _____

3. The big tennis tournament was <u>last weekend</u>.

   (yes-no) _____

   _____

   (when) _____

   _____

EXERCISE 7. Writing *where* Questions

Write a yes-no question, and give a short answer. Then write a *wh-* question using *where,* and give a short answer.

1. You live <u>on Miller Street</u>.

   (yes-no) _____

   _____

   (where) _____

   _____

2. They watched a movie <u>at Carl's house</u>.

   (yes-no) _____

   _____

   (where) _____

   _____

3. The books were <u>in the desk drawer</u>.

   (yes-no) _____

   _____

   (where) _____

   _____

ONE-MINUTE LESSON

at/on/in for place: The three sentences in Exercise 7 are good examples of **at/on/in.** We use **on** with street names (*you live on Miller Street*), **at** with a person's house to talk about an action there (*they watched a movie at Carl's house*), and **in** for the inside part of something (*the books were in the desk drawer*). For information about **at/on/in** for *place,* see pp. 268–70 in Unit 10.

Do Online Exercise 7.4. My score: _____ /10. _____ % correct.

EXERCISE 8. Writing *why* Questions

Write a yes-no question, and give a short answer. Then write a *wh-* question using *why,* and give a short answer.

1. Victor speaks French well <u>because he lived in France</u>.

   (yes-no) _____

   _____

   _____

   (why) _____

   _____

2. Mark stayed home <u>because it was too cold to go outside</u>.

   (yes-no) _____

   _____

   _____

   (why) _____

   _____

3. You like volleyball <u>because it has a lot of quick points</u>.

   (yes-no) _____

   _____

   _____

   (wh) _____

   _____

ONE-MINUTE LESSON
Because is followed by a subject and a verb. Don't forget to include the second subject: *I passed the test* **because** *I studied hard.*

EXERCISE 9. Writing *which* Questions

Write a yes-no question, and give a short answer. Then write a *wh-* question using *which,* and give a short answer.

1. The teacher's book is the book <u>on the table</u>.

    (yes-no)   Is the book on the table the teacher's book?

    Yes, it is.

    (which)   Which book is the teacher's book

    The book on the table. (OR: The one on the table.)

2. Emily wants the <u>green cotton</u> t-shirt.

    (yes-no)   _____

    _____

    (which)   _____

    _____

3. The most difficult question was question <u>number seven</u>.

    (yes-no)   _____

    _____

    (which)   _____

    _____

4. You like <u>grammar</u> class the best.

    (yes-no)   _____

    _____

    (which)   _____

    _____

> **ONE-MINUTE LESSON**
> We use **one** or **ones** in place of a noun. We usually use **one** or **ones** when identifying which person or thing we are talking about. We use **ones** before a descriptive adjective or after *which: Which **one** do you want? The green **one**?*

✓ **EXERCISE 10. Editing. Is It correct?**

If the sentence is correct, write a check mark (✓) on the line. If it is not correct, write X on the line and circle the mistake. Then change the sentence to make it correct. Write the change above the sentence. (*Hint:* There are twelve sentences. Two are correct, but ten have mistakes.)

Ordering Pizza by Phone

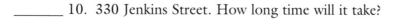

_____ 1. "Hi, this is Giovani's Pizzeria. What you would like?"

_____ 2. I would like to order a cheese pizza.

_____ 3. We have small, medium, large, and extra large. Which size you want?

_____ 4. How much people is a large pizza for?

_____ 5. I think about three people.

_____ 6. Ok, then I want two large pizzas. And this is for delivery. Are you understand?

_____ 7. Where you live?

_____ 8. Excuse me? What you said?

_____ 9. Where is your address?

_____ 10. 330 Jenkins Street. How long time will it take?

_____ 11. About 30 minutes. Are you have any other questions?

_____ 12. Yes. How much money do these two pizzas cost?

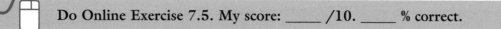

Do Online Exercise 7.5. My score: _____ /10. _____ % correct.

Who/Whom

Who is for people. In informal English, we can say Who lives in that house? or Who did you call? However, in formal English, we use whom for the object of a verb or a preposition. If you want to write academic English, you may need to know about whom. If you only want conversational English, you probably do not need to know about whom. Ask your teacher what you need to know about who and whom.

Who + verb		Whom + do/does/did + subject + verb			
Who	used	my cell phone?	Whom	did	you	call?
Who	needs	a pencil?	Whom	does	Pamela	work with?

function	informal or spoken English	formal or written English
subject	Who *lives there?*	Who *lives there?*
object of verb	Who *did you call?*	Whom *did you call?*
object of preposition	Who *did you talk to?*	Whom *did you talk to?*

__Rule 1__. In a question, who is the subject.

__Rule 2__. In a question, whom is the object.

__Rule 3__. Who can be singular or plural.

__Rule 4__. Whom can be singular or plural.

__Rule 5__. Most people use who all the time, especially in speaking.

 BE CAREFUL!

Common Learner Errors	Explanation
1. ~~Whom~~ Who wrote this contract?	Always use who for the subject, not whom.
2. ~~Who~~ Whom did the main character in this story fall in love with?	In academic writing, use whom as the object of a verb or a preposition.
3. ~~Whom~~ Who do you want to marry?	In informal language, especially speaking, it is unusual to use whom at any time.

EXERCISE 11. Writing *who/whom* Questions

WHO/WHOM: Make a question with *who* and then a question with *whom*. Write the answers too.

Example: Mr. Al-Asmar called Mr. Baez.

Who called Mr. Baez?   (Mr. Al-Asmar)

Whom did Mr. Al-Asmar call?   (Mr. Baez)

1. Ayako invited Junichi and Sam to the party.

(who) _____

(whom) _____

_____

2. Ana usually studies vocabulary with Joshua and Elizabeth.

(who) _____

(whom) _____

_____

3. The company director hired a new secretary.

(who) _____

(whom) _____

_____

4. Mario gave a concert ticket to Zeke.

(who) _____

(whom) _____

_____

ONE-MINUTE LESSON

With the verb **give**, we have two possible sentences. We can say, *Mario* **gave** *a concert ticket to Zeke* (**give** + [object] + *to* + [person]) or *Mario* **gave** *Zeke a concert ticket* (**give** + [person] + [object]). Both sentences are correct. Six common verbs that permit these two ways are: **give, lend, pass, show, teach, tell.**

Do Online Exercise 7.6. My score: _____ /10. _____ % correct.

Asking Questions about Meaning, Pronunciation, and Spelling

To ask about . . .	Questions
meaning	*What does _____ mean?* *What is the meaning of _____?*
pronunciation	*How do you say _____?* *How do you pronounce _____?* *What is the pronunciation of _____?*
spelling	*How do you spell _____?* *What is the spelling of _____?*

BE CAREFUL!

Common Learner Errors	Explanation
1. ~~What means "dozen"~~ What does "dozen" mean?	For meaning, do not say What means ___? The correct question is What does ___ mean?
2. ~~What says "dozen"~~ How do you pronounce "dozen"?	For pronunciation, do not say What says ___? The correct question is How do you say ___? or How do you pronounce ___?

EXERCISE 12. Questions about Meaning

Write a question and answer about the meaning of each word. If you do not know a word, use a dictionary or ask an English speaker.

1. dozen Q: _What does dozen mean?_

    A: _Dozen means twelve._

2. sour Q: _____

    A: _____

3. might Q: _____

    A: _____

4. a few Q: _____

    A: _____

For Numbers 5 and 6, find a word that you do not know. Then find the meaning in a dictionary or from a native speaker.

5. _____ Q: _____

    A: _____

6. _____ Q: _____

    A: _____

EXERCISE 13. Informal Questions

Make a question by substituting *who,* * *why, what, when,* and *where* for the underlined words. Follow the examples.

Example: <u>Mary</u> called John.   _____

He speaks <u>English</u> at home.   _____

1. She arrives <u>at 8 AM</u>.   _____

2. Mary learned French <u>in Paris</u>.   _____

3. She asked <u>John</u>.   _____

4. <u>Rick</u> wants a new car.   _____

5. Jane has <u>a new watch</u>   _____

6. The boys are <u>in the kitchen</u>.   _____

7. <u>The boys</u> are in the kitchen.   _____

8. They go <u>to Florida</u> every summer.   _____

9. They go to Florida <u>every summer</u>.   _____

10. You played football with <u>Mike</u>.   _____

11. Yuri walks to school <u>because she likes the exercise</u>.   _____

12. Fiesta means <u>a party</u>.   _____

ONE-MINUTE LESSON
If we don't know if **who** refers to one person or several people, we use singular. If someone knocks at your door, you ask, **Who** *is it?* before opening the door. Even if you think there is more than one person outside the door, the question is still the same.

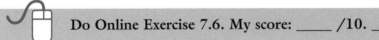

Do Online Exercise 7.6. My score: _____ /10. _____ % correct.

*These questions are for informal spoken English. *Whom* is very rare in this kind of conversational language.

EXERCISE 14. Review of Different Question Words

Review of question words. Make questions according to the underlined words. Follow the example.

1. <u>Mary</u> studied <u>French</u> with <u>Paul and Sue</u> <u>last night</u>.
      A   B   C   D

   a. Who studied French with Paul and Sue last night? _____

   b. _____

   c. _____

   d. _____

2. Hilarious <u>means very funny</u>.

   _____

3. <u>Jill and Zina</u> listen to the radio every night. They do this
        A

   <u>because they want to learn new English words</u>.
                                  B

   a. _____

   b. _____

4. <u>Thomas Edison</u> invented the <u>lightbulb</u>. He was born <u>in Ohio</u>. He died <u>in 1931</u>.
         A   B   C   D

   a. _____

   b. _____

   c. _____

   d. _____

EXERCISE 15. Speaking Practice: Who Is Who?

Five students from five different countries are studying English in the U.S. Some of the information about the students is missing.

Student A

Step 1. Work with a partner. You are Student A, and your partner is B.
Step 2. Student A works on this page, but Student B works on page 199.
Step 3. Take turns asking information questions to fill in the missing information.

Name	Student Number	Country	Place of Birth	Arrived in U.S.	Teacher
Susan Johnson	228441		Stockholm		Mr. Currier
Kerry Gomez			Lima		
Battulga Liam	219558		Ulan Bator	March 2007	
Paulo Rossi	223819	Brazil			Mr. Kennedy
Emi Tanaka		Japan		last October	

Student B

Step 1. Work with a partner. You are Student B, and your partner is A.

Step 2. Student B works on this page, but Student A works on page 198.

Step 3. Take turns asking information questions to fill in the missing information.

Name	Student Number	Country	Place of Birth	Arrived in U.S.	Teacher
Susan Johnson		Sweden		January 2010	
Kerry Gomez	228497	Peru		last year	Mrs. Montluzin
Battulga Liam		Mongolia			Mrs. Little
Paulo Rossi			Sao Paolo	two years ago	
Emi Tanaka	228114		Nagoya		Mrs. Valen

EXERCISE 16. Sentence Study for Critical Reading

Read the numbered question. Then read the three answer choices, and place a check mark in the yes or no boxes in front of each sentence to show if that answer is true based on the information in the original sentence. If there is not enough information to mark something as yes, then mark it as no. Remember that more than one true answer is possible.

1. Where did Susan go?

   ☐ yes ☐ no   a. To the airport.

   ☐ yes ☐ no   b. To a meeting.

   ☐ yes ☐ no   c. From her house.

2. When did you get home?

   ☐ yes ☐ no   a. Because it rained really hard for a long time.

   ☐ yes ☐ no   b. All of the stores closed.

   ☐ yes ☐ no   c. A little after seven.

3. What did he study in his first year in college?

   ☐ yes ☐ no   a. History.

   ☐ yes ☐ no   b. English and science.

   ☐ yes ☐ no   c. International business.

4. Why did you come to class late?

   ☐ yes ☐ no   a. By bike.

   ☐ yes ☐ no   b. I am not a morning person, so it's hard for me to get up on time.

   ☐ yes ☐ no   c. My alarm clock was broken.

5. Which exercise did we do in the last class?

   ☐ yes ☐ no   a. The exercise about question words.

   ☐ yes ☐ no   b. In the back of the book.

   ☐ yes ☐ no   c. The one at the top of page 437.

6. When did Michael come to the United States?

   ☐ yes ☐ no   a. For a year.

   ☐ yes ☐ no   b. In 1997.

   ☐ yes ☐ no   c. Next month.

7. Where did the boys go last weekend?

   ☐ yes ☐ no   a. Because they had a vacation.

   ☐ yes ☐ no   b. To the zoo.

   ☐ yes ☐ no   c. At approximately 8:00 PM.

8. Which movie did you see last night?

   ☐ yes ☐ no   a. With several of my closest friends.

   ☐ yes ☐ no   b. The comedy.

   ☐ yes ☐ no   c. In the theater at the mall.

EXERCISE 17. Review Test 1: Multiple Choice

Circle the letter of the correct answer to complete these conversations.

1. "Mark, _____ do you live now?"

   "I live near Miami, Florida."

       a. Who   b. When   c. Where   d. How long

2. "_____ did you stay in Paris when you were there for vacation last summer?"

   "About 2 weeks. I wanted to stay longer, but it wasn't possible."

       a. How much   b. How many   c. How long   d. Why

3. "_____ were you late to class?"

   "Because I woke up late this morning. "

       a. Why   b. How   c. When   d. Which

4. " What _____?   "

   "It's the number 1 and 100 zeros."

       a. means google?   c. google means?
       b. does google mean?   d. is meaning google?

5. "Friday, Saturday, or Sunday — _____ day is best for you?"

   "I prefer Friday if that's OK with you."

       a. When   b. Why   c. How many   d. Which

6. "I can't pronounce the difference between L and R well."

   "Ok, so how _____ the words *far* and *fall*?"

       a. you pronounce   c. do you pronounce
       b. pronounce you   d. are you pronounce

7. "Who _____ a class right now?"

   "Mark has English class, and Susan and I have French class."

       a. have   b. has   c. does   d. do

8. "How much _____?

   "That shirt is $47."

       a. does that shirt cost?   c. costs that shirt?
       b. money is that shirt?   d. does cost that shirt?

REVIEW **EXERCISE 18. Review Test 2: Production and Evaluation**

Part 1.
Fill in the blanks with the question words from this word list. Use each word/phrase once.

word list	how long how many	how old what	how much which	why how many

---

Sami,

I was very happy to get your last e-mail. I am really glad to have you as a new friend in Korea. Next year my family will live in Korea, so we have many questions about Korea. Here are some questions that I hope you can answer for me.

❶ _____ is the largest city in Korea? Between Seoul and Busan,

❷ _____ city is better for us?

❸ _____ seasons does Korea have? I live in Florida, and we have only two seasons. We have a long summer and a short winter.

Someone told me that the winter weather is very cold. ❹ _____ does the cold weather last in Korea?

Someone told me that Korean is a very difficult language for foreigners to learn. Do you agree with this? ❺ _____ do you have this opinion?

❻ _____ people live in Korea? Is it very crowded?

My daughter is five years old. In America, children begin school at age 6.
❼ _____ are children when they start school in Korea?

We want to rent a small apartment. ❽ _____ does it cost to rent a small apartment?

Thank you very much for your help. I hope to read your answers very soon.

Scott

Part 2.

Read each sentence carefully. Look at the underlined part. If the underlined part is correct, circle the word *correct*. If it is wrong, circle the word *wrong* and the wrong part. Then write the correction above.

correct   wrong   1. A: <u>Where was</u> the meeting?

B: It was at 8 AM.

correct   wrong   2. A: <u>What means huge</u>?

B: It means very, very big.

correct   wrong   3. A: Who <u>wants</u> some coffee?

B: Mehdi and I want some coffee, please.

correct   wrong   4. A: <u>You study English so hard why</u>?

B: Because I need better English to get a great job later.

correct   wrong   5. A: <u>Where does Mariana live</u>?

B: In an apartment near the university.

correct   wrong   6. A: <u>What do Victor has</u> in that bag?

B: A new cell phone.

EXERCISE 19. Reading Practice: A Webpage

Read this encyclopedia entry about Google, and then answer the ten comprehension questions on page 205. The grammar from this unit is underlined for you.

---

vocabulary – Google Search

◄ ► + 🔖 http://www.google.com/search?hl=en&source=hp&q=vocabulary&aq=f&aqi=g10&oq=   ⟳   Q⟩ Google

📖 ▦   eBook Archit...on Services   Stock Photos...s Unlimited   Welcome To t...s FTP Site!   Welcome To t...s FTP Site!   Apple   Yahoo!   Google Maps   YouTube   Wikipedia   »

Web   Images   Videos   Maps   News   Shopping   Gmail   more ▾   Web History | Search settings | Sign in

Google | vocabulary | Search   Advanced Search

What is Google?

Web ⊞ Show options...   Results **1 - 10** of about **38,800,000** for **vocabulary** [definition]. **(0.13 seconds)**

Google is a U.S. company. Its most well-known product is its search engine, which is a system that helps people search for information on the Internet. Google is a name that everyone knows because Google is the most popular search engine in the world.

Who started Google?

Larry Page and Sergey Brin started Google.

Where did Page and Brin start this famous business?

Page and Brin began their research about the Google search engine at Stanford University, where they were Ph.D. students.

When did Page and Brin start Google?

While he was a Ph.D. student in 1996, Larry Page began working on a research project about searching for information on different websites. Shortly after he started this research project, Sergey Brin, who was also a Ph.D. student at Stanford, joined the project. In September 1997, Page and Brin started google.com. One year later, they started the Google company.

How many people use Google every day?

Google is the most popular search engine in the entire world, so millions of people use it every day. According to ask.com, there are more than two billion (2,000,000,000) searches per day. This means that probably more than 300 million (300,000,000) people use Google every day. The actual number is probably much higher.
(Source: *http://wiki.answers.com/Q/How_many_people_use_the_search_engine_'Google'_everyday_day,* accessed on January 19, 2010)

Where did the name Google come from? What does Google mean?

The name Google comes from the word "googol." Googol is a huge number. Googol is 10^{100}, which means the number one followed by one hundred zeros.

Is Google a noun? Or is it a verb?

At first, Google was only a noun. It was the name of something, so that made it a noun. However, people began to use Google as a verb. For example, they might say, "Google that topic to see how much information you can get." In 2006, the verb *google* appeared in several famous dictionaries. Now we know Google to be both a noun and a verb.

1. What happened in 1996? _____

   _____

2. What is Google? _____

   _____

3. Who are Larry Page and Sergey Brin? _____

   _____

4. What does the name Google mean? _____

   _____

5. When did google.com begin? _____

6. How many people use Google daily? _____

7. In current English usage, is Google a noun or a verb? _____

8. When did Google become a company? _____

9. What were Page and Brin doing at Stanford? _____

   _____

10. When did Google enter the dictionary as a verb? _____

EXERCISE 20. Vocabulary Practice: Word Knowledge

Circle the word or phrase that is most closely related to the word or phrase on the left. Use a dictionary to check the meaning of words you do not know.

Vocabulary	Answer Choices	
1. worst	very bad	very good
2. a season	winner	winter
3. to end	to cook	to finish
4. dozen	10	12
5. where	place	person
6. a drawer	in a desk	in a computer
7. well-known	intelligent	famous
8. a race	learning	running
9. would rather	bring	prefer
10. agree with	have different ideas	have the same idea
11. when	time	reason
12. entire	one	all
13. a price	$10	10%
14. a subject	second or third	math or science
15. recommend	suggest	try
16. an ad	to sell a car	to drive a car
17. a total	$48 + 6 = 54$	$48 - 6 = 42$
18. a cruise	in a hotel	on a ship
19. Person 1 killed Person 2	Person 1 died	Person 2 died
20. sure	certain	perhaps
21. one letter is missing	a blac_ cat	a black _____
22. main	most important	not possible
23. scramble	look	mix
24. hilarious	very funny	very hungry
25. too cold	very cold	also cold
26. kids	children	clothing
27. to order	to ask for	to say again
28. points	in a game	in a mystery
29. how many	length of time	number of something
30. alphabet	A to Z	1 to 100
31. to hire	for a sport	for a job
32. I guess	I promise	I think
33. be out of money	not need money	not have money
34. to discover	to find	to rent

EXERCISE 21. Vocabulary Practice: Collocations

Fill in each blank with the answer on the right that most naturally completes the phrase on the left. If necessary, use a dictionary to check the meaning of words you do not know.

Phrase	Answer Choices	
1. on _____	August	Monday
2. _____ the dishes	brush	wash
3. a _____ pizza	cheese	scrambled
4. How long does your class _____?	end	last
5. dark _____	green	warm
6. _____ own car	I	my
7. second, _____, fourth	third	fifth
8. _____ Green Street	in	on
9. How _____ did it cost?	many	much
10. I don't know _____.	correctly	exactly
11. _____ five days	for	with
12. _____ Room 126	in	on
13. an alarm _____	clock	watch
14. The movie _____ at nine.	ended	turned
15. Thank you so much _____ your help.	by	for
16. _____ you go.	Here	This
17. your _____ name	end	last
18. a piece of _____	idea	meat
19. a list of _____	names	pencils
20. _____ married	get	take
21. Who should I ask _____?	for	without
22. to rain _____	hard	little
23. my _____ friend	closest	deadest
24. to _____ in one place	need	stay
25. go to the _____	beach	flight
26. _____ large	extra	more
27. to _____ at a store	kill	shop
28. according _____	for	to
29. What are your _____?	plan	plans
30. _____ the top drawer	at	in
31. _____ a new job	run	take
32. at _____ six	age	old
33. the _____ character	friend	main
34. _____ shopping	go	make
35. _____ a word correctly	spell	think
36. he scored 95 _____ the exam	in	on
37. a cotton _____	coat	t-shirt

EXERCISE 22. Writing Practice: Details about an Animal or a Thing

Part 1. Editing Student Writing.

Read these sentences about an animal. Circle the 15 errors. Then write the number of the sentence with the error next to the type of error. (Some sentences may have more than one error.)

_____ a. no subject   _____ e. singular-plural

_____ b. no verb   _____ f. verb tense

_____ c. *is/are* (wrong form)   _____ g. capital letter

_____ d. question

Giraffes
1. What is a giraffe? A giraffe is one of the tallest animal in the world.
2. where do giraffes live? Giraffes live in open areas of Africa. You can find them from Chad to South Africa.
3. What giraffes eat? They liked to eat leaves from trees. Giraffes are very tall, so can reach the trees easily.
4. How long time do giraffes sleep? Giraffes are special. In one day, sometimes sleep only ten minutes. The average time about two hours per day.
5. How many giraffes there in africa? There is approximately 130,000 giraffes in Africa.
6. Which countries have the most giraffes? The three country with the most giraffes are Kenya, Tanzania, and Botswana.
7. How many years are most giraffes? Griaffes in a zoo can live to age 25, but giraffes in the wild lived to about age 13.
8. Where does the English name "giraffe" come from? The name giraffe comes from the Arabic word for this animal, which are "ziraafa."

Part 2. Original Student Writing.

Now write a short paragraph (or some questions and answers) about an animal, a thing, or a person. Use 5 words from the vocabulary pages. Underline the 5 words. Use 2 new words from your dictionary. Put a circle around the 2 dictionary words.

Greetings from Paris

Unit 8

Present Progressive

Discover the Grammar

Ann and Matt are vacationing in Paris. Mary is in charge of their apartment while they are staying in Paris. Read this postcard that they wrote to their good friend Mary.

Line	
1	Dear Mary,
2	Scott and I are visiting Paris!!! We are spending
3	7 days here. I'm doing fun things. I'm eating and
4	shopping, and Scott is relaxing. We are enjoying
5	this great weather. We're staying at the Royal
6	Jardin Hotel. What a great place! I really like it a
7	lot. Right now I'm sitting at a cafe, and I'm writing
8	this card. We are having a great time. I work every
9	day in Fairfax, but I'm not working here!
10	Love, Ann
11	P.S. Are you watering our plants? We hope so! ☺

Mary Sawyer
833 Elm St.
Fairfax, VA 22033

1. Underline these 14 verbs in the postcard. (Some verbs appear twice.)

do	have	shop	stay	work
eat	like	sit	visit	write
enjoy	relax	spend	water	

2. Put a box around *-ing* verbs and the form of *be* that comes before it. For example, put a box around *are* <u>*visiting*</u> in Line 2. The combination of verb *be* plus the *-ing* form of a verb is called **present progressive**. When do you think we use present progressive?

   _____

   _____

   _____

3. Study the verbs that end in *-ing*. Circle the verbs (for example, *shopping*) that double the last letter when you add *-ing*. Why do you think these verbs double the last letter but other verbs (for example, *eat*) do not?

   _____

   _____

   _____

   _____

4. Find the one example of a question from the postcard. If you want to make a question with present progressive tense, how do you form the question?

   _____

   _____

5. What questions do you have about this grammar?

   _____

   _____

   _____

Grammar Lesson

Present Progressive: Affirmative

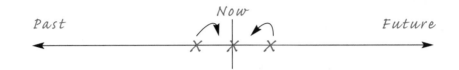

Example	subject	*be*	VERB + -ing
I am watching TV now.	I	am	watching
You're using the computer at this	moment.	you	're
using	He is living	in a house	in Los
Angeles.	he	is	living
She's renting an apartment in Burbank.	she	's	renting
It is raining right now.	it	is	raining
We are studying present progressive now.	we	are	studying

<u>**Rule 1**</u>. In present progressive tense, a verb has three forms: am VERB + -ing, is VERB + -ing, are VERB + -ing.

<u>**Rule 2**</u>. We use am VERB + -ing with *I*; is VERB + -ing with *he, she, it*; are VERB + -ing with *you, we, they*.

<u>**Rule 3**</u>. It is necessary to include a subject (noun or pronoun) before the verb.

<u>**Rule 4**</u>. Use simple present tense for actions that are happening now. Common time expressions for present progressive tense include **now, right now, today, tonight,** and this _____ (this year).

<u>**Rule 5**</u>. We can use present progressive tense with action verbs like *eat, do, read,* and *cry*. We do not use this tense with verbs that do not show an action. Four kinds of verbs that do not usually occur in present progressive tense are: senses (*hear, see, smell, feel, sound*), emotions (*like, love, need, prefer, want*), mental states (*believe, forget, remember, seem, think*), and possession (*belong, have, own, possess*).

> *Exception:* You can say *I'm having a good time* or *We're having a test* because *have* is an action in these two examples. You cannot say *I'm having a book* or *She's having a green pen* because *have* is not a real action here.

<u>**Rule 6**</u>. For verbs that end in -e, drop the final -e before adding -ing: take → taking.

<u>**Rule 7**</u>. If a one-syllable verb ends in consonant + vowel + consonant, double the final consonant before adding *-ing*: cut → cu<u>tt</u>ing (but read → reading).

Rule 8. If a two-syllable verb ends in consonant + vowel + consonant, we double the final consonant before adding *–ing* if the pronunciation stress is on the second syllable:

open → opening	*begin → beginning*
(o) pen [1st] 2nd	be (gin) 1st [2nd]
because we stress the 1st syllable	because we stress the 2nd syllable

 BE CAREFUL!

Common Learner Errors	Explanation
1. Laura ~~cooks~~ is cooking scrambled eggs for breakfast now.	Remember to use present progressive when the action is happening now.
2. The earth ~~is taking~~ takes one year to go around the sun.	Don't use present progressive for actions that happen every day or all the time.
3. My baby sister ~~crying~~ is crying now. I don't know why.	Use a form of be with present progressive tense.
4. My baby sister is ~~cry~~ crying now. I don't know why.	You must use -ing with present progressive tense.
5. ~~eatting~~ eating ~~helpping~~ helping ~~takking~~ taking ~~openning~~ opening ~~cuting~~ cutting ~~comming~~ coming	Be careful with the spelling of the -ing verb.
6. I ~~am owning~~ own an old gold truck.	Use present progressive only when the verb shows action.

EXERCISE 1. Affirmative Present Progressive

Fill in the blanks with the correct forms of the verbs.

take	run	begin
I _am taking_____	I _____	I _____
you _are taking_____	you _____	you _____
he _____	he _____	he _____
she _____	she _____	she _____
it _____	it _____	it _____
we _____	we _____	we _____
they _____	they _____	they _____
Jo _____	Jo _____	Jo _____
Jo and I _____	Jo and I _____	Jo and I _____

Do Online Exercise 8.1. My score: _____ /10. _____ % correct.

EXERCISE 2. Comparing Simple Present and Present Progressive

Write the forms of *work* in simple present and present progressive. Notice the time words in each sentence.

Simple Present Tense	Present Progressive Tense
1. I ____work____ every day.	8. I __am working__ now.
2. You _____ at night.	9. You _____ right now.
3. He _____ all of the time.	10. He _____ today.
4. She _____ every day.	11. She _____ this week.
5. It _____ most of the time.	12. It _____ now.
6. We _____ every Monday.	13. We _____ hard this semester.
7. They _____ here every day.	14. They _____ here this morning.

15. Now match these time expressions from Numbers 1–14 with the correct verb form.

at night	*every afternoon*	*every day*
all of the time	*right now*	*this week*
most of the time	*now*	*this semester*
today	*this morning*	*every Monday*

simple present	present progressive

EXERCISE 3. Present Progressive in Context

Fill in the blanks with the correct forms of the verbs.

A Busy Place

1. An airport _____is_____ (be) a very busy place.

2. Many things _____ (happen) there now.

3. Many flights _____ (take) off right now.

4. At the same time, many other flights _____ (land).

5. Some passengers _____ (arrive) home after a long trip.

6. They look tired, but they _____ (think) about their great vacations!

7. These passengers' family members _____ (wait) for them at the airport.

8. However, many other passengers _____ (leave) now.

9. These passengers _____ (begin) their trips now.

10. Security people _____ (check) these passengers' IDs.

11. A pilot _____ (buy) a cup of coffee before her flight.

12. The co-pilot _____ (talk) to her about the flight.

13. Some people _____ (eat) today at the many restaurants in the airport.

14. Airport workers _____ (clean) the airport.

15. They _____ (pick) up newspapers and other garbage every day.

Connecting Grammar and Vocabulary

Verbs like *own* and *seem* that do not show action are not used in present progressive tense. Most verbs are action verbs, so most verbs can be in present progressive tense. This means that there are thousands of possible verbs for you to learn, but this is not a good strategy. You should focus on the most commonly used verbs in present progressive tense. Study this list of common verbs for present progressive tense.

10 Frequent Verbs in Present Progressive Tense				
make	stand	live	put	try
do	work	get	say	think

<u>Source</u>: Based on information in the Corpus of Contemporary American English: www.americancorpus.org/.

EXERCISE 4. Spelling *-ing* Forms of 30 Common Verbs in Context

Complete these sentences with the correct *–ing* spelling of these 30 very common English verbs.

1. (do) What are you _____?

2. (say) What are you _____?

3. (make) Is Maznah _____ a tuna sandwich or a chicken sandwich?

4. (go) They are _____ to Dallas by car.

5. (take) I'm _____ some medicine for my cold.

6. (come) He is _____ here now.

7. (use) This math homework is difficult. I'm _____ a pencil so I can erase any mistakes that I make.

8. (get) Wow! It's windy, and now the weather is _____ cold.

9. (work) We are _____ harder than ever.

10. (give) Yousef is _____ an important speech now.

11. (look) What are you _____ at?

12. (tell) You have to believe me! I'm _____ you the truth!

13. (write) The students are _____ a short paper about a book.

14. (show) Why are you _____ me your brother's ID card?

15. (call) Fatimah, who are you _____?

16. (move) We are _____ all of these boxes today.

17. (begin) Oh, no! It is _____ to rain.

18. (turn) It's fall, and the tree leaves are _____ red and yellow.

19. (leave) Why are you _____ your job now?

20. (ask) I'm _____ you to help me, ok?

21. (end) The movie is _____ now.

22. (open) It's Giovana's birthday, and now she's _____ her presents.

23. (follow) Are we _____the directions exactly?

24. (present) What new information is the boss _____to us today?

25. (hold) Johnny is right-handed, but he's _____ his pen in his left hand.

26. (plan) Larissa is busy with her sister and mom. They're _____ her wedding.

27. (run) Look at that mouse! It's _____ behind that tree.

28. (keep) I'm putting my coins in this box, but Matt's _____ his coins in a secret place.

29. (play) Kevin and my cousin Ahmad are at the park. They're _____ softball today.

30. (stand) Look at those monkeys! One is sitting by the tree, and another is _____ by those bushes.

ONE-MINUTE LESSON
The word **get** has many different meanings. One common usage is **get** + adjective. In this case, **get** means "become." If it's almost noon, you can say, *I'm getting hungry.* If Mary put on a sweater, she can say, *I'm getting cold.* Use **get**, not *become.*

Do Online Exercise 8.2. My score: _____ /10. _____ % correct.

EXERCISE 5. Speaking Practice: Charades

Step 1. Work in groups of three to five. Each person makes a list of at least three activities he or she has done in the last few months (for example, *miss the bus*, *go rollerskating*, *watch a basketball game*). Don't show your list to the other group members.

Step 2. Take turns acting out the activities. Student A acts out the first activity. The group members try to guess what A is doing. Student A can only answer "Yes, I am" or "No, I'm not."

<u>Example</u>: (Student A acts out an activity; Students B, C, D try to guess the activity.)

B: Let's see . . . are you jogging?

A: No, I'm not.

C: Are you running away from somebody?

A: No, I'm not.

D: Are you carrying your books to school?

A: No, I'm not.

C: I know! Are you walking your dog?

A: Yes, I am! Now it's your turn.

EXERCISE 6. Action vs. Non-Action Verbs

Write each expression in the present progressive tense. Put an X by the verbs that are not usually used in present progressive.

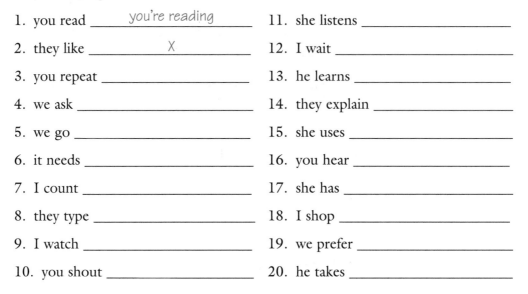

1. you read _____ you're reading _____
2. they like _____ X _____
3. you repeat _____
4. we ask _____
5. we go _____
6. it needs _____
7. I count _____
8. they type _____
9. I watch _____
10. you shout _____

11. she listens _____
12. I wait _____
13. he learns _____
14. they explain _____
15. she uses _____
16. you hear _____
17. she has _____
18. I shop _____
19. we prefer _____
20. he takes _____

Do Online Exercise 8.3. My score: _____ /10. _____ % correct.

EXERCISE 7. Simple Present and Present Progressive in Context

Write the correct form of the verb in each sentence.

(read)   1. After I eat breakfast, I usually _____ the newspaper.

          2. This week I _____ a book by Stephen King. It's scary.

(study) 3. Susan is busy now. She _____ math.

          4. Susan _____ math for an hour every day.

(play)   5. Mark and I _____ tennis after school.

          6. I can't play today, so Mark _____ with someone else.

(like)   7. Jenny didn't like coffee when she was a child, but now she really
                  _____ it a lot.

          8. Jenny _____ to drink orange juice for breakfast.

(have) 9. New York _____ many people.

       10. New York _____ many tourists
            this week.

(cook) 11. I can't play checkers with you now.
            I _____ dinner.

       12. I sometimes _____ rice with vegetables.

Do Online Exercise 8.4. My score: _____ /10. _____ % correct.

Present Progressive: Negative

Making a negative statement with present progressive is very easy. You just follow the same rules for making the verb **be** negative. (See Unit 1 for a reminder if you need it.) You add **not** after the form of **be**. You can also use contractions for informal language.

Other examples:

Statement		Question
I am sitting in your chair.	→	I am **not** sitting in your chair. I'm **not** sitting in your chair.
You are helping Mike.	→	You are **not** helping Mike. You aren't helping Mike. You're **not** helping Mike.
Maria is working at the bank this month.	→	Maria is **not** working at the bank this month. Maria isn't working at the bank this month. Maria's **not** working at the bank this month.

<u>Rule 1</u>. We use the word **not** to make a negative sentence with the verb **be** in present progressive: am not, is not, are not.

<u>Rule 2</u>. There is no contraction for **am not**. It is possible to use contractions for **is not** and **are not**: isn't, aren't.

<u>Rule 3</u>. It is also possible to make a contraction with the subject and **be** before the word **not**: I'm not, you're not (you aren't), she's not (she isn't), etc. There is no difference in meaning between these two forms of contractions.

EXERCISE 8. Mini-Conversations

Circle the correct words in these eight mini-conversations.

1. A: Your food looks good.

   B: Yes, it's very delicious. I (like, am liking) it a lot.

2. A: Can your teacher speak Chinese?

   B: Yes, she (speaks, is speaking) Chinese, English, and French.

3. A: Can I use your computer?

   B: Yes, but it (doesn't run, isn't running) very fast today.

4. A: Where (do you go, are you going)?.

   B: To the mall. (Do you want, Are you wanting) to go with me?

5. A: I'm glad the rain finally stopped.

   B: Yes, but now it (gets, is getting) colder. Can't you feel it?

6. A: Oh, the baby (cries, is crying). Is everything OK?

   B: Yes, everything is fine. She (needs, is needing) to eat now.

7. A: Which is better for math class—a pen or a pencil?

   B: Most people (prefer, are preferring) to use a pencil.

8. A: What's wrong with your car?

   B: I don't know. It (makes, is making) a noise. I'm not sure what's up.

ONE-MINUTE LESSON

One of the most common words in English is **up**, but it almost never means "opposite of down." Any phrase with **up** usually has a special meaning. **What's up?** means "hi" or "hello" in informal language. It also means "what is happening?" and "what is the problem?" You will also find **up** with many verbs, and these have special meanings: *the baby didn't* **throw up** *(vomit)*, *she will* **take up** *tennis (start to learn)*, *I never* **get up** *before 8 (be awake)*, and *the little boy* **made up** *a story (created)*. (These verbs are called *phrasal verbs* and are in *Clear Grammar, Book 3.*)

Do Online Exercise 8.5. My score: _____ /10. _____ % correct.

EXERCISE 9. Simple Present and Present Progressive Forms

Write the correct forms of these verbs for simple present tense and present progressive tense. If a form is not usual, write *not possible* in the box.

	Simple Present		Present Progressive	
	Affirmative	Negative	Affirmative	Negative
1. I/work	I work	I don't work	I am working	I'm not working
2. he/like	he likes	he doesn't like	not possible	not possible
3. they/want				
4. Ana/call				
5. we/watch				
6. you/get				
7. she/do				
8. it/begin				
9. they/sing				
10. he/explain				

Present Progressive: Making a Question

Making a question with present progressive is easy. You just follow the same rules for making a question with the verb *be*. (See Unit 1 for a reminder if you need it.) You move the form of *be* before the subject.

Examples:

Statement	Question
She's driving to the bank. →	**Is** she driving to the bank? Where **is** she driving to the bank?
You and Jenna are eating fried fish. →	**Are** you and Jenna eating fried fish? What **are** you and Jenna eating?

EXERCISE 10. Questions in Simple Present and Present Progressive

Make a question from each statement. Circle the time words (if they are there). Decide if the verb in the statement is simple present tense or present progressive. This will help you write the question.

1. A. Jill is swimming in the pool (now.)   Is Jill swimming in the pool now?

   B. Jill swims five laps (every day.)   Does Jill swim five laps every day?

2. A. Mr. Yoshida teaches history. _____

   B. Mr. Yoshida is teaching Sue now. _____

3. A. They're having a good time there. _____

   B. They have a good time in that class. _____

4. A. It's snowing heavily now. _____

   B. It snows a lot in January. _____

5. A. Josh takes a shower at night. _____

   B. Josh is taking a shower now. _____

6. A. Mr. Po is preparing lunch. _____

   B. Mr. Po prepares lunch every day. _____

7. A. Henry and Mark study together. _____

   B. Henry and Mark are studying. _____

8. A: It's raining now. _____

   B: It rains a lot in summer. _____

EXERCISE 11. Information Questions in Context

Use these words to make a *wh-* question with *you* according to the answer that is given. Be sure to end each question with a question mark.

word list	call	~~cook~~	go	hurry	work	write

1. Q: What ___are you cooking?___

   A: Scrambled eggs.

2. Q: Where _____

   A: At First Country Bank on Lincoln Avenue.

3. Q: Why _____

   A: Because I'm late for work.

4. Q: Who _____

   A: Susan. I want to talk to her about the homework.

5. Q: What _____

   A: A short email to my best friend from college.

6. Q: Where _____

   A: To the bank. I have to get some cash.

ONE-MINUTE LESSON

One of the most common verbs in the English language is **get**. You need to learn to use this word if you want your English to sound natural. We say *I'm going to the bank to* **get** *some cash,* not *take.* Common meanings of **get** are: "take or receive" (*Did you* **get** *your pay check?*), "become" (*When I hear that song, I always* **get** *sad*), and "arrive" (*What time do you* **get** *to the office?*).

Do Online Exercise 8.6. My score: _____ /10. _____ % correct.

EXERCISE 12. Editing. Is It Correct?

If the sentence is correct, write a check mark (✔) on the line. If it is not correct, write X on the line and circle the mistake. Then make the change above the sentence. (*Hint:* There are eight sentences. Two are correct, but six have mistakes.)

An Email to a Friend

_____ 1. I'm writing you this email now because I am have some good news.

_____ 2. I am have a new place, and I want to give you my new address.

_____ 3. Are you remember my old apartment?

_____ 4. Well, it really was no so nice, and the rent was pretty high.

_____ 5. I finally decide to move.

_____ 6. My new address is 1706 East Jasmine Avenue, Apartment 121.

_____ 7. I had a roommate before, but in my new place, I am living alone.

_____ 8. I'm so much happier in this new apartment, and I'm wanting you to visit me as soon as possible.

EXERCISE 13. Sentence Study for Critical Reading

Read the numbered sentences. Then read the three answer choices, and place a check mark in the yes or no boxes in front of each sentence to show if that answer is true based on the information in the original sentence. If there is not enough information to mark something as yes, then mark it as no. Remember that more than one true answer may be possible.

1. Brian works for the police department.

   ☐ yes ☐ no   a. This verb is talking about the future.

   ☐ yes ☐ no   b. This verb is talking about the past.

   ☐ yes ☐ no   c. This verb is talking about every day.

2. Charlie is making a sandwich, so he can't answer the phone.

   ☐ yes ☐ no   a. This action is true all of the time.

   ☐ yes ☐ no   b. This action is happening now.

   ☐ yes ☐ no   c. This action is finished.

3. Nancy took that photo with her cell phone.

   ☐ yes ☐ no   a. This verb is talking about the future.

   ☐ yes ☐ no   b. This verb is talking about the past.

   ☐ yes ☐ no   c. This verb is talking about every day.

4. Fred walks to school because he doesn't live far away.

   ☐ yes ☐ no   a. This action is true all of the time.

   ☐ yes ☐ no   b. This action is happening right now.

   ☐ yes ☐ no   c. This action is finished.

5. In June and July, it rains a lot in Florida.

   ☐ yes ☐ no   a. The weather there is wet in these months.

   ☐ yes ☐ no   b. It rains more in June and July.

   ☐ yes ☐ no   c. July has more rain than any other month.

6. My sister's computer is having some problems.

   ☐ yes ☐ no   a. This action is true all of the time.

   ☐ yes ☐ no   b. This action is happening now.

   ☐ yes ☐ no   c. This action is finished.

7. Kelly studied creating websites for eight months.

    ☐ yes ☐ no a. This action is true all of the time.

    ☐ yes ☐ no b. This action is happening now only.

    ☐ yes ☐ no c. This action is finished.

8. Kevin is holding the baby until Sharon opens the car door.

    ☐ yes ☐ no a. This action is true all of the time.

    ☐ yes ☐ no b. This action is happening now.

    ☐ yes ☐ no c. This action is finished.

EXERCISE 14. Speaking Practice: Questions about Photos

Step 1. Look at the photos. Write ten questions about the people and things in the photos. Use present progressive tense when possible.

Step 2. Write five questions that have a yes answer. Write five questions that have a no answer.

Step 3. Then work with a partner. Take turns asking each other questions.

Yes Answers	No Answers
Are the students in Photo 1 learning?	Is the teacher in Photo 2 sitting down?
1.	1.
2.	2.
3.	3.
4.	4.
5.	5.

Present Progressive for Future Time

We use present progressive for actions that are happening now, but it is also common to use present progressive for future actions, especially in conversation. In this case, it is important to say the time of the action. Compare the difference between the time of A–B and C–D.

Example	Form	Time
A: What **are** you **doing** now? B: We're **helping** our dad with yard work.	*present progressive* *present progressive*	**now** **now**
C: What **are** you **doing** next Saturday? D: We're **helping** our dad with yard work.	*present progressive* *present progressive*	**future** **future**

Other examples of future time actions:

E: What time is Colin **coming**? F: He's **arriving** at 8.	*present progressive* *present progressive*	**future** **future**
G: Let's play tennis tomorrow, ok? H: Sorry, I can't. I'm **studying** with Lena tomorrow.	*present progressive*	**future**

<u>**Rule 1.**</u> It is possible to use present progressive for current actions and for future actions: I'<u>m reading</u> this book now because we'<u>re having</u> a test on it tomorrow.

<u>**Rule 2.**</u> Another way to talk about future actions is to use be going to + VERB: I'<u>m reading</u> this book now because we'<u>re going to have</u> a test on it tomorrow. (*Note:* This grammar is explained in detail in Unit 11.)

<u>**Rule 3.**</u> The types of mistakes for present progressive for future actions are the same as those for present progressive for current actions, so study the mistakes on page 213 again.

ONE-MINUTE LESSON

It is common and polite to offer an excuse when you do not accept an invitation for the future. If a friend invites you to a party by saying, *Can you come to my party tomorrow night?* it is strange to only say, *No, I can't.* It is usual to add an excuse with **No, I can't because I have to study tomorrow night.**

EXERCISE 15. Comparing Tenses and Times

Identify the form and the time of the underlined verbs. For verb form, write simple present, simple past, or present progressive. For verb time, write present, past, or future.

Example	Form	Time
Arif: What <u>did</u> you <u>make</u> on your history test?	1. simple past	2. past
Masahiro: I <u>got</u> a 97. What about you?	3.	4.
Arif: I <u>was</u> absent.	5.	6.
Masahiro: So now what? <u>Are</u> you <u>taking</u> it?	7.	8.
Arif: Yes, I<u>'m taking</u> the test next week.	9.	10.
Masahiro: Really? <u>Did</u> you <u>study</u> for the test?	11.	12.
Arif: Of course. I <u>study</u> every night.	13.	14.
Masahiro: Why <u>did</u> you <u>miss</u> the test?	15.	16.
Arif: I<u>'m</u> not <u>feeling</u> well this week.	17.	18.
Masahiro: Really? What<u>'s</u> up?	19.	20.
Arif: I <u>have</u> the flu.	21.	22.
Masahiro: <u>Did</u> you <u>go</u> to the doctor?	23.	24.
Arif: No, but my dad <u>is taking</u> me to the doctor's tomorrow.	25.	26.

EXERCISE 16. Review Test 1: Multiple Choice

Circle the letter of the correct answer in these conversations.

1. "Excuse me. Is this bus going to the mall?"

    "Yes, _____, but Bus 62 or Bus 88 can take you there faster.

        a. it is   b. they are   c. it does   d. they do

2. "_____ Karen and Sandra study together every day?"

    "No, because they live in different parts of the city."

        a. Are   b. Do   c. Is   d. Does

3. "Do you spend a lot of time watching TV?"

    "Yes, we do. For example, my brother and sister _____ a horror movie right now."

        a. watch   b. don't watch   c. are watching   d. aren't watching

4. "Listen! I think _____ to rain now."

    "Yes, I can hear it now."

        a. is beginning   b. it's begining   c. is beginning   d. it's beginning

5. "Wait a minute! Mark wants to go with us."

    "Why _____?"

        a. is he coming   b. is he come   c. do he comes   d. does he come

6. "Where _____, Matt? I need you to help me."

    "Don't worry. I'll be back in a minute."

        a. do you go   b. are you go   c. do you going   d. are you going

7. "Is Neal busy now?"

    "Yes, he is _____."

        a. openning his mail   c. getting dressed

        b. begining his work   d. fixxing the TV

8. "Where is Kevin?"

    "He's at Greg's house. They _____ football."

        a. are playing   b. is playing   c. playing   d. play

REVIEW ▶   **EXERCISE 17. Review Test 2: Production and Evaluation**

Part 1.

Fill in the blanks with one of the words from the word list. Use each word one time. You might have to make some changes in the form of the word.

word list	be	blow	catch	drink	eat	fly	have
	laugh	like	play	shine	sit	sleep	throw

There are six people in the park. It ❶ _____ a beautiful day.

The sun ❷ _____, and the wind ❸ _____ lightly.

There is a little girl with her mother. They ❹ _____ next to

each other on a bench. The girl ❺ _____ an ice cream cone. Her

mother ❻ _____ a soft drink. She doesn't have an ice cream cone

because she doesn't ❼ _____ ice cream.

There is an old man with a long beard. His eyes are closed. Yes, he

❽ _____ on the bench.

There are two children near a big tree. They ❾ _____ with a ball.

One of them ❿ _____ the ball, and the other one

⓫ _____ it. They ⓬ _____ because they

⓭ _____ a great time. They are really happy.

Finally, there is a teenager on the other side of the park. He

⓮ _____ a kite.

Part 2.

Look at the underlined part in each sentence. If the underlined part is correct, circle the word *correct*. If it is wrong, circle the word *wrong* and the wrong part. Then write the correction above.

correct   wrong   1. Mark likes TV. He's <u>watch</u> a TV show right now.

correct   wrong   2. <u>Does Linda going</u> to the bank now?

correct   wrong   3. Mr. Wendell <u>teaches</u> French in room 301 right now.

correct   wrong   4. The boys <u>are no doing</u> their homework now.

correct   wrong   5. People in Canada <u>drive</u> on the right-hand side of the road.

EXERCISE 18. Reading Practice: Emails from Famous Places

Read these six postcards from international destinations. Then answer the five comprehension questions on page 235. The grammar from this unit is underlined for you.

❶

Dear Mom,

We took the kids to a nearby park. They saw kangaroos and koala bears! Josh and Amber <u>are having</u> a great time. They<u>'re learning</u> a lot about this place. They want to speak Australian. They<u>'re saying</u> g'day (hello) and mate (friend).

Love,

Janet

❷

Mark,

Wow! It's hard for me to believe it, but I<u>'m sitting</u> by the pool at the hotel. From here, I can see a pyramid! Yes, right now I<u>'m looking</u> at the Great Pyramid. You know how I love history, and I<u>'m learning</u> so much about this place.

See you,

Keith

❸

Dear Ann,

We hope you<u>'re watching</u> TV or doing something fun. We<u>'re working</u> a lot here, but we<u>'re</u> also <u>enjoying</u> this huge city. So many people . . . so many buildings…

We<u>'re learning</u> a few Japanese words and how to use chopsticks!

Take care,

Mary and Pablo

❹

Dear Ben,

You were right. This city is beautiful. I<u>'m writing</u> this card in a small café. I<u>'m drinking</u> some strong coffee, and I<u>'m listening</u> to French conversations. I don't understand anything, but it sounds so pretty. I wish you were here now!

Miss you,

Susan

❺

Laura,

What an interesting city! I<u>'m taking</u> a special class here. I<u>'m improving</u> my Spanish because I<u>'m practicing</u> every day. I'm studying a lot, but I<u>'m</u> also <u>visiting</u> places in the city. Oh, the food… I<u>'m eating</u> great meat and fresh pasta!

Your friend,

Tina

❻

Dear Grandma,

We<u>'re having</u> a great time here. The weather is sunny all the time, and the beaches are so beautiful. The water is warm. There are palm trees everywhere. In fact, I<u>'m writing</u> this card while I<u>'m sitting</u> on the beach under a palm tree.

Love,

Kara

1. What is the probable destination city for each postcard?

   Buenos Aires, Argentina   *Cairo, Egypt*   *Honolulu, Hawaii, USA*

   Paris, France   *Sydney, Australia*   *Tokyo, Japan*

Postcard 1	Postcard 2
Postcard 3	Postcard 4
Postcard 5	Postcard 6

2. Which travelers are not traveling alone?

   _____

3. Which travelers talked about language?

   _____

4. Do you know these six destinations? When did you go there? What was it like?

   _____

   _____

   _____

   _____

5. If you could go anywhere in the world, where would you go? Why?

   _____

   _____

   _____

   _____

   _____

ONE-MINUTE LESSON

In Postcard 4, Susan writes, *I wish you were here now!* It may seem strange to use past tense (*were*) for present (*now*), but this is normal after the verb **wish**. To wish for the present, use past tense.

EXERCISE 19. Vocabulary Practice: Word Knowledge

Circle the word or phrase that is most closely related to the word or phrase on the left. Use a dictionary to check the meaning of words you do not know.

Vocabulary	Answer Choices	
1. a bush	an animal	a plant
2. to own	do	have
3. a secret	everyone gives	no one knows
4. at this moment	now	then
5. to move	change places	change prices
6. scary	afraid	awake
7. the mall	feeling	shopping
8. to relax	enjoy	happen
9. to take off	arrive	leave
10. a yard	inside the house	outside the house
11. around	a circle	a line
12. to turn red	become red	lose your money
13. passengers	people	things
14. behind	in back of	in front of
15. to feed	ask questions	give food
16. to sing	history	music
17. a flight	travel by car	travel by plane
18. absent	not happy	not present
19. I wish you were here.	You are here now.	You are not here now.
20. your boss	at home	at work
21. an address	for a place	for a time
22. to fix	to repair	to give your idea
23. Hold my hand!	Look at my hand!	Take my hand!
24. a bench	for cutting	for sitting
25. a kite	in the air	in the water
26. to possess	have	make
27. a destination	a person	a place
28. get up	after sleeping	before sleeping
29. to improve	become better	become bigger
30. tuna	a kind of fish	a kind of music
31. to land	to begin a flight	to end a flight
32. jogging	eating	running

EXERCISE 20. Vocabulary Practice: Collocations

Fill in each blank with the answer on the right that most naturally completes the phrase on the left. If necessary, use a dictionary to check the meaning of words you do not know.

Phrase	Answer Choices	
1. at this _____	day	moment
2. _____ take off	automobiles	airplanes
3. _____ you the truth	say	tell
4. _____ a mistake	belong	erase
5. _____-handed	right	wrong
6. work _____ First National Bank	at	to
7. all of _____	time	the time
8. Which is better _____ you?	for	from
9. What's _____ with your car?	problem	wrong
10. _____ a shower	make	take
11. pick _____ from the floor	down	up
12. _____ lunch	prepare	repair
13. stay _____ a hotel	at	on
14. Can you help _____ now?	me	to me
15. it's _____ noisy	quiet	quite
16. _____ hard	call	work
17. I made 100 _____ my test	in	on
18. _____ a speech	get	give
19. it's _____ heavily	snowing	windy
20. go around a _____	seed	tree
21. _____ directions	follow	wish
22. arrive _____ noon	at	in
23. check _____	an I.D.	a restaurant
24. I _____ 97 on the test.	did	got
25. have the _____	flu	horror
26. the wind's blowing _____	heavy	lightly
27. What's _____?	down	up
28. cook eggs _____ breakfast	for	in
29. she missed the _____	airport	meeting
30. _____ a long beard	have	wear
31. not _____	still	yet
32. have a _____ time	fast	great
33. _____ night	at	in
34. _____ pasta	fresh	palm

EXERCISE 21. Writing Practice: Explaining Actions in a Painting

Part 1. Editing Student Writing

Read these sentences about Mona Lisa, a famous painting by Leonardo da Vinci. Circle the 15 errors. Then write the number of the sentence with the error next to the type of error. (Some sentences may have more than one error.)

_____ a. no subject   _____ e. singular-plural

_____ b. no *-ing*   _____ f. negative

_____ c. word order   _____ g. no verb

_____ d. possessive adjectives   _____ h. verb tense

Mona Lisa
1. I'm write about a famous painting named the "Mona Lisa."
2. This painting by da Vinci one of my favorite paintings.
3. In this painting, a girl smiles a little. His smile is so interesting.
4. She is stand in front of some hills or some mountains.
5. She has beautiful eyes brown and long black hair.
6. Her eye are look to the right.
7. What is looking at? We don't know.
8. Who is she looking at? We aren't know.
9. What does she think about?
10. Maybe is thinking about her family.
11. Maybe she thinking about a problem in his life.
12. Maybe she is worrying about something, but she is not frown. She is smiling!

Part 2. Original Student Writing

Use the Internet or library to find a famous painting or scene (from a movie). Write some sentences or a paragraph about what you see. Use present progressive tense when possible.

Unit 9

Count and Non-Count Nouns

Discover the Grammar

A grandfather and granddaughter are discussing food for dinner. Read their conversation.
Then answer the six questions.

Line	
1	**Grandpa:** Hey, Rita, what are you up to?
2	**Rita:** Well, that's a good question. Tonight I want to cook chili for
3	dinner, and you know that I really love yours. Tell me, what do you
4	put in your chili?
5	**Grandpa:** Ah, the first ingredient is easy. I start with some ground beef.
6	**Rita:** Right. Um, how much ground beef do you recommend?
7	**Grandpa:** Well, it depends. How many people are you cooking this chili for?
8	**Rita:** Just three.
9	**Grandpa:** Ok, then add about one pound of ground beef.
10	**Rita:** OK. And your chili has some vegetables in it, right? How many
11	kinds of vegetables do you use?
12	**Grandpa:** Well, let's see. I use onions, a green pepper, a few hot chilies, some
13	tomatoes. What else? OK, some pinto beans and some carrots, so
14	that's six.

15	**Rita**:	I had no idea your chili had so many types of vegetables in it.
16	**Grandpa**:	I think it's healthy, and they taste great together.
17	**Rita**:	Carrots in chili? That's a surprise.
18	**Grandpa**:	I guess so.
19	**Rita**:	So how many carrots do you put in your chili? I don't remember
20		seeing carrots in your chili.
21	**Grandpa**:	Just one carrot. I like to think it's my secret ingredient! And, Rita,
22		you don't see it because you have to chop it up into small pieces.
23	**Rita**:	Is there anything else I should know?
24	**Grandpa**:	Let's see. Yes, I always add some sugar to the chili about ten
25		minutes before I serve it.
26	**Rita**:	Um, sugar? Really? How much sugar?
27	**Grandpa**:	Just a little. Perhaps two tablespoons. Try it. It's really delicious!
28	**Rita**:	Well, OK. I'll do that. Thanks, grandpa.
29	**Grandpa**:	You're welcome, but I'm expecting you to bring me some chili
30		tomorrow!

1. Underline the three examples of *how many* in the conversation. What word comes after *how many*? Put a box around that word. Write the line numbers on the left and that word on the lines to the right.

   <u>Line</u>   <u>Noun</u>

   _____   *how many* _____

   _____   *how many* _____

   _____   *how many* _____

2. Underline the two examples of *how much* in the conversation. What food comes after *how much*? Put a box around that word. Write the line numbers on the left and that word on the lines to the right.

   <u>Line</u>   <u>Noun</u>

   _____   *how much* _____   _____

   _____   *how much* _____

3. What do you think the difference between *how many* and *how much* is?

   _____

   _____

4. Can you write eight new examples with these two expressions? Compare your
   answers with a partner or your classmates.

   <u>*how many*</u>   <u>*how much*</u>

   how many _____   *how much* _____

   how many _____   *how much* _____

   how many _____   *how much* _____

   how many _____   *how much* _____

5. Circle the two examples of *a few* and *a little* in the conversation. Study the word
   that comes after each. Do you have any ideas about when we use these two
   expressions?

   _____

   _____

   _____

6. What questions do you have about *how many, how much, a few,* or *a little?*

   _____

   _____

   _____

Grammar Lesson

Types of Nouns

Count Nouns		Non-Count Nouns
singular	*plural*	
a coin	coins	money
one coin	some coins	some money
	a few coins	a little money
	many coins	much money
	a lot of coins	a lot of money
	How many coins?	How much money?

There are two groups of nouns: **count** and **non-count.**

Count nouns are nouns that we can count. The word *coin* is a count noun because we can say *1 coin, 2 coins, 10 coins.* Count nouns have two forms: a singular form (*coin*) and a plural form (*coins*).

Non-count nouns are nouns that we cannot count. The word *money* is a non-count noun because we cannot say *3 moneys* or *8 moneys.* Non-count nouns have only one form (*money*).

Categories of Non-Count Nouns	
FOODS	*butter, bread, cheese, chocolate, fish, flour, fruit, macaroni, meat, mustard, pasta, pepper, rice, salt, soup, spaghetti, spinach, sugar*
LIQUIDS	*coffee, cream, ice, juice, milk, oil, tea, water*
IDEAS	*honesty, importance, intelligence, peace, wisdom*
NATURE	*lightning, rain, scenery, snow, sunlight, thunder*
"GROUP" NOUNS*	*advice, cash, clothing, equipment, fruit, furniture, hair, homework, information, luggage, makeup, money, news, research, traffic, vocabulary*

*A group noun is a singular noun that has many different parts. For example, we say, *My advice is for you to take the job and move to New York.* We can say that *advice* is a group noun. We use *is*, but I am giving two ideas.

Rule 1. The plural of most **count** nouns is with *-s: car* → *cars; book* → *books.* However, some count nouns have irregular plural forms and do not use *-s.*

man → *men*	*shelf* → *shelves*	*foot* → *feet*	*loaf* → *loaves*
child → *children*	*mouse* → *mice*	*box* → *boxes*	*fish* → *fish*
tooth → *teeth*	*woman* → *women*		

Rule 2. We use **a** or **an** with a **singular count noun.** If that noun has an adjective before it, we still use *a* or *an* with it. We use *an* before words that begin with a **vowel sound** (*an apple, an open window*). We use *a* before words that begin with a **consonant sound** (*a vegetable, a closed window*). Problems sometimes happen with words beginning with *h* or *u. A* or *an* depends on the sound of the next word, not its letter.

words beginning with the letter *h*		words beginning with the letter *u*	
a house	*an hour*	*a university*	*an umbrella*

Rule 3. If you want to talk about the quantity of a **non-count noun**, sometimes we can use a special quantity word:

a loaf of bread	*a glass of milk*	*a bottle of oil*	*a bag of sugar*
a sheet of paper	*a piece of furniture*	*a cup of coffee*	*a piece of advice*
a slice of pie	*a piece of cake*		

Rule 4. Some words can be count and non-count, but the meanings are different:

Word	Count	Non-Count
chicken	*a chicken* (an animal)	*some chicken* (meat from a chicken)
coffee	*3 coffees* (3 cups of coffee)	*some coffee* (the dark powder or the drink)
Time	*2 times* (2 occasions)	*some time* (duration)
Cake	*1 cake* (1 whole cake)	*some cake* (a piece of cake)

Rule 5. The word **some** means the number or amount is not important or we do not know the number. It is common to use **some** in front of a non-count noun or a plural count noun. For example, we usually say, *Please give me some water.* It is not so common to say, *Please give me water* because it is very direct and sounds like a command. Another possibility is, *We need some books,* instead of just *We need books.* Using *some* before a non-count noun or a plural count noun sounds more formal and more polite.

BE CAREFUL!

Common Learner Errors	Explanation
1. There are 20 ~~student~~ students in my class.	Use the correct plural form of a count noun.
2. ~~Computer~~ A computer has ~~mouse~~ a mouse and ~~keyboard~~ a keyboard.	Do not use a singular count noun alone. You need a, an, my, the, this, etc.
3. We have a lot of ~~homeworks~~ homework for tomorrow.	Non-count nouns do not have a plural form.
4. I have ~~a homework~~ homework to do now.	Non-count nouns do not have a singular form.
5. I want ~~fries~~ some fries with my burger.	It often sounds more polite to use some before a non-count noun or a plural count noun.

EXERCISE 1. Using *a/an* in Context

Write *a* or *an* in front of these singular count nouns.

My Apartment

1. My apartment has four rooms. It is a _____ large place for one person.

2. My apartment has _____ nice kitchen. It has everything I need. The kitchen has _____ refrigerator, _____ dishwasher, _____ stove, and _____ oven. It also has _____ microwave.

3. My bedroom has _____ really big closet for all of my clothes. The bedroom also has _____ bed, _____ dresser, and _____ bookcase.

4. My bathroom is small. It doesn't have _____ bathtub. Instead, it has _____ shower. It has _____ closet where I keep towels and wash rags, and it has _____ medicine cabinet with _____ antique mirror.

5. The living room is my favorite room. In my living room, there is _____ sofa, _____ easy chair, _____ coffee table, _____ floor lamp, two table lamps, and of course _____ large TV. I just got my TV last year, so it's still pretty new.

ONE-MINUTE LESSON
The word **pretty** has two meanings: "beautiful" (*your ring is* **pretty**) or "very" (*the test was* **pretty** *difficult*). This second meaning of **pretty** is very common in informal language. Do not use **pretty** for *very* in formal or academic writing.

EXERCISE 2. *a? an? some?*

Read the list of words. If the word is a count noun, write *a* or *an* on the line. If the word is a non-count noun, write *some* on the line.

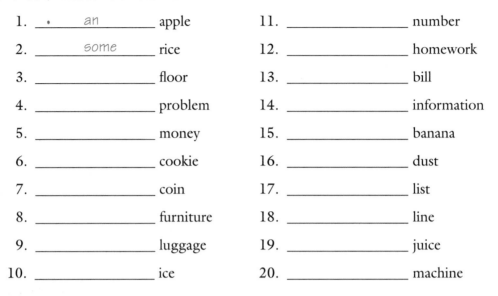

1.	*an*	apple	11.	_____	number
2.	*some*	rice	12.	_____	homework
3.	_____	floor	13.	_____	bill
4.	_____	problem	14.	_____	information
5.	_____	money	15.	_____	banana
6.	_____	cookie	16.	_____	dust
7.	_____	coin	17.	_____	list
8.	_____	furniture	18.	_____	line
9.	_____	luggage	19.	_____	juice
10.	_____	ice	20.	_____	machine

EXERCISE 3. Phrases with Count and Non-Count Nouns

Read the list of words. If the word is a count noun, write any number greater than 1 on the line, and add an *-s*. If the word is a non-count noun, write *some* on the line.

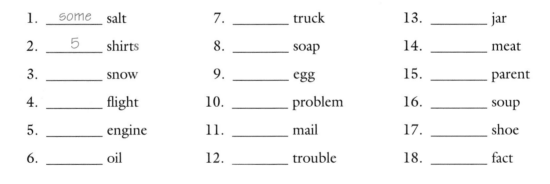

1.	*some*	salt	7.	_____	truck	13.	_____	jar
2.	*5*	shirts	8.	_____	soap	14.	_____	meat
3.	_____	snow	9.	_____	egg	15.	_____	parent
4.	_____	flight	10.	_____	problem	16.	_____	soup
5.	_____	engine	11.	_____	mail	17.	_____	shoe
6.	_____	oil	12.	_____	trouble	18.	_____	fact

Do Online Exercise 9.1. My score: _____ /10. _____ % correct.

EXERCISE 4. Editing. Is it Correct?

If the sentence is correct, write a check mark (✓) on the line. If it is not correct, write X on the line and circle the mistake. Then change the sentence to make it correct. Write the change above the sentence. (*Hint:* There are eight items. Two are correct, but six have errors.)

My Sister's Hobby

_____ 1. My sister has a interesting hobby.

_____ 2. She likes to collect stamp.

_____ 3. She has stamps from more than 100 countries.

_____ 4. She has a stamp from every countries in South America.

_____ 5. She has a special stamp book where she keeps just her South American stamps.

_____ 6. She has a stamps that are from before 1900. They are awesome.

_____ 7. She has Argentinean stamp from 1870. It is extremely valuable now.

_____ 8. In my opinion, stamp collecting is great hobby.

EXERCISE 5. Speaking Practice: Nouns from the Alphabet

Step 1. Make a list of count nouns that begin with the letters listed. If you cannot think of a count noun, then write a count noun with an adjective that begins with that letter. For example, for E, you could write *egg* or *excellent student*.

T _____   D _____   L _____

U _____   B _____   S _____

C _____   E _____   M _____

A _____   I _____   R _____

N _____   W _____   G _____

O _____   H _____   P _____

Step 2. Now work with a partner. Student A will name one of the letters from Step 1 of Exercise 5. Student B will say the noun he or she wrote for that letter. Then Student A has to make a true sentence about the quantity of that item in a place.

A: "P"

B: pen

A: There are about 17 pens in this room. Now it's your turn.

B: "D"

A: duck

B: There isn't a duck in this room. Now it's your turn.
 (There are no ducks in this room OR There aren't any ducks in this room.)

A: "T"

B: teacher

A: There is only one teacher in this room.

Some/Any (polite, quantity)

	Plural Count Nouns	Plural Non-Count Nouns
affirmative	I want some fries.	Your plant needs some water.
negative	I don't want any fries.	Your plant doesn't need any water.
question	Do you want some fries? Do you want any fries?	Does your plant need some water? Does your plant need any water?

<u>Rule 1</u>. We use some and any with plural count nouns and with non-count nouns.

<u>Rule 2</u>. We use some and any when the number is not known or is not important.

<u>Rule 3</u>. We use some in affirmative, any in negative. In a question, both some and any are possible with no real difference in meaning.

<u>Rule 4</u>. Sometimes we do not use some or any, but this is common with people that we know well. "I want fries" may be OK to say to a friend but too strong to say to someone you do not know.

Any (it makes no difference)

	any + noun	meaning
affirmative	You can use this card at **any** bank.	You can go to Bank A or Bank B and use your card there.
	Any supermarket sells bread.	It does not matter which supermarket you enter; you will find bread there.
	Well, you can sit **anywhere** you want.	You can choose any chair. It does not matter which chair you select.

Rule 1. Be careful with **any** because **any** has another meaning, which is completely different. The word **any** also means "it makes no difference which one." When **any** is used in affirmative sentences, it has this special meaning.

 BE CAREFUL!

Common Learner Errors	Explanation
1. We have ~~any~~ some more time.	Do not use **any** for quantity in an affirmative statement.
2. A: May I help you? B: Yes, give me ~~fries~~ some fries.	For quantity, add **some** or **any** in front of nouns when you don't know the person.
3. Is it ok for me to sit in ~~some~~ any chair?	Use **any** in an affirmative statement when you mean the choice doesn't matter. Don't use **some** here.
4. ~~Any~~ No people live on the moon.	The word **any** in the subject position is not negative. To express a negative idea before a noun subject, we use **no** with an affirmative verb.

 Do Online Exercise 9.2. My score: _____ /10. _____ % correct.

EXERCISE 6. Mini-Conversations

Circle the correct words in these eight mini-conversations, For some, both answers are possible.

1. A: I cooked fried chicken for dinner. Do you want (any, some)?

   B: No, thanks. I had (any, some) potato salad just a little while ago, so I'm still full.

2. A: Excuse me. I'd like to buy (any, some) Swiss cheese.

   B: Oh, I'm sorry, but we don't sell (any, some) cheese at all here.

3. A: Hi, come on in and sit down! Would you like (any, some) coffee? It's fresh.

   B: Well, to tell you the truth, I would love (any, some) coffee right now, but no thanks. I can't drink (any, some).

   A: I don't get it. What do you mean? You love coffee.

   B: Yes, but my doctor told me not to have (any, some) drinks with caffeine.

4. A: Did Kevin buy (any, some) apples yesterday?

   B: I don't think so. There aren't (any, some) in the kitchen.

   A: Hey, are you going to the store later?

   B: Maybe. Why?

   A: If you go, please get (any, some) green apples for me. I'll pay you back later.

5. A: Do you want (any, some) chicken salad. I just made (any, some).

   B: Yes, that sounds good. I'd like to have mine with (any, some) bread, ok?

6. A: When can we go in the theatre?

   B: Let's see. The show starts at 8 PM and the doors open at 6 PM.

   A: So we can go in (any, some) time between 6 and 8?

   B: Yes, (any, some) person with a ticket can enter then.

7. A: Sue went to the store.

   B: For what?

   A: To get (any, some) cookies.

   B: But we have (any, some) on the top shelf of the cabinet.

   A: Uhm. . . . Actually, no, we don't. Sorry, I ate all of them last night!

8. A: I want to buy a soft drink.

   B: There's a drink machine over there.

   A: Yes, but I don't have (any, some) change. Do you?

   B: No, but ask that woman over there. Maybe she has (any, some).

A lot, Many, Much

		Count Nouns		Non-Count Nouns
question	a lot of	Were there a lot of people at the meeting?	a lot of	Was there a lot of food at the party?
	many	Were there many people at the meeting?	much	Was there much food at the party?
affirmative	a lot of	There were a lot of people at the meeting.	a lot of	There was a lot of food at the party.
	many	There were many people at the meeting.		
negative	a lot of	There weren't a lot of people at the meeting.	a lot of	There wasn't a lot of food at the party.
	many	There weren't many people at the meeting.	much	There wasn't much food at the party.

<u>Rule 1.</u> We can use a lot of with count and non-count nouns. We can use a lot of in questions, affirmatives, and negatives.

<u>Rule 2.</u> We use many with plural count nouns. We can use many in questions, affirmatives, and negatives.

<u>Rule 3.</u> We use much with non-count nouns. We can use much for questions and negatives, but it is not common in affirmatives.

<u>Rule 4.</u> We use how many for count nouns and how much for non-count nouns when we want to ask about quantity.

 ## BE CAREFUL!

Common Learner Errors	Explanation
1. There are ~~much~~ many Japanese students in my class.	Use many with count nouns and much with non-count nouns.
2. This sandwich has ~~much~~ a lot of mustard.	Do not use much in simple affirmative statements.
3. This soup has ~~a lot~~ a lot of salt.	You must include of before a noun or pronoun.
4. Bob: Do you want some sauce on your spaghetti? Tim: Yes, give me ~~a lot of~~ a lot.	Don't use of if there is no noun or pronoun.

Connecting Grammar and Vocabulary

Don't learn the phrases *how many* and *how much* alone. Instead, you should learn these phrases with the nouns that most commonly follow them. If you learn the nouns that often occur with these phrases, it can help your speaking and listening a lot. Learn these two lists by heart.

10 Nouns Frequently Used with *How many* and *How much*	
how many _____	*how much* _____
1. people	1. money
2. times	2. time
3. years	3. damage
4. hours	4. trouble
5. children	5. water
6. kids	6. pressure
7. women	7. work
8. days	8. information
9. votes	9. difference
10. men	10. pain

Source: Based on information in the Corpus of Contemporary American English: www.americancorpus.org/.

ONE-MINUTE LESSON

An **idiom** is a group of words that has a different meaning from the meanings of the words in the phrase. The word *heart* is part of your body, but in the phrase "learn something **by heart**," we are not talking about your body. If you learn something **by heart**, it means you memorize the information. If something is **a piece of cake**, it is very easy to do. If a company is **in the red**, it means the company is broke.

Do Online Exercise 9.3. My score: _____ /10. _____ % correct.

EXERCISE 7. *A lot, many, much* in Context

Put a check mark (✓) in the column to indicate which quantity words are possible. Remember that sometimes more than one answer is possible.

		many	*much*	*a lot of*	
1	I have				good friends from Brazil.
2	We want				people to attend next month's meeting.
3	Roses need				sunshine.
4	Potato chips have				salt, so I don't eat them every day.
5	I never take				cash with me on trips.
6	Plants that don't require				light can grow in this spot.
7	Ben doesn't have				good reasons for quitting school.
8	Sorry, but I don't have				time to talk right now.
9	Are there				passengers on today's flight?
10	Did you spend				time with your grandparents?
11	Do you usually listen to				different singers? Or do you have one favorite artist?
12	Was there				information on that website?

13. What can you say about your answers for Numbers 1, 2, 3, 4? What about for Numbers 5, 6, 7, 8? What about for Numbers 9, 10, 11, 12? How are these groups similar?

_____

_____

 Do Online Exercise 9.4. My score: _____ /10. _____ % correct.

A few, A little

	Count Nouns		Non-Count Nouns
a few	I have a few coins. I don't have a few coins. Do you have a few coins?	**a little**	I have a little change. I don't have a little change. Do you have a little change?

__Rule 1.__ We use a few with plural count nouns. We can use a few for questions, affirmatives, and negatives.

__Rule 2.__ We use a little with non-count nouns. We can use a little for questions, affirmatives, and negatives.

BE CAREFUL!

Common Learner Errors	Explanation
1. I have ~~a little~~ a few problems with English pronunciation.	Use a few with count nouns and a little with noncount nouns.

EXERCISE 8. Phrases with *a few* or *a little*

Write *a few* or *a little* on the lines.

1. _____ tea		7. _____ countries		13. _____ people	
2. _____ time		8. _____ homework		14. _____ questions	
3. _____ tests		9. _____ pencils		15. _____ bread	
4. _____ ink		10. _____ children		16. _____ times	
5. _____ paper		11. _____ classes		17. _____ water	
6. _____ cream		12. _____ money		18. _____ furniture	

Do Online Exercise 9.5. My score: _____ /10. _____ % correct.

EXERCISE 9. Mini-Conversations

Circle the correct quantity words in these eight mini-conversations.

1. A: Could I borrow (a few, a little) coins? I need to make a phone call.

   B: How much money do you want?

   A: Just (a few, a little). I'm only going to talk for three minutes. I only need about 75 cents.

2. A: How did you do on yesterday's test?

   B: I understood only (a few, a little) questions, so I guess I failed. How about you?

   A: I had (a few, a little) trouble with the first part, but I think I did OK on the second part. I didn't ace it, but I think I did pretty well.

3. A: What did you buy at the store?

   B: (A few, A little) ground beef and (a few, a little) vegetables.

4. A: How does Susana take her coffee?

   B: I'm not 100% sure, but I think she likes (a few, a little) milk in it.

5. A: What's Billy going to do this weekend?

   B: He might read (a few, a little) books.

   A: Read books on the weekend? Are you kidding? Why would he do that?

   B: Well, his research paper is due next Thursday. That means he only has (a few, a little) days to finish reading the books and then write the paper.

6. A: Do you have any plans for tomorrow?

   B: No, not yet. Why do you ask?

   A: Well, I'm going to the beach with (a few, a little) friends. Would you like to come with us?

   B: Gee, that sounds great. Thanks for inviting me.

   A: Be sure to bring (a few, a little) money so you can buy something to eat there. We'll be there all day long.

7. A: How (many, much, a lot of) cousins do you have?

   B: I'm not 100% sure. I think I have more than 20 cousins.

8. A: What's your favorite snack?

   B: Well, sometimes I like to eat (a few, a little) cookies.

EXERCISE 10. Quantity Words in Context

Circle the correct quantity words in this conversation between a doctor and a patient.

At the Doctor's Office

Doctor: Well, Mr. Williams. How are you these days?

Patient: Not so good. I'm tired all the time. I can't sleep.

Doctor: Oh, really?

Patient: Yes, and I watch TV all the time.

Doctor: Ok, tell me something. How (many, much) hours of television do you usually watch every day?

Patient: Oh, not so (many, much). . . . ust six or seven during the day and then five or six at night.

Doctor: Are you kidding? That's too (many, much) hours of TV! It's OK to watch just (a few, a little) hours every day, but not that (many, much).

Patient: OK, I know you're right, but at night I have a hard time falling asleep.

Doctor: Really? Hmmmm. Tell me, how (many, much) soda do you drink every day?

Patient: Oh, not (many, much) really. . . . about three liters.

Doctor: No wonder you can't sleep! That's too (many, much) soda and too (many, much) caffeine! It's OK to drink just (a few, a little) soda, but not that (many, much).

Patient: OK, I know you're right.

 Do Online Exercise 9.6. My score: _____ /10. _____ % correct.

ONE-MINUTE LESSON

There is a big difference in meaning between **a few / few** and **a little / little** for quantity.

One is positive; one is negative. The positive meaning is more common.

+ *She has a few friends.* = some friends; positive meaning

– *She has few friends.* = almost no friends; negative meaning

+ *He did a little work.* = some work; positive meaning

– *He did little work.* = almost no work; negative meaning

EXERCISE 11. Sentence Study for Critical Reading

Read the numbered sentences. Then read the three answer choices, and place a check mark in the yes or no boxes in front of each sentence to show if that answer is true based on the information in the original sentence. If there is not enough information to mark something as yes, then mark it as no. Remember that more than one true answer is possible.

1. Kurt finally bought some new furniture for his house. He said that there isn't much open space in his house now.

   ☐ yes ☐ no a. Kurt probably bought only one or two pieces of furniture.

   ☐ yes ☐ no b. We don't know what kind of furniture he bought.

   ☐ yes ☐ no c. The new furniture takes up a lot of space.

2. My flight from Germany to the U.S. was good because there weren't many passengers on it. In fact, the plane was less than half full.

   ☐ yes ☐ no a. More than fifty percent of the seats were open.

   ☐ yes ☐ no b. I liked my flight from Germany.

   ☐ yes ☐ no c. There weren't many passengers on the flight.

3. To cook jambalaya, Lisa needs rice, shrimp, sausage, and tomatoes, but she doesn't need any cabbage, potatoes, or chicken.

   ☐ yes ☐ no a. Lisa needs shrimp and tomatoes to cook jambalaya.

   ☐ yes ☐ no b. She doesn't need any chicken, but she needs sausage.

   ☐ yes ☐ no c. There is meat in jambalaya.

4. A few students arrived late, but the teacher didn't say anything to them.

   ☐ yes ☐ no a. Many students were late to class.

   ☐ yes ☐ no b. A lot of students were late to class.

   ☐ yes ☐ no c. The teacher told the students not to come late again.

5. There is not much water in the river this year.

   ☐ yes ☐ no a. The water level in the river now is low.

   ☐ yes ☐ no b. The water level in the river was low last year.

   ☐ yes ☐ no c. Right now there is no water in the river. It is completely dry.

6. Julia, if you want any ice cream, we have a little vanilla ice cream in the freezer. We also have a little chocolate sauce in a bowl on the top shelf in the refrigerator.

   ☐ yes ☐ no a. There is a lot of chocolate sauce.

   ☐ yes ☐ no b. There isn't much vanilla ice cream.

   ☐ yes ☐ no c. Both the ice cream and the chocolate sauce are in the freezer.

7. When he was in Los Angeles last week, Mark got some new shirts and some new shoes.

   ☐ yes ☐ no   a. Mark likes any new shirt.

   ☐ yes ☐ no   b. Mark got some new shoes in Los Angeles.

   ☐ yes ☐ no   c. Many of Mark's shirts came from Los Angeles.

8. Many people love to eat pizza. A few of the most popular toppings for pizzas are pepperoni, mushrooms, and sausage. Other popular toppings include green peppers, onions, and extra cheese.

   ☐ yes ☐ no   a. A lot of people love pizza.

   ☐ yes ☐ no   b. Any vegetable is a very popular pizza topping choice.

   ☐ yes ☐ no   c. A few people like pepperoni as a pizza topping.

EXERCISE 12. Speaking Practice: A Shopping List

Work with a partner. You are going to go grocery shopping for five items that you need, but first you have to make your shopping list. Try to guess the items on your partner's shopping list.

Step 1. Your list is on the left. Write any five items next to the five quantity words. This will make your list unique. (Be careful with count and non-count items.)

Step 2. Student A will begin by asking a yes-no question about Student B's list. For example, you can ask, *Do you need some rice?*

Step 3. If the answer is yes, then Student A continues with a yes-no quantity question such as, *Do you need a little rice?* If the answer is yes, Student A continues. If the answer is no, then Student B can ask a question.

Step 4. The winner is the first person to guess the other student's entire list.

ITEMS:						
mustard	meat	bread	spaghetti	onions	flour	doughnuts
apples	oranges	potatoes	cookies	pickles	rice	cookies

Your List

1. a lot of _____
2. a little _____
3. many _____
4. a few _____
5. a lot of _____

Your Partner's List

1. a lot of _____
2. a little _____
3. many _____
4. a few _____
5. a lot of _____

REVIEW

EXERCISE 13. Review Test 1: Multiple Choice

Circle the letter of the correct answer in these conversations.

1. "Do you like coffee?"

   "Oh, yes. I drink _____ coffee every day."

   a. a lot of   b. much   c. many   d. a lot

2. "Do you need a lot of sugar?"

   "No, I only need _____ sugar."

   a. a few   b. a little   c. any   d. much

3. "Would you like some tea?"

   "Yes, but just _____ please."

   a. some   b. any   c. a few   d. a little

4. "You look tired."

   "Yes, I ran here. I'd really like _____ water."

   a. much   b. a lot   c. a few   d. some

5. "What did you buy?"

   "I bought a loaf of _____."

   a. bread   b. meat   c. cheese   d. sugar

6. "Who drew this picture?"

   "My son did. He's only four years old. In the picture, you can see two _____."

   a. rice   b. mice   c. tooth   d. foot

7. "Which teacher can explain this grammar to me?"

   "Well, all of the teachers in this school know English grammar very well, so you can ask _____ teacher you want."

   a. any   b. some   c. no   d. all

8. "I need a pencil for my test."

   "Oh, I think there is _____ pencil in my briefcase. Let me check."

   a. a   b. any   c. some   d. a lot of

ONE-MINUTE LESSON

The word **let** is a common verb. The grammar is **let** + [person] + VERB.
Common examples are **let** *me check* and **let** *me see*. Here **let** has the same meaning
as **allow** or **permit**, but **let** is much more common and has a different grammar.
We say, *I can't* **let** *you* _use_ *my car* but *I can't* **allow** *you* _to use_ *my car* and
I can't **permit** *you* _to use_ *my car.*

REVIEW ▶ **EXERCISE 14. Review Test 2: Production and Evaluation**

Part 1.

Fill in the blanks with one of the quantity words from the word list. Sometimes more than one answer is possible.

word list	many	much	a few	a little
	some	any	a lot	a lot of

Jim: "Did you go to the bank this morning?"

Ben: "No, I went to the grocery store to get ❶ _____ food."

Jim: "Hey, did you remember to buy ❷ _____ potato chips for me?"

Ben: "Sorry, I didn't buy ❸ _____ potato chips. I forgot."

Jim: "That's OK. I'll get ❹ _____ the next time I go to the store."

Ben: "I think there are ❺ _____ chips in the cabinet."

Jim: "No, I looked this morning. There aren't ❻ _____ chips in the cabinet."

Ben: "Well, if you're just looking for a salty snack, I think we have ❼ _____ whole wheat crackers."

Jim: "You know, that's a really popular snack these days, and ❽ _____ people like them. I'd like to try them."

Part 2.

Look at the underlined part in each sentence. If the underlined part is *correct*, circle the word *correct*. If it is wrong, circle the word *wrong* and the wrong part. Then write the correction above.

correct	wrong	1. She has <u>many</u> good friends at that school.
correct	wrong	2. Would you <u>like any cheese now</u>?
correct	wrong	3. He worked very hard, and now he <u>has much money.</u>
correct	wrong	4. The science teacher gave us <u>a little homeworks</u>.
correct	wrong	5. Kevin gave <u>Jim many old</u> magazines.
correct	wrong	6. There's <u>a slice of</u> cherry pie in the refrigerator.
correct	wrong	7. Linda <u>has beautiful new car.</u>
correct	wrong	8. She didn't <u>buy some fruit</u> at the store.

EXERCISE 15. Reading Practice: A Political Candidate

Read the information in this flyer from a politician who is running for mayor. Then answer the five comprehension questions on page 262. The grammar from this unit is underlined for you.

VOTE FOR BERT HARRIS!!!

Dear Citizens of Lakewood,

My name is Bert Harris, and I am running for the position of Mayor of Lakewood, and I would sincerely appreciate your vote. In these difficult <u>times</u>, we have <u>many problems</u> facing our lovely town. For one thing, we have <u>too much traffic</u>. There are <u>too many cars and trucks</u> on the road, and there isn't enough public transportation. I would add <u>many more bus routes</u>, especially in the mornings and afternoons and <u>a few more bus routes</u> out to the airport.

There is also <u>too much pollution</u>. And even <u>a little pollution</u> is <u>too much</u>! I think we need <u>a few more laws</u> – stronger laws – to stop factories from polluting our air and water. There are <u>many ways</u> to protect the environment and still make the products we need, but we don't have <u>much time</u>. We need to control the factories now—before it's too late.

Finally, I think we need to spend more money on education. Our schools don't have <u>much funding</u>, and even <u>a little increase</u> in spending can help a lot of children. Do you know that some schools don't even have enough money for books for our students?

<u>Some</u> of my opponents say that I will raise taxes to pay for these programs. However, I propose to save money that is being wasted on <u>some unnecessary programs</u> that help only <u>a few people</u>. My ideas would help <u>many people</u>—heavy traffic affects <u>a lot of</u> us, we all breathe the air and drink the water, and we all care about our children and their future.

If you elect me, I promise to work hard to help all citizens of Lakewood, not just <u>a few</u> of them. If you have <u>any concerns</u>, please let me know. I want to be YOUR mayor! Help me help our town! Vote for me! I will not let you down.

Sincerely,

Bert Harris

1. Put a check mark (✓) by the four topics that Mr. Harris mentioned in his flyer.

___ traffic   ___ new businesses   ___ pollution

___ homeless people   ___ schools   ___ city parks

___ police officers   ___ crime   ___ free lunches

___ taxes   ___ weather   ___ vacations

2. What is the name of the town? _____

3. Why does Mr. Harris talk about factories? _____

_____

_____

_____

_____

4. What is Mr. Harris's plan for schools? _____

_____

_____

_____

_____

5. What does Mr. Harris's last sentence, *I will not let you down* mean?

_____

_____

_____

_____

EXERCISE 16. Vocabulary Practice: Word Knowledge

Circle the word or phrase that is most closely related to the word or phrase on the left. Use a dictionary to check the meaning of words you do not know.

Vocabulary	Answer Choices	
1. a carrot	a ticket	a vegetable
2. a briefcase	for animals	for people
3. a snack	eat	play
4. perhaps	maybe	welcome
5. a mayor	of a city	of a country
6. an ingredient	when you're cooking	when you're working
7. What's he up to?	What's he doing?	What's he saying?
8. snow	summer	winter
9. recommend	change	suggest
10. mustard	green	yellow
11. a keyboard	a computer	a flight
12. wisdom	equipment	intelligence
13. kidding	adding	joking
14. flour	to make bread	to make peace
15. to vote	to forget	to select
16. thunder	you hear it	you see it
17. a topping	in a pizza	on a pizza
18. towels	in a bathroom	in a library
19. a jar	made of glass	made of paper
20. spinach	green	yellow
21. a hobby	fun	work
22. a stove	for cooking	for painting
23. shelves	apples	books
24. pickles	green	red
25. traffic	cars and trucks	cats and dogs
26. passengers	airport	supermarket
27. quit	start	stop
28. ace a test	a good score	a great score
29. cabbage	a fruit	a vegetable
30. raise	go down	go up

EXERCISE 17. Vocabulary Practice: Collocations

Fill in each blank with the answer on the right that most naturally completes the phrase on the left. If necessary, use a dictionary to check the meaning of words you do not know.

Phrase	Answer Choices	
1. a little _____ ago	time	while
2. you _____ tired	look	take
3. ___ me check	let	permit
4. many _____	person	people
5. _____ chips	onion	potato
6. a popular _____	brand	homework
7. I _____ no idea	had	was
8. _____ else	anything	one thing
9. one pound _____	chicken	of chicken
10. just _____	a little	a lot
11. very heavy _____	hair	luggage
12. in these difficult _____	time	times
13. a green _____	mayor	pepper
14. give me some _____	advice	traffic
15. a slice of _____	bread	library
16. I guess _____	so	yes
17. the _____ level	sausage	water
18. He finished _____ the book.	reading	to read
19. _____ much traffic	to	too
20. _____ beef	floor	ground
21. _____ lot of money	a	the
22. _____ up an onion	chop	cry
23. a piece of _____	furniture	alphabet
24. it's _____ new, right?	beautiful	pretty
25. How many _____ do you have?	change	coins
26. _____ valuable	extreme	extremely
27. _____ mice	one	ten
28. _____ some fries for me	get	give
29. _____ and lightning	darkness	thunder
30. a _____ lamp	chair	table
31. it _____ matter	doesn't	isn't
32. to _____ you the truth	say	tell

EXERCISE 18. Writing Practice: Completing Your Wish List

Part 1. Editing Student Writing

Read this short wish list of six things that the writer would like to be different. Circle the 14 errors. Then write the number of the sentence with the error next to the type of error. (Some sentences may have more than one error.)

_____ a. no verb		_____ e. *a few/a little*	
_____ b. *many/much*		_____ f. verb tense	
_____ c. singular-plural		_____ g. *a lot/a lot of*	

My Wish List
1. I drink too many coffee. I think coffee very delicious, but I want to stop drinking so much coffee.
2. My brother doesn't have many patience, so I want him to have more patience. He always got angry so quickly, and he can't wait for anything.
3. I have a few money, but I would like to have a lot money. Some people say money is bad, but I think money important for many reason.
4. My car is old, and it has a little scratches on it. I wanted my car to look good again.
5. I always made a lot of mistake in my English writing. I want to improve my English writing.
6. I have a few friend, but I would like to have more friends. Yes, I really want to have a lot of.

Part 2. Original Student Writing

Now write your wish list of things you would like to change about yourself, your life, or anything or anyone in your life.

Unit 10

Prepositions: *at, on, in*

Discover the Grammar

Read this information about a teacher's school year, and then answer the five questions.

Line	
1	I'd like to explain a little bit about my schedule in the school year. Our
2	school year now starts in August. When I started teaching in 2006, our school
3	year started in September. The same was true in 2007, but it changed in 2008
4	and now begins in August. Some parents don't like school to start in this
5	month because they think it is too early. However, this is the official school
6	calendar now. We begin the school year now in August, and the school year
7	finishes in early June.
8	My week is pretty crazy. I have a full schedule on three days (Monday,
9	Tuesday, and Thursday). On Wednesday, I finish at 2:00 instead of at 3:00.
10	On Friday, my last two classes do not meet, so I have two hours for planning.
11	What does a typical day look like? My school day begins at 7:45 every
12	morning. At 8:00, I have my first class. At 9:00, I have my second class, and at
13	10:00, I have a break. At 11:00, I have my third class. I eat lunch with some of
14	my students at noon. I have a reading class at 1:00 and then another reading

15	class at 2:00. All of the students go home at 3:00. This is my schedule on three
16	days of the week. I have a different schedule on Wednesday and on Friday.
17	Students love holidays, but teachers do, too! Our school holidays change a
18	little every year, but three holidays never change. We don't have school on
19	Thanksgiving, which is in November, on Christmas, which is on December 25,
20	or on New Year's Day, which is of course on January 1.

1. Underline the 11 examples of *at*. Write the 11 nouns that follow *at*. Write the line number in parentheses.

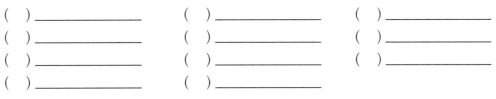

2. Put a box around the 11 examples of *on*. Write the 11 nouns that follow *on*. Write the line number in parentheses.

3. Put a circle around the 12 examples of *in*. Write the 12 nouns that follow *in*. Write the line number in parentheses.

4. Look at your answer to Questions 1–3. How do you think we use *at/on/in* with time words? _____

_____

5. What questions do you have about this grammar?

_____

_____

_____

Grammar Lesson

Prepositions

Prepositions are small words that show the relationship between a noun (or pronoun) and the rest of the sentence. Prepositions can show **place** (*on the rug*), **time** (*at 8:30*), **movement** (*to the bank*), and other meanings.

| The cat is sleeping ON THE RUG. | The class begins AT 8:30. | She is driving TO THE BANK. |

There are more than 100 prepositions in English, but 9 of the most common prepositions are of, in, to, for, with, on, at, by, and about. Prepositions are one of the most difficult aspects of learning any language, especially English. (*Note:* You can see a longer list of prepositions in Appendix 4.)

One problem is that an English preposition may not exist in your language, and your language may have a preposition that English does not have.

Another problem is that one preposition may have many different meanings. For example, the word *on* can have more than 10 or 15 different meanings in a dictionary! *On Monday* is not the same meaning as *on the table*, but both are correct.

Finally, prepositions are used in idioms (special expressions) like *do something on purpose* or *your sandwich is on the house.*

Prepositions: *at, on, in*

Of the 100+ prepositions in English, three prepositions that are difficult for many learners are **at, on, in**. In Unit 10, you will study these three prepositions because they are so common and hard to master.

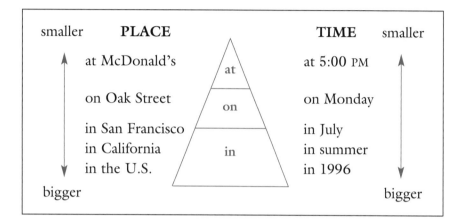

Rule 1. Use **at** for very specific places or times.
      Place Use **at** with the name of a place or with an address with a number: **at** Boston University, **at** 653 Maple Drive.
      Time Use **at** with clock times: **at** noon, **at** 1:20.

Rule 2. Use **on** for medium-sized places or times.
      Place Use **on** for just the name of streets, roads, avenues, etc.: **on** Maple Drive, **on** Pacific Avenue.
      Time Use **on** with days and dates: **on** March 15, **on** Saturday.

Rule 3. Use **in** for larger size places or times.
      Place Use **in** for cities, counties, regions, states, and countries: **in** Cincinnati, **in** Ohio, **in** Honduras, **in** Central America.
            We also use **in** for all rooms: **in** the kitchen, **in** Room 117.
      Time Use **in** for months, seasons, years, periods of time, decades, etc.: **in** July, **in** summer.

Rule 4. Prepositions have many exceptions. Remember these four prepositional phrases for parts of the day: **in the morning, in the afternoon, in the evening, at night.**

BE CAREFUL!

Common Learner Errors	Explanation
1. My sister is ~~England~~ in England now.	Do not forget to use a preposition.
2. My trip is ~~in~~ on June 17th.	Don't use in with days or dates.
3. My cousin works ~~in~~ at that bank.	Don't use in with specific places.
4. I like to watch TV ~~in~~ at night.	Be careful with prepositions for parts of a day.

EXERCISE 1. *at/on/in* in Phrases

Underline the correct prepositions.

1. (at, on) Monday
2. (at, in) night
3. (at, on) Central Street
4. (at, on) 445 Central Street
5. (in, on) my birthday
6. (in, at) the morning
7. (at, in) 9:00
8. (at, in) 9:00 in the morning
9. (in, on) Saturday
10. (at, in) March
11. (at, on) 12:30
12. (at, on) Friday night
13. (in, on) 1995
14. (on, at) Lake Street
15. (at, on) March 17th
16. (at, in) the English Institute

EXERCISE 2. More *at/on/in* in Phrases

Underline the correct prepositions.

1. (at, on) Saturday
2. (at, in) the winter
3. (at, on) Brown Road
4. (at, on) 200 Brown Road
5. (in, on) the first day
6. (in, at) the afternoon
7. (at, in) 3:00
8. (at, in) 3:00 in the afternoon
9. (in, on) Tuesday
10. (at, in) September
11. (at, on) noon
12. (at, on) Monday night
13. (in, on) 1996
14. (on, at) my street
15. (at, on) January 1st
16. (at, in) Blankner High School

Do Online Exercise 10.1. My score: _____ /10. _____ % correct.

EXERCISE 3. Reviewing *at/on/in*

Write the correct prepositions. When you finish, copy your answers on the correct lines. Then write the rules in the box.

1. __in__ Canada   8. _____ Paris   15. _____ 1993

2. _____ Main Street   9. _____ the summer   16. _____ ten past two

3. _____ the kitchen   10. _____ May 11   17. _____ your birthday

4. _____ McDonald's   11. _____ Highway 993   18. _____ Texas

5. _____ Monday   12. _____ Burger King   19. _____ December

6. _____ 10:00   13. _____ 803 Main St.   20. _____ Bob's Used Cars

7. _____ noon   14. _____ Oak Lane   21. _____ October 25th

at	on	in
at _____	on _____	in ___Canada___
at _____	on _____	in _____
at _____	on _____	in _____
at _____	on _____	in _____
at _____	on _____	in _____
at _____	on _____	in _____
at _____	on _____	in _____

Rules:	
Use **at** with	
Use **on** with	
Use **in** with	countries,

 **Do Online Exercise 10.2. My score: _____ /10. _____ % correct.**

EXERCISE 4. Editing. Is It Correct?

If the sentence is correct, write a check mark (✓) on the line. If it is not correct, write X on the line and circle the mistake. Then change the sentence to make it correct. Write the change above the sentence. (*Hint:* There are eight sentences. Two are correct, but six have mistakes.)

My Friends

_____ 1. My best friend Susan lives at Toronto.

_____ 2. She works in Taco Express Restaurant.

_____ 3. My good friend Jeanine lives in Florida.

_____ 4. She teaches in the University of Central Florida.

_____ 5. My oldest friend Paolo works at Europe.

_____ 6. He was born in January 1, 1976.

_____ 7. My friend James likes to run in the morning.

_____ 8. He wakes up really early because he likes to go running in 6 o'clock.

ONE-MINUTE LESSON
There are a few special expressions that use **go + VERB + -ing**: **go shopping, go swimming, go running, go fishing**. It is more common to say, *She didn't go shopping* than *She didn't shop*. Learn these special **go + VERB + -ing** idioms and use them in your English conversations.

Review of *at/on/in* for Time

- **At** is used with clock time (a specific time): *at noon, at 4:30.*

  also: *at night, at the beginning, at the end*

- **On** is used with days: *on Monday, on July 7th.*

  also: *on Friday morning, on Friday night*

- **In** is used with months, seasons, and years: *in May, in spring, in 1995.*

  also: *in the morning, in the afternoon, in the evening*

EXERCISE 5. *at/on/in* for Time in Context

Complete the sentences with the correct prepositions.

When?

1. She was born _____ December 9th _____ 1889.

2. In history class, we always have a test _____ Friday.

3. I still can't believe that he called me _____ 3:30 _____ the morning!

4. The trees this year were especially beautiful. _____ August, they were full of green leaves, but _____ the fall, they turned red or yellow.

5. Our English class starts _____ eight and ends _____ eight-fifty.

6. Many people take vacation _____ the summer, but I prefer to take mine _____ October.

7. The next big sale will take place _____ the third Saturday _____ February.

8. The meetings are usually held _____ the morning, but the next one will be _____ night.

9. The treaty between Russia and the U.S. will expire _____ midnight _____ the last day of this year.

10. When I saw Tina _____ lunch today, she looked very worried, but when I talked to her later _____ the afternoon, she said nothing was wrong.

 Do Online Exercise 10.3. My score: _____ /10. _____ % correct.

Review of *at/on/in* for PLACE

- **At** is used with specific places, including street addresses: *at McDonald's, at 704 Green Street, at the corner of Green and Main.*

- **On** is used with street names: *on Green Street, on Kennedy Avenue.*

- **On** is used when something touches a surface: *on the wall, on the floor.*

- **In** is used with towns, cities, states, and countries: *in Los Angeles, in Texas.*

- **In** is used when something is inside: *in the box, in my pocket.*

EXERCISE 6. *at/on/in* for Place in Context

Complete the sentences with the correct prepositions. Some of these are difficult.

Where?

1. The new post office is _____ Elm Road, but the old one was _____ the downtown area.

2. She was born _____ a suburb of Boston, but she grew up _____ Los Angeles.

3. He put his credit card _____ his wallet, and then he put his wallet _____ his back right pocket.

4. The saucers are _____ the top shelf of the white cabinet _____ the kitchen.

5. He used to live _____ 536 Goode Street, but now he lives _____ a different address.

6. I know you can get a money order _____ a bank, and I think you can get one _____ a convenience store, too.

7. Disney World is _____ Orlando, which is _____ Florida, but Disney Land is _____ Anaheim, which is _____ California.

8. Susan did a crossword puzzle on the bus today. She wrote the last word _____ the correct squares just as the bus arrived _____ her stop.

9. She put the turkey _____ the oven and then checked the two pots _____ the stove.

10. I have worked _____ the appliance store _____ Mills Avenue for six years.

11. _____ that country, the people who live _____ the central part and the people who live _____ the coast speak with very different accents.

Do Online Exercise 10.4. My score: _____ /10. _____ % correct.

EXERCISE 7. Speaking Practice: Student Information

This chart has information about five people. The information includes people's names, birth year, birthplace, workplace, location, and starting time. Some information is missing. Work together with a partner to find the missing information.

Student A

Step 1. Work with a partner. You are A, and your partner is B.

Step 2. Student A works on this page, and Student B works on page 276.

Step 3. Take turns asking information questions to complete the chart.

Examples: When was (Paul) born?
What does (Paul) do?

Name	Year Born	Where Born	Workplace	Location	Starting Time
Vic	1980				7:00 AM
Paul		New York		Ben Road	
Tasha		Atlanta		Peach Street	3:00 PM
	1983		Star Taxi Co.*		11:00 PM
Marjory	1960		Nation's Bank	Branch Road	

*Co. is the abbreviation (short form) of company.

Student B

Step 1. Work with a partner. You are B, and your partner is A.

Step 2. Student B works on this page, and Student A works on page 275.

Step 3. Take turns asking information questions to complete the chart.

<u>Examples:</u> When was (Vic) born?

What does (Hank) do?

Name	Year Born	Where Born	Workplace	Location	Starting Time
Vic		Miami	McDonald's	Main Street	
Paul	1970		Nation's Bank		9:00 AM
Tasha	1985		Delta Airlines		
Hank		Dallas		Coral Street	
		Memphis			9:00 AM

EXERCISE 8. Mini-Conversations

Circle the correct words in these eight mini-conversations.

1. A: When were you born?

   B: (At, On, In) 1992.

2. A: Where is Cancun?

   B: It's (at, on, in) Mexico.

   A: I know that, but what part of Mexico is it (at, on, in)?

   B: I think it's (at, on, in) the southeastern area. It's (at, on, in) the coast.

3. A: I'm surprised you're still here. What time is your meeting?

   B: It begins (at, on, in) 7. I can't be late, so I have to go now.

4. A: Is she living (at, on, in) Apartment 212?

   B: I'm not sure. All I know for sure is that she lives (at, on, in) the second floor.

5. A: Didn't you go to Puerto Rico last summer?

   B: Yes, I did. It was my first time to visit any place (at, on, in) that area.

6. A: Was George Washington born (at, on, in) February 21st?

   B: No, he was born (at, on, in) February but not (at, on, in) that date. He was born (at, on, in) the 22nd.

7. A: Susan teaches (at, on, in) Highline Community College.

   B: Yes, that's right, and she lives (at, on, in) downtown Seattle.

8. A: Was your flight on time?

   B: Yes, we landed (at, on, in) 9:30 or so, which was close to the scheduled time.

 Do Online Exercise 10.1. My score: _____ /10. _____ % correct.

 ONE-MINUTE LESSON
The idiom **or so** means "approximately." If you arrive at 9:30 **or so**, it means you arrived near 9:30 but not exactly at 9:30. If someone asks, *How many people were at the meeting?* you can answer **50 or so** if you do not know the exact number.

EXERCISE 9. Sentence Study for Critical Reading

Read the numbered sentences. Then read the three answer choices, and place a check mark in the yes or no boxes in front of each sentence to show if that answer is true based on the information in the original sentence. If there is not enough information to mark something as yes, then mark it as no. Remember that more than one true answer is possible.

1. Susan is in her bedroom, and her cousin Jill is in the kitchen.
   - [ ] yes [ ] no   a. Susan is not in the kitchen.
   - [ ] yes [ ] no   b. These two girls are in the same building.
   - [ ] yes [ ] no   c. Susan is in the left part of the house.

2. The party begins at 9:00, and it's almost 7:30 now.
   - [ ] yes [ ] no   a. A few people are at the party now.
   - [ ] yes [ ] no   b. The party begins about 90 minutes from now.
   - [ ] yes [ ] no   c. The party is on Saturday night.

3. Bui has a pain in his foot.
   - [ ] yes [ ] no   a. Bui is wearing white socks today.
   - [ ] yes [ ] no   b. Bui's foot hurts him.
   - [ ] yes [ ] no   c. Bui's shoes are too big. He needs to buy a smaller size.

4. Maria lives in Madrid now, but she worked in New York from 2007 to 2009.
   - [ ] yes [ ] no   a. She is in the United States now.
   - [ ] yes [ ] no   b. She worked in the United States in 1999.
   - [ ] yes [ ] no   c. She did not work in New York in 2009.

5. Sam finished eating dinner five minutes ago, so he put his dirty dishes on the counter next to the sink.
   - [ ] yes [ ] no   a. The dishes are dirty.
   - [ ] yes [ ] no   b. The dishes are wet now.
   - [ ] yes [ ] no   c. The dishes are in the sink.

6. The weather yesterday wasn't so nice, but today it is incredible. We had two inches of rain yesterday, but today it is sunny. The children are playing in the park.
   - [ ] yes [ ] no   a. Today's rain is extremely heavy.
   - [ ] yes [ ] no   b. It is a great day to be outside.
   - [ ] yes [ ] no   c. The children played in the park yesterday.

7. I wrote the plumber's telephone number on a small piece of yellow paper, and then I put it on the refrigerator. You can see it now.

   ☐ yes ☐ no a. The note is cold now.

   ☐ yes ☐ no b. The plumber wrote a note on yellow paper.

   ☐ yes ☐ no c. The note is on yellow paper.

8. Nina, Salina, and Rafaela are in class today. Their teacher is at the board explaining something. Nina isn't paying attention, but Salina and Rafaela are.

   ☐ yes ☐ no a. Salina's chair is in the middle of the room.

   ☐ yes ☐ no b. Nina is wearing a silver bracelet on her left wrist.

   ☐ yes ☐ no c. The teacher is using a computer right now.

ONE-MINUTE LESSON
We use **on** to talk about things you wear on your body. We say, *She is wearing her watch* **on** *her right wrist* or *He has a silver ring* **on** *his left hand.* Don't use **in** with these examples.

EXERCISE 10. Speaking Practice: Partner Drill for *at/on/in*

Step 1. Student A completes the left box; Student B completes the right box.

Step 2. Write the numbers 1 to 12 on the first blanks. Mix up the numbers (so everyone is not doing the same question at the same time).

Step 3. Write the prepositions for *one* of the groups (A or B) in the second blank. Check your answers with another student who also did the same work.

Step 4. Then work with a partner who did not do the same group. Take turns asking each other your questions. The listener should not see the book.

Step 5. When you finish, work with a different partner.

Example of Student A asking Student B:

A: "December"

B: "in December"

A: "That's right."

B: "night."

A: "in night"

B: "No, that's not right. Try again: night."

A: "at night"

B: "Yes, that's right."

Student A	Student B
_____. _____ 1997	_____. _____ Monday
_____. _____ night	_____. _____ 2 PM
_____. _____ the shelf	_____. _____ May
_____. _____ the evening	_____. _____ January
_____. _____ winter	_____. _____ 1945
_____. _____ the afternoon	_____. _____ 6 AM
_____. _____ the kitchen	_____. _____ First Union Bank
_____. _____ midnight	_____. _____ 1776
_____. _____ Miller Road	_____. _____ Ponte Street
_____. _____ Young Avenue	_____. _____ Sam's Market
_____. _____ the last day	_____. _____ summer
_____. _____ December	_____. _____ Friday

REVIEW

EXERCISE 11. Review Test 1: Multiple Choice

Circle the letter of the correct answer. Some are conversations.

1. "When do you usually call Susan?"

   "She works during the day, so I call her _____."

       a. in the night   b. in night   c. at the night   d. at night

2. "Where is Joe now?'

   "He's at the bank on _____."

       a. New York City   b. California   c. State Street   d. Nation's Bank

3. "Where do you work?"

   "_____ Lucky Travel Agency."

       a. In   b. At   c. On   d. To

4. "Let's play tennis at _____."

   "OK, that sounds like a good idea to me."

       a. 5:30   b. Saturday   c. the morning   d. June 15

5. "Where are Mark and Katie?"

   "They're _____ the kitchen."

       a. in   b. at   c. on   d. to

6. "What do students usually do _____ the first day of school each year?"

   "Sometimes they write essays about what they did in the summer."

       a. in   b. at   c. on   d. to

7. "Where does Benjamin live?"

   "He lives on _____."

       a. 536 Broad Street   b. Broad Street   c. Miami   d. Miami, Florida

8. Which of these is correct?

       a. at spring   b. at noon   c. at Friday night   d. at June 17th

REVIEW **EXERCISE 12. Review Test 2: Production and Evaluation**

Part 1.

Fill in each blank with a phrase from the word list that makes sense. Use each phrase one time.

word list	the morning a very busy neighborhood	a very busy street the kitchen table	6 o'clock Saturday

Today is the beginning of the weekend, but I woke up

really early. In fact, I got up at ❶ _____.

This is unusual for me because I usually get up much later on

❷ _____. My husband tried to tell

me something, but I couldn't listen to him because I can't

think in ❸ _____ until I have a cup of

coffee. I got a cup of coffee for myself and sat at

❹ _____. I could hear cars racing by, but this is usual because

we live on ❺ _____ in ❻ _____.

Part 2.

Look at the underlined part in each sentence. If the underlined part is correct, circle the word *correct*. If it is wrong, circle the word *wrong* and the wrong part. Then write the correction above.

correct   wrong   1. Vancouver is a city <u>on</u> British Columbia.

correct   wrong   2. Do you think the best cheeseburgers are <u>in</u> McDonald's?

correct   wrong   3. It's impossible for her to arrive here <u>in</u> the afternoon.

correct   wrong   4. John is my best friend. I met him <u>in</u> 2002.

correct   wrong   5. I'm going to visit my aunt <u>in Dallas in</u> Friday.

correct   wrong   6. They have a TV <u>in the living room and another in</u> the kitchen.

correct   wrong   7. Fatima studied French <u>in</u> a small town near Paris.

correct   wrong   8. My first class is early <u>on</u> the morning.

correct   wrong   9. Flight 337 to Madrid left <u>in</u> 10:38 on the dot.

correct   wrong   10. The TV commercial said, "<u>In</u> Bob's Used Cars, we have the very best prices for you!"

EXERCISE 13. Reading Practice: 15 Capital Cities

Read the information about these capital cities. Then fill in the chart, and answer the seven comprehension questions on page 285. The grammar from this unit is underlined for you.

- Beirut, Jakarta, and Tokyo are in different countries in the same continent.
- Accra is in Ghana, Vienna is in Austria, and Quito is in Ecuador.
- The largest city in Argentina is Buenos Aires.
- Bucharest is located on the Danube River.
- Ottawa is the capital of Canada.
- The largest city in any country is usually the capital as well. In this chart, if the city is not the largest city, that information is provided.

Capital City	Country	Continent	City Population	Interesting Facts
Abu Dhabi	United Arab Emirates	Asia	900,000	1. the name means "Father of Gazelle" 2. the 2nd largest city in the country 3. a port on the Persian Gulf
Accra		Africa	2,800,000	the name comes from a word meaning "ants"
Beirut	Lebanon		2,200,000	a port on the Mediterranean Sea
Belgrade	Serbia	Europe	1,500,000	1. the name means "white city" 2. located on the Danube River
Bratislava	Slovakia	Europe	500,000	located on the Danube River
	Romania	Europe	2,400,000	located on the Danube River
Budapest	Hungary	Europe	2,000,000	1. located on the Danube River 2. originally Buda and Pest were two cities on different sides of the river
	Argentina	S. America	12,000,000	1. the name means "good airs" 2. located on a river 3. the 2nd largest city in S. America
Jakarta	Indonesia		9,000,000	a port on the island of Java
Tokyo	Japan	Asia	12,000,000	1. the name means "Eastern Capital" 2. the population of the Tokyo area is about 37,000,000
Libreville	Gabon	Africa	600,000	1. the name means "Free Town" 2. located on the Komo River near the Gulf of Guinea
	Canada	N. America	1,100,000	1. the 4th largest city in the country 2. the name comes from the name of the original people there, the Odawa 3. located on the Ottawa River

Quito		S. America	1,500,000	1. the 2nd largest city 2. located in the Andes Mountains 3. the 2nd highest capital city in the world (at 9,186 feet above sea level)
Rabat	Morocco	Africa	700,000	1. the 2nd largest city in the country 2. located on the Atlantic Ocean and the Bou Regreg River
Vienna		Europe	1,900,000	located on the Danube River

1. Can you name three of these capital cities that are located on a river? Which are they? _____

   _____

2. How many of the cities in this chart are in Africa? _____

3. How many capital cities have a population that is less than half a million? _____

4. Are both South American capital cities located in the Andes Mountains? _____

5. Can you name the three Canadian cities that are larger than the capital city? Ask a classmate or use the Internet if you need help. _____

   _____

   _____

6. Circle the two statements that are true.
   a. _____ More people live in the capital of Canada than in Accra, Ghana.
   b._____ The capital of Indonesia, Jakarta, is on an island.
   c. _____ Abu Dhabi is an important city in the United Arab Emirates.
   d._____ The capital of Morocco is the largest city in the country as well.

7. Was there any information in this chart that is surprising to you? Why?

   _____

   _____

   _____

   _____

EXERCISE 14. Vocabulary Practice: Word Knowledge

Circle the word or phrase that is most closely related to the word or phrase on the left. Use a dictionary to check the meaning of words you do not know.

Vocabulary	Answer Choice	
1. a continent	France or Spain	Asia or Europe
2. a guarantee	a promise	a relationship
3. less than 80	77 or 78 or 79	79 or 80 or 81
4. a square	3 sides	4 sides
5. a decade	10 years	100 years
6. an essay	you cook it	you write it
7. turned (red)	became (red)	found (red)
8. a plumber	a person	a thing
9. a surface	a box	a wall
10. a schedule	a place	a plan
11. expire	begin	finish
12. at 8 on the dot	8:00	7:55–8:05
13. exist	there are	we need
14. an agency	a place	a time
15. however	but	so
16. provide	give	take
17. an idiom	English or Japanese	raining cats and dogs
18. a wallet	for babies	for money
19. a puzzle	a place	a thing
20. an accent	reading	speaking
21. have to go	need to go	want to go
22. an oven	in the bathroom	in the kitchen
23. a neighborhood	a place	a time
24. an appliance	in the garden	in the kitchen
25. a bracelet	prefer	round
26. as well	and	but
27. 5 minutes from now	in the future	in the past
28. at sea level	every beach	every capital
29. a sink	in a car	in a house
30. an avenue	a person	a street

EXERCISE 15. Vocabulary Practice: Collocations

Fill in each blank with the answer on the right that most naturally completes the phrase on the left. If necessary, use a dictionary to check the meaning of words you do not know.

Phrase	Answer Choices	
1. a _____ bit	few	little
2. instead _____	of	to
3. a full _____	corner	schedule
4. in early _____	May	Monday
5. _____ September	in	on
6. an _____ fact	outside	interesting
7. the capital _____ a country	of	on
8. have something in _____	common	course
9. _____ of water	empty	full
10. as we can see _____ this chart	at	in
11. _____ the middle shelf	in	on
12. a typical _____ in my home	day	furniture
13. a _____ in my foot	hurt	pain
14. if you _____ help	let	need
15. she _____ born	did	was
16. do something _____ purpose	in	on
17. on the _____	coast	country
18. I _____ my vacation	make	take
19. it _____ like a good idea	listens	sounds
20. my _____ expires soon	exam	license
21. a _____ commercial	newspaper	television
22. put it on the _____	counter	drawer
23. in the southern _____	area	country
24. write an essay _____ a person	about	to
25. it's difficult _____ us	for	to
26. the _____ shelf	suburb	top
27. at _____	none	noon
28. on the _____	oven	stove
29. during the _____	day	dry
30. we finished _____ at 8	eating	to eat

EXERCISE 16. Writing Practice: Specific Details about a Past Event

Part 1. Editing Student Writing

Read these sentences with specific details about one student's favorite trip. Underline the 15 errors. Then write the number of the sentence with the error next to the type of error. (Some sentences may have more than one error.)

_____ a. *at/on/in*   _____ d. negative

_____ b. no verb   _____ e. verb tense

_____ c. word order   _____ f. no subject

My Favorite Place to Visit
1. One of my cities favorite is New Orleans. It is a wonderful place to visit.
2. New Orleans is at Louisiana, which is a state in the southern part of the United States.
3. People like to visit New Orleans because has an interesting history and because the food local is so good.
4. When I a young child, my family go to New Orleans four or five times.
5. Sometimes we went in June or in July. The weather in New Orleans is very hot and humid at summer, so I am not recommend that you went there then.
6 . In 1999, we were there for my birthday, which is on February. Was also Mardi Gras, which is a huge celebration in New Orleans.
7. My family let me choose where we ate dinner in that special day, so I choose to eat at a special restaurant in the historic French Quarter.
8. New Orleans is a place marvelous to visit, and know you will enjoy it, too.

Part 2. Original Student Writing

Now write some sentences about a favorite trip. Give advice to your readers about whether they should or should not visit this place. Underline all examples of prepositions.

Unit 11

Be going to + VERB

Discover the Grammar

Today is Wednesday, and Kevin is calling friends because he needs their help. On Saturday, he is going to move from his old apartment to a new house. Kevin does not have a car, so he needs someone to help him. He needs a friend who has a big car or truck who can help him on Saturday. Read his two phone calls, and then answer the nine questions.

Line	Call 1	Call 2
1	**Mike:** Hello.	**Jeff:** Hello.
2	**Kevin:** Mike, hi. It's me, Kevin.	**Kevin:** Jeff, hey, this is Kevin. How's it
3	How's it going?	going?
4	**Mike:** Great. How have you been?	**Jeff:** Pretty good. I haven't heard
5	**Kevin:** Great. Hey, I'm calling now	from you in a long time.
6	because I have a favor to ask	**Kevin:** Yeah, I know. I've been really
7	of you.	busy with work and other stuff.
8	**Mike:** Ok.	**Jeff:** Cool.
9	**Kevin:** Well, I am going to move to a	**Kevin:** Well, my big news is I'm going
10	new place on Saturday, and	to move to a new place next
11	I'm looking for someone with	weekend.
12	a car who can help me.	**Jeff:** Really? Which part of town?

13	**Mike:**	Wow, I wish I could help you,
14		Kevin, but I already have
15		plans. Brittany and I are
16		going to visit her parents in
17		Brookfield.
18	**Kevin:**	Ok, no problem. Hey, please
19		tell Brittany I said hello, ok?
20	**Mike:**	Ok, I'll do that. Hey, why
21		don't you ask Jeff? I'm pretty
22		sure he has a truck.
23	**Kevin:**	I didn't think of Jeff. That's a
24		good idea. This move is going
25		to be a lot easier if I can use
26		his truck.
27		
28		
29		
30		
31		
32		

Kevin: To a house near the airport. It's a lot bigger than where I am now.

Jeff: That sounds great.

Kevin: Hey, is there any chance you can help me move on Saturday?

Jeff: Oh, wow. I can't do that. On Saturday, I'm going to paint my mom's house. She asked me to do this a long time ago, but I kept saying no until now.

Kevin: It's ok. To tell you the truth, painting a house sounds easy. Moving all my furniture is going to be a lot of hard work.

Jeff: Well, I wish I could help, but I have to help my mom on Saturday.

Kevin: No problem.

ONE-MINUTE LESSON
The word **keep** has two common meanings: "have" amd "continue." When it means "have," the next word is a noun or pronoun: *I* **keep** *my wallet in my desk.* When it means "continue," it must have **VERB + -ing:** *I* **kept** *saying no.* If you want your English to sound better, use **keep + VERB + -ing.**

1. In Call 1, underline all the examples of *going to*. How many did you find? _____

2. Now circle all of the words to the left of *going to* in Call 1. Write the words here:
   _____, _____, _____

3. Now put a box around the word that comes after *going to*. Write those words here.

   _____   _____   _____

4. What do you notice about all the words in Number 3? What part of speech are they? _____ How many of these words end in suffixes such as *-s, -es, -ing,* or *-ed*? _____

5. Combine your information from Numbers 1, 2, 3, and 4. What is the pattern here for this lesson?

   subject + _____ + *going to* + _____

6. When do we use *be going to* + VERB? Is it for present time, past time, or future time? _____

7. Find three examples of the present progressive. Write them here. What time are these verb examples talking about?

   _____   _____   _____

   _____

8. Now put two lines under all examples of *be going to* + VERB in Call 2. How many examples did you find? _____

9. Are all the examples of *be going to* + VERB for the future time? _____

10. What questions do you have about this grammar before we study this unit?

    _____

    _____

    _____

Grammar Lesson

Be Going To

Past   Now   Future

X

Examples	subject	*be going to*	VERB
I'm going to take a trip to Miami in two more days.	I	'm going to	take
You're going to have a great time tonight.	you	're going to	have
At this rate, he is never going to graduate.	he	is going to	graduate
She's going to call you at noon.	she	's going to	call
Do you think it's going to rain?	it	's going to	rain
We are going to eat dinner at Jack's later.	we	are going to	eat
They're going to get together at 6 tonight.	they	're going to	get

Rule 1. One usage of **be going to** + **VERB** is to talk about future plans.

Rule 2. We can use **be going to** + **VERB** to talk about predictions based on current evidence. (A: "Oh, the sky is really dark." B: "Yes, it's going to rain soon.")

Rule 3. We use **will** + **VERB** to talk about future time, but the usage is more limited than **be** + **going to**. For example, you cannot use **will** for future intentions that you have already planned. We ask, *What are you going to do tomorrow?* not *What will you do tomorrow?* In contrast, if the phone rings right now, you could say, *I'll answer it* (not *I'm going to answer it*) because you have no prior plan to answer the phone.

Rule 4. We use **am** with *I*; **is** with *he, she, it*; **are** for *you, we, they.*

Rule 5. It is necessary to include a subject (noun or pronoun) with this expression.

Rule 6. Common time expressions for **be going to** include *tomorrow, next* _____ (*next week*), and *in* _____ (*in 5 minutes*).

Rule 7. The negative of **be going to** is the same for all **be** verbs. Use *not* or a contraction *n't.* (*We aren't going to drive there* OR *We're not going to drive there*)

Rule 8. Questions for **be going to** are the same for all *be* verbs. Move *be* before the subject. (*Are most people going to vote tomorrow?* OR *Where is the meeting going to be?*)

Rule 9. In spoken language, **going to** before VERB often sounds like "gonna." This is ok in informal spoken language, but we never write "gonna" in academic writing.

Connecting Grammar and Vocabulary

It is possible to use any verb after *be going to*, but you cannot learn thousands of verb combinations. You need the most common verbs for this grammar point. Memorize these two lists.

The 15 Most Commonly Used Verbs (in order frequency) after *be going to*					
Spoken English			**Academic English**		
1. be	6. take	11. come	1. be	6. make	11. give
2. have	7. happen	12. give	2. have	7. take	12. change
3. do	8. make	13. talk	3. do	8. go	13. say
4. get	9. see	14. try	4. get	9. see	14. use
5. go	10. say	15. tell	5. happen	10. die	15. come

<u>Source</u>: Based on information in the Corpus of Contemporary American English: www.americancorpus.org/.

BE CAREFUL!

Common Learner Errors	Explanation
1. Laura ~~going~~ is going to study with Ana and Carla tonight.	Use a form of be with going to verb.
2. If we don't hurry up, we're going ~~be~~ to be late.	Don't forget the word to.
3. Your application for a new passport is going to ~~takes~~ take four to six weeks.	The verb after be going to is the base simple form. Don't use -s or -ed or -ing with the verb after to.
4. Written language example: Many people think those new laws are ~~gonna~~ going to be good for the environment.	We often pronounce going to as *gonna*, but don't write *gonna*. It is not a written word.
5. Spoken language example: I really think it's ~~gonna to~~ gonna OR going to rain soon.	If you want to say *gonna*, don't say *gonna to*. The pronunciation *gonna* meaning *going to*, so the error *gonna to* really means *going to to*.
6. Spoken language example: We're ~~gonna~~ going to New York tomorrow.	We never say *gonna* with a place. The pronunciation *gonna* in informal spoken English tells us that a verb follows.

EXERCISE 1. Scrambled Sentences about the Future

Unscramble these words to produce common examples of *be going to* in sentences. Use each word only one time, but use all the words. Add end punctuation. Sometimes more than one combination is possible.

Predictions about the Year 2025

1. going expensive in prices to be much gas more are 2025

   Gas prices are going to be much more expensive in 2025 .

2. cars than smaller people going to are now drive

   _____

3. to be a little average now temperature warmer than the is going it is

   _____

   _____

4. write English am I to going perfectly speak and

   _____

5. to get until their 30s married are are in most they people going not

   _____

   _____

6. find a doctors are to cancer or another cure for disease serious going

   _____

   _____

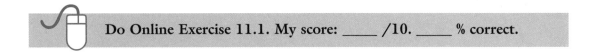

Do Online Exercise 11.1. My score: _____ /10. _____ % correct.

EXERCISE 2. *Be going to* in Context

Circle *be going to* + VERB in each sentence. Then consult your favorite Internet travel site to add the missing information.

Air Travel

1. To fly from Miami to Paris round-trip next week, the cheapest ticket is going to cost _____ .

2. To fly one-way from Los Angeles to Tokyo in business class tomorrow, the fare is going to cost

    _____.

3. If your friends want to fly from Moscow to New York next month, it is going to take approximately

    _____ hours for them to reach their destination.

4. There are no nonstop flights from Mexico City to Singapore. How many stops is an air traveler on this route going to have to make? _____ Where is he or she going to stop? _____

5. If you plan to travel from Dallas to Tokyo, how many meals are you probably going to receive? _____ Which meals are you going to get?

    _____

Do Online Exercise 11.2. My score: _____ /10. _____ % correct.

EXERCISE 3. Questions with *be going to*

Write a yes-no question, and give a short answer. Then write a *wh-* question for the underlined word, and give a short answer. (*Hint:* Look at the words in italics.)

1. Karen is going to write <u>a letter to the president</u>.

   (yes-no) Is Karen going to write a letter to the president?

   Yes, she is.

   (wh) What is Karen going to write?

   A letter to the president.

2. We are going to give Jeremy <u>a trip to Paris</u> for his birthday.

   (yes-no) _____

   _____

   (wh) _____

   _____

3. The current problem is going to continue <u>because people do not care</u>.

   (yes-no) _____

   _____

   (wh) _____

   _____

Do Online Exercise 11.3. My score: _____ /10. _____ % correct.

ONE-MINUTE LESSON
The adjective **current** is a difficult word for some learners. The word **current** means "now" or "at the present time." We say, *The* **current** *price is $500* and *Did you vote for our* **current** *president?* Do not use the word **actual** for this meaning. That is a different word with a different meaning. Learn to use the word **current**.

EXERCISE 4. Speaking Practice: Guessing Game about Your Plans

Step 1. There are six actions and six future times given. Use them to write your schedule for tomorrow.

Step 2. After you finish your plans, work with a partner. Take turns asking questions to try to guess your partner's schedule. If the answer to a question is yes, then that person can continue asking. If the answer is no, the turn passes to the other student. The first partner to finish is the winner! When you finish, try it with another student.

Actions	Times
go to the library	at 10 AM tomorrow
do the dishes	at 5 PM tomorrow
wash clothes	at 8 PM tomorrow night
make soup	at 2 PM tomorrow
watch a movie on TV	at noon tomorrow
call Paula	at 4 PM tomorrow

Your Schedule

Actions	Times
I'm going to	
I'm going to	
I'm going to	
I'm going to	
I'm going to	
I'm going to	

Your Partner's Schedule

Actions	Times
I'm going to	
I'm going to	
I'm going to	
I'm going to	
I'm going to	
I'm going to	

EXERCISE 5. Mini-Conversations

Circle the correct words in these eight mini-conversations.

1. A: When are you going (get, getting, to get) a present for Joseph?

   B: Tomorrow I'm going (go, going, to go) shopping at the mall.

2. A: Can your sister speak German?

   B: No, but she (takes, is going to take) a German course before her trip.

3. A: Are you busy now?

   B: Yes, I am, but I'm (having, have, going to have) some free time after 5. Can you come back then?

4. A: What's wrong with your car?

   B: I don't know. (It makes, It's making, It's going to make) a strange noise, so I'm going to take it to the garage tomorrow morning.

5. A: Wow, today's weather was great, wasn't it?

   B: Yes, but I think (it rains, it's going to rain) tomorrow.

6. A: Why are you crying? Is everything ok?

   B: Yes, everything is fine. I'm just cutting up onions now because (I make, I'm going to make, I will make) onion soup for dinner.

7. A: How long (are you going to study, do you study) tonight?

   B: For about two or three hours. If I study more than that, (I go, I'm going, I'm gonna) to get really tired and then I am not going to (am, is, be) able to concentrate.

8. A: Where are your sisters going to go for vacation?

   B: Sarah (am, is, are) not going to go anywhere, but Christine (visit, goes to visit, visits, is going to visit) our grandfather in Maine.

 Do Online Exercise 11.4. My score: _____ /10. _____ % correct.

EXERCISE 6. Editing. Is It Correct?

If the sentence is correct, write a check mark (✓) on the line. If it is not correct, circle the mistake and write X on the line. Then change the sentence to make it correct. Write the change above the sentence. (*Hint*: There are eight sentences. Two are correct, but six have mistakes.)

Tomorrow's Weather Map

_____ 1. The weather in New York City today was very wet, but tomorrow it's going to sunny.

_____ 2. The high temperature in Los Angeles going to be 85 tomorrow.

_____ 3. The high temperature in Dallas going to be the same as the temperature in Los Angeles.

_____ 4. It's going to be extremely windy tomorrow in northern Arizona.

_____ 5. If you live in Detroit, you're probably not going like the weather report for tomorrow because it's going to be rainy and quite cool.

_____ 6. Residents of Denver are gonna be very happy with the beautiful weather they're going to have tomorrow.

_____ 7. There is going to be very heavy showers and some severe thunderstorms tomorrow afternoon in New Orleans and Houston.

_____ 8. Atlanta is going to have one more day of sunshine tomorrow before bad weather arrives the next day.

EXERCISE 7. Sentence Study for Critical Reading

Read the numbered sentences. Then read the three answer choices and place a check mark in the yes or no boxes in front of each sentence to show if that answer is true based on the information in the original sentence. If there is not enough information to mark something as yes, then mark it as no. Remember that more than one true answer may be possible.

1. The grammar test is going to have two sections with twenty questions each.
   - [ ] yes [ ] no a. The test will have twenty questions.
   - [ ] yes [ ] no b. The test will have more than one section.
   - [ ] yes [ ] no c. The number of questions will be less than fifty.

2. Charlie is going to cook dinner tonight, so Chelsea doesn't have to do it.
   - [ ] yes [ ] no a. Chelsea is not going to cook dinner.
   - [ ] yes [ ] no b. Charlie is going to cook steaks with potatoes.
   - [ ] yes [ ] no c. Tonight's cook is Charlie.

3. I'm going to make some tea. Maybe that will help me feel better.
   - [ ] yes [ ] no a. The person drank some tea a little while ago.
   - [ ] yes [ ] no b. The person is drinking tea right now.
   - [ ] yes [ ] no c. The person will drink some tea in a little while.

4. Because of the bad weather, our flight isn't going to take off on time.
   - [ ] yes [ ] no a. Our flight will leave late.
   - [ ] yes [ ] no b. We are going to take off on time.
   - [ ] yes [ ] no c. The weather is going to be bad after our flight.

5. Getting a visa is going to get harder after the new rules are in place next month.
   - [ ] yes [ ] no a. Now it is very difficult to get a visa.
   - [ ] yes [ ] no b. It will be easier in the future to get a visa.
   - [ ] yes [ ] no c. Next month no one will be able to get a visa.

6. The doctor told her patient, "You must take these vitamins and exercise every day. You have to walk a lot more and do more things. Stay active! At your age, you're going to lose muscles really quickly if you don't work out."
   - [ ] yes [ ] no a. The doctor is a man.
   - [ ] yes [ ] no b. We can't tell if the patient is a man or a woman.
   - [ ] yes [ ] no c. The doctor is talking about the past.

7. According to the report in yesterday's newspaper, the new government plan is going to give more money for schools in poor neighborhoods.

   ☐ yes ☐ no   a. The plan will give money for some schools.

   ☐ yes ☐ no   b. This information came from a newspaper report.

   ☐ yes ☐ no   c. The newspaper company wrote the plan.

8. After the police get all the facts, they're going to try to figure out exactly why this bus crash happened.

   ☐ yes ☐ no   a. A police car and a bus had an accident.

   ☐ yes ☐ no   b. The police want to know why there was an accident.

   ☐ yes ☐ no   c. Right now they don't know why the accident happened.

ONE-MINUTE LESSON

The verb **figure out** is very common. We say, *I can't* **figure out** *the meaning of this word, so I need a dictionary* or *She* **figured out** *the price of the order.* Don't use the words **know** or **learn** for these examples. Learn to use the verb **figure out**.

EXERCISE 8. Speaking Practice: Future Travel Plans

Five friends are talking about their plans for the Thanksgiving holidays. This chart has some information about their plans, but some of the information is missing. Work with a partner to find out the missing information.

Student A

Step 1. Work with a partner. You are A, and your partner is B.

Step 2. Student A works on this page, but Student B works on page 304.

Step 3. Take turns asking information questions to fill in the missing information. Use *be going to* in your conversations.

Name	Plan	Where	When
Joy	watch old movies on TV		
Kerry	visit her grandparents	Minneapolis, Minnesota	
Maria		her parents' house in Miami	on Thursday
Lindsay	go to the beach	in Los Angeles	
Jason			on Friday, Saturday, and Sunday

Student B

Step 1. Work with a partner. You are B, and your partner is A.

Step 2. Student B works on this page, and Student A works on page 303.

Step 3. Take turns asking information questions to fill in the missing information. Use *be going to* in your conversations.

Name	Plan	Where	When
Joy		her apartment	on Friday
Kerry			on Thursday and Friday
Maria	eat a big dinner with her parents		
Lindsay		in Los Angeles	on Friday
Jason	visit his family and write a report for school	in Seattle	

REVIEW **EXERCISE 9. Review Test 1: Multiple Choice**

Circle the letter of the correct answer. Some are conversations.

1. "Is our ticket to Mexico and Guatemala going to cost more than $400?"

   "Yes, _____, but you're going to visit two cities in Mexico and three cities in Guatemala.

       a. it is   b. they are   c. you are   d. we are

2. "Are you busy tomorrow?"

   "No, I _____ anything."

       a. am not do   b. do not do   c. am not going to do   d. did not do

3. "_____ work every day?"

   "No, I work from Tuesday to Saturday. I don't work on Sunday and Monday.

       a. Are you going to   b. Do you   c. Are you   d. Did you

4. No one is free next week, so we _____ be able to get together.

       a. don't go to   b. don't go   c. aren't going to   d. aren't going

5. "I'm really hungry. Is dinner almost ready?"

   "Look, I just put the chicken in the oven, so you're _____ for another 30 minutes at least. Why don't just have a snack if you can't wait?"

       a. have to wait   c. have waiting
       b. go to have to wait   d. going to have to wait

6. "_____ go swimming today?"

   "No, I'm going to go swimming tomorrow afternoon with Rae and Martina."

       a. Did you   b. Do you   c. Are you going to   d. Were you

7. "Wow, don't you think it's hot in here?"

   "Yes, it is. I _____ turn on the air conditioner right now."

       a. am   b. want   c. am going to   d. am going

8. I see you have three suitcases. You're allowed two bags for free, so _____ going to have to pay $75 for the third bag.

       a. you're   b. you do   c. you   d. you will

REVIEW > **EXERCISE 10. Review Test 2: Production and Evaluation**

Part 1.

Fill in each blank with one of the words from the word list. Use each word one time. You might have to make some changes in the form of the word.

word list	present be	open talk	be able to like

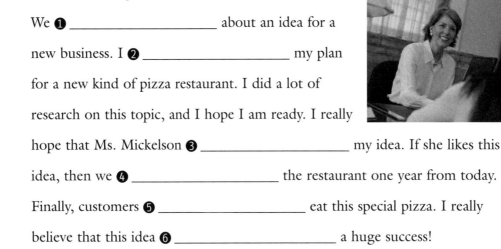

I have a meeting with Ms. Mickelson in 10 minutes.

We ❶ _____ about an idea for a

new business. I ❷ _____ my plan

for a new kind of pizza restaurant. I did a lot of

research on this topic, and I hope I am ready. I really

hope that Ms. Mickelson ❸ _____ my idea. If she likes this

idea, then we ❹ _____ the restaurant one year from today.

Finally, customers ❺ _____ eat this special pizza. I really

believe that this idea ❻ _____ a huge success!

Part 2.

Look at the underlined part in each sentence. If the underlined part is correct, circle the word *correct*. If it is wrong, circle the word *wrong* and the wrong part. Then write the correction above.

correct   wrong   1. John, Sue, and I <u>are going to watch</u> TV last night.

correct   wrong   2. Those shirts <u>are going to be</u> on sale next week.

correct   wrong   3. I was late for work today, but tomorrow I'm <u>going be</u> on
                        time for sure.

correct   wrong   4. She always eats eggs for breakfast, but <u>tomorrow she's going
                        to starts</u> a new diet that does not any include eggs.

correct   wrong   5. We're going <u>go</u> to France next year, but we want to go
                        sooner.

correct   wrong   6. <u>Do Mike and John going</u> to go jogging tomorrow?

correct   wrong   7. Why are they going to <u>doing</u> their homework with a red pen?

correct   wrong   8. <u>Laura going</u> to make salad, and I'm going to make cheese
                        sandwiches.

EXERCISE 11. Reading Practice: Future Schedules

Read the four schedules for these four people for next month. Then answer the three comprehension questions on page 308. The grammar from this unit is underlined for you.

Kaley	Next Month's Planner
2nd	doctor's appointment @ 8:45 AM
8th	lunch with Mrs. Wilson at Tavern on the Green, 12:30 PM, reconfirm on the 7th
9th–13th	visit Aunt Sue in Boston; flight on 9th at 10:15 AM; flight on 13th at noon
15th	Jackie's birthday; 7 p.m. surprise party
23rd	shop for new car at Greenway Autos all day
28th	dinner with Shelia and Grant
30th	take cat to the veterinarian's office

Jacob	Next Month's Planner
4th	dentist's appointment @ 9 AM
6th–11th	sister and kids visit
12th	birthday party for Kurt
15th	doctor's appointment @ 2 PM; get medical records from Mom
20th	football game at the college
23rd–25th	trip to visit grandparents
28th	our 8th anniversary! get flowers; dinner at Limoncello's @ 7 PM

Brian	Next Month's Planner
1st	meet with Mark's teacher @ 4 PM
2nd	Mark's class play @ 7 PM
9th	concert at 7 PM
13th	football game @ 6 PM
15th	dentist's appointment @ 7:30 AM
20th	plant sale at church all morning
27th	meet with Jill's teacher @ 3 PM
28th	dinner with Renee's parents @ their house @ 6 PM

Tina	Next Month's Planner
3rd–7th	business trip to Miami; out flight @ 7 AM; return flight @ 5 PM
10th	pick up new work uniforms
11th	take dog to veterinarian's office @ noon
12th	meeting with boss @ 2 PM
15th	dentist's appointment; verify exact time?
27th	meet with bank person about home loan @ 9 AM
28th	dinner with Alan and Cindy; verify time?

1. Put a check mark (✔) in the column of the person who can say these statements. Sometimes more than one answer is possible.

	Kaley	Jacob	Brian	Tina
a. I'm going to see my dentist on the 15th.				
b. My sister and her kids are going to visit me.				
c. I'm going to take my pet to the veterinarian's office.				
d. I am not going to do anything on the 4th.				
e. I'm going to meet with my two children's teachers.				
f. I'm going to fly somewhere.				
g. I'm going to attend a concert.				
h. I'm going to see a football game.				

2. Write full sentences to tell what these people *are going to do* on these dates.

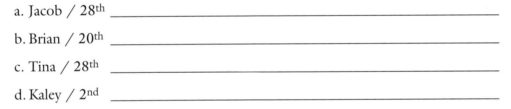

a. Jacob / 28th _____

b. Brian / 20th _____

c. Tina / 28th _____

d. Kaley / 2nd _____

3. In your opinion, who is going to do the most things? In other words, who is going to have the busiest schedule? Explain your opinion.

_____

_____

_____

EXERCISE 12. Vocabulary Practice: Word Knowledge

Circle the word or phrase that is most closely related to the word or phrase on the left. Use a dictionary to check the meaning of words you do not know.

Vocabulary	Answer Choices	
1. at noon	in the day	at night
2. I wish I could help	I can help	I can't help
3. in 5 hours	in the past	in the future
4. hurry	go fast	go slow
5. stuff	actions	things
6. a meal	eating	sleeping
7. keep writing	continue writing	stop writing
8. current	in the past	in the present
9. a chance	a person	a possibility
10. quite	something	very
11. move	change places	meet a new person
12. verify	check information	make an appointment
13. let's get together	let's enjoy	let's meet
14. prior	in the future	in the past
15. take off	a flight begins	a flight ends
16. X looks like Y	X and Y look similar	X looks better than Y
17. average	at the top	in the middle
18. severe	bad	good
19. approximately 100	103	153
20. get harder	difficult → easy	easy → difficult
21. a cure	for a disease	for a temperature
22. the mall	where you cook	where you shop
23. a patient	at a banker's office	at a doctor's office
24. a fare	a president	a ticket
25. be a success	something bad	something good
26. a snack	you eat it	you open it
27. a destination	an accident	a trip
28. be on sale	it's cheaper	it's not so cheap
29. a route	a problem	a road
30. a veterinarian	animals	restaurants

EXERCISE 13. Vocabulary Practice: Collocations

Fill in each blank with the answer on the right that most naturally completes the phrase on the left. If necessary, use a dictionary to check the meaning of words you do not know.

Phrase	Answer Choices	
1. scrambled _____	eggs	onions
2. pretty _____	all right	sure
3. _____ weekend	ago	next
4. it _____ four days	does	takes
5. _____ have you been?	How	What
6. much _____ expensive	extremely	more
7. I have a favor to _____ of you	ask	say
8. _____ up	hurry	pronounce
9. to _____ you the truth	say	tell
10. _____ a good idea	Is	That's
11. come _____	back	that
12. _____ it going?	How's	What's
13. take care _____	of	on
14. _____ tired	get	give
15. _____ wrong with your car?	What's	Why's
16. have a great _____	occasion	time
17. it happened _____ 4:30	at	to
18. _____ married	do	get
19. make _____	pan	soup
20. a present _____ you	for	to
21. figure out _____	the answer	the office
22. a lot _____	bigger	imporant
23. _____ Monday	in	on
24. a current _____	animal	problem
25. _____ noises	doing	making
26. _____ all the facts	get	take
27. cutting _____ onions	on	up
28. _____ to the news report	according	based
29. the average _____	cure	temperature
30. _____ a destination	make	reach
31. the flight _____ off	gave	took
32. I hate to _____ the dishes	do	make
33. I _____ heard from you in a long time	don't	haven't

EXERCISE 14. Writing Practice: Future Plans

Part 1. Editing Student Writing

Read these sentences about one student's future. Circle the 15 errors. Then write the number of the sentence with the error next to the type of error. (Some sentences may have more than one error.)

_____ a. *be going to*   _____ e. singular-plural

_____ b. prepositions   _____ f. no *a*

_____ c. word order   _____ g. *much/a lot of*

_____ d. no subject   _____ h. capital letters

My Future
1. Is difficult to say what I'm going to do in the future because I want to do so many thing. I have many plans.
2. I think I'm going to finish my degree university first.
3. Of course I'm going to work hard for improve my english.
4. After graduation, I'm go to get a good job with a big international company. this is a very important goals for me.
5. I'm go to make much money because I'm really good worker.
6. I'm gonna get married to my girlfriend Susana.
7. We're going to buy a house very beautiful at california.
8. Susana already told me that we going to have a big family.

Part 2. Original Student Writing

Now write about your future. What are your plans? Write some sentences or a paragraph about what you want to do. Use *be going to* when possible.

Unit 12

Review of Verb Tenses from Book 1

 Grammar Review

KEYS
2
3
4

In this book, we have studied three verb tenses and one verb expression: **simple present** (Units 1 and 3), **simple past** (Units 5 and 6), **present progressive** (Unit 8), and *be going to* for future time (Unit 11).

Verb Tense/Expression	Example	Units
simple present tense	My father is a taxi driver.	1
	The machine takes only coins.	3
simple past tense	Last night's dinner was delicious.	5
	I called the police when someone took my wallet.	6
present progressive tense	Why is the baby crying now?	8
be going to	I think it's going to rain very soon.	11

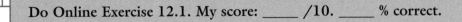

Do Online Exercise 12.1. My score: _____ /10. _____ % correct.

312

EXERCISE 1. Verb Forms

Fill in the blanks with the correct form of the verb *work*.

Simple Present

1. I _____work_____ all of the time.
2. You _____ every day.
3. He _____ most of the time.
4. She _____ every morning.
5. It _____ most of the time.
6. We _____ all week.
7. They _____ every day.

Present Progressive

15. I _____am working_____ right now.
16. You _____ today.
17. He _____ now.
18. She _____ this month.
19. It _____ now.
20. We _____ this week.
21. They _____ right now.

Simple Past

8. I _____worked_____ yesterday.
9. You _____ last night.
10. He _____ a year ago.
11. She _____ last Monday.
12. It _____ yesterday.
13. We _____ in 1974.
14. They _____ last summer.

be going to

22. I _____am going to work_____ next week.
23. You _____ tomorrow.
24. He _____ in five minutes.
25. She _____ next year.
26. It _____ tomorrow.
27. We _____ next Monday.
28. They _____ next summer.

 **Do Online Exercise 12.2. My score: _____ /10. _____ % correct.**

EXERCISE 2. Using *does* and *doesn't*

Circle the correct negative form of these simple present verbs.

1. The students (don't, doesn't) have class now.

2. Jonathan (don't, doesn't) speak French very well.

3. Students (don't, doesn't) go to class on Sunday.

4. In North America, people (don't, doesn't) drive on the left side of the road.

5. In Canada and the U.S., people (don't, doesn't) use Mexican pesos or Japanese yen.

6. Vegetarians (don't, doesn't) eat meat.

7. I (don't, doesn't) wear jeans to my office because the boss (don't, doesn't) allow it.

8. You (don't, doesn't) arrive in class late because you get up so early every day.

9. April (don't, doesn't) have 31 days.

10. Every year (don't, doesn't) have 366 days.

11. Rick and I (don't, doesn't) understand the teacher's explanation.

12. The food (don't, doesn't) taste good. It is too spicy!

EXERCISE 3. Verbs and Time in Context

Circle the correct form of the verb. Sometimes more than one answer is possible.

1. The boys (are going to work, are working, worked, work) here tomorrow.

2. Jose (is going to play, is playing, played, plays) the piano at our party last week.

3. Ryan and Lee (are going to study, are studying, studied, study) vocabulary next week.

4. We (are going to be, are being, were, was) on the plane in one hour from now.

5. Susan (attends, attend) class every day.

6. They (are needing, needed, need) a camera right now.

7. John and Susan (are listening, listened, listen) to the radio right now.

8. I (am going to assist, am assisting, assisted, assist) the doctor yesterday.

9. You need your umbrella if you're going outside because it (is raining, rained, rains) right now.

10. Kirk and I (are going to visit, are visiting, visits, visit) Mrs. Jones in two more weeks.

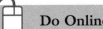 **Do Online Exercise 12.3. My score: _____ /10. _____ % correct.**

Present Perfect Tense: An Introduction

There is one other verb tense that was used in this book a few times, but you did not study it: present perfect tense. Present perfect tense is covered in Book 2 of *Clear Grammar*. Here is a brief introduction to present perfect tense.

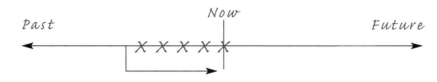

Example	subject	*have/has*	past participle
I have lived in this apartment for ten years.	I	have	lived
You have worked at the bank since 2007.	you	have	worked
He has been here since 8 AM today.	he	has	been
She's taught at Lincoln High since 1995.	she	'	taught
It has taken me six years to learn English.	it	has	taken
We've known Susan for about four years.	we	've	known
They've played the piano since they were ten.	they	've	played

<u>Rule 1</u>. The present perfect tense of a verb is **have** or **has** + **past participle** of a verb. (Contractions with *'ve* and *'s* are possible.)

<u>Rule 2</u>. The past participle of a regular verb is the same as its past tense: VERB + -ed. The past participle of an irregular verb has many forms, but a common ending is VERB + -en. You can find examples of past participle forms in Appendix 3.

<u>Rule 3</u>. Use present perfect tense for a past action that continues to be true now. (This tense has several different uses, but this one is a good start.) Common time expressions for simple past tense include for _____ (for ten years), since _____ (since 2000), so far, and until now.

ONE-MINUTE LESSON
The idiom **so far** means "until now." It is common to use present perfect tense with **so far**: *We have finished 11 units* **so far** or *I've liked this class* **so far**.

EXERCISE 4. Comparing Verb Forms

Write the correct form of the verb on the line.

1. *play*

   a. They _____ chess now.

   b. We _____ chess yesterday.

   c. He _____ chess tomorrow.

   d. She _____ chess every day.

   e. I _____ chess since I was ten years old.

2. *study*

   a. She _____ grammar now.

   b. They _____ vocabulary last night.

   c. He always _____ spelling.

   d. I _____ grammar tomorrow.

   e. We _____ English for more than twenty years.

3. *do*

   a. You _____ the homework last night.

   b. I _____ the exercises every day.

   c. Last night they had a party for all their neighbors. They

      _____ the same thing on the first day of June since

      1975!

   d. We _____ Lesson 5 right now.

   e. She _____ her homework tomorrow morning before

      class begins.

4. *need*

   a. We _____ some help last week.

   b. We _____ a car next week for our trip to San Diego.

   c. I always _____ more money.

   d. I _____ money right now.

   e. Since I first met Christina, she _____ a better job

      with a higher salary, but she still doesn't have a good job.

EXERCISE 5. Verb Forms

Write the correct form of the verb to fill each blank.

1. *be*

    a. I _____ a doctor. I work at the hospital.

    b. I _____ in Venezuela last year.

    c. I _____ in France next month.

    d. I _____ in Canada now.

    e. I _____ in this room for more than an hour, and I want to leave.

2. *work* (use *you* in the questions)

    a. _____ every day?

    b. How long _____ here? Do you like it?

    c. _____ in a nice office now?

    d. _____ in Korea last year?

    e. _____ there next month?

3. *rain* (use *it* in the questions)

    a. _____ tomorrow?

    b. _____ yesterday?

    c. _____ every day in August?

    d. _____ right now?

4. *have* (use *you* in the questions)

    a. When _____ a car accident?

    b. _____ any free time next week? I'd like to see you.

    c. _____ a good time now? Or do you want to go home?

    d. _____ any questions? The teacher can explain the lesson again.

    e. _____ that same car since you got your license?

Do Online Exercise 12.4. My score: _____ /10. _____ % correct.

EXERCISE 6. Identifying Errors

Circle the mistake, and write the correction above it. Check the verbs carefully.

1. When my mother and I <u>went</u> to the movies, she <u>liked</u> the movie, but <u>I no like</u> it.
                      A   B   C

   It <u>was</u> too violent.
      D

2. I <u>met</u> my friend at school today and <u>say</u> hello to her. She <u>was happy</u> to <u>see</u> me.
    A   B   C   D

3. <u>Those</u> cake is very <u>expensive</u>. I <u>bought</u> two cakes <u>for</u> the same price last week.
    A   B   C   D

4. My brother <u>wanted</u> to take a vacation. He <u>didn't have</u> any money, so <u>I offered</u> to
               A   B   C

   give <u>him</u> any.
      D

5. Brett <u>washed</u> his car, <u>cut</u> the grass, and <u>cleaned</u> the house, so now <u>he is sleeps</u>.
         A   B   C   D

6. <u>In</u> April 15, 1912, the Titanic <u>sank</u> to the bottom of the sea. Many people <u>died</u> <u>on</u>
   A   B   C D

   that night.

7. My doctor <u>asked</u> me where the pain <u>was</u>, and I <u>tell</u> him it <u>was</u> in my shoulder.
             A   B   C   D

Do Online Exercise 12.5. My score: _____ /10. _____ % correct.

EXERCISE 7. Multiple Choice

Circle the letter of the correct answer in these conversations.

1. "Did you call your mom and dad yesterday?"

   "Yes, I did, but they _____ home when I called."

       a. am not   b. weren't   c. don't   d. didn't

2. "Janice lives in an apartment."

   "Actually, that _____ true. Janice lived in an apartment before, but now she lives in a house."

       a. isn't   b. aren't   c. don't   d. doesn't

3. "How was your test?"

   "Well, I _____ study, so my score was really bad."

       a. wasn't   b. am not   c. isn't   d. didn't

4. "How was your vacation? Did you like Toronto?"

   "We _____ stay there very long, but it was great!"

       a. doesn't   b. am not   c. weren't   d. didn't

5. "Was the test very long?"

   "No, it wasn't. It _____ have many questions at all."

       a. didn't   b. wasn't   c. isn't   d. weren't

6. "That word is really long, and it's tough to spell."

   "Yes, it's tough to spell, but no, I don't think that word _____ have many letters."

       a. am not   b. doesn't   c. don't   d. isn't

7. "OK, let's go to the game room. I have one dollar."

   "Only one dollar? One dollar _____ enough money."

       a. doesn't   b. am not   c. isn't   d. don't

8. "_____ you study for the grammar test last night?"

   "Yes, of course. Grammar class is difficult, so I studied for about 3 hours."

       a. Were   b. Was   c. Do   d. Did

9. "Were you and Sally at the meeting last night?"

"No, we _____. Sally was sick, and I was tired."

    a. didn't   b. wasn't   c. weren't   d. don't

10. "Excuse me. _____ you know what time it is now?"

"Yes, it is exactly 11 AM."

    a. Is   b. Did   c. Do   d. Are

11. "_____ you and your parents travel to France last year?"

"Yes, it was a great trip."

    a. Did   b. Was   c. Are   d. Were

12. "_____ the word *dozen* mean the same as *twelve*?'

"Yes, those two words mean the same thing."

    a. Is   b. Are   c. Does   d. Do

13. "Do people in Brazil speak Spanish?"

"No, _____. Portuguese is the national language."

    a. it isn't   b. they don't   c. it doesn't   d. they aren't

14. "_____ your score on the test the best in your class?"

"No, Jane had 10 more points than I did."

    a. Had   b. Were   c. Was   d. Did

15. "_____ British Columbia and Ontario part of Canada in 1800?"

"No, I don't think so."

    a. Were   b. Do   c. Was   d. Did

Do Online Exercise 12.6. My score: _____ /10. _____ % correct.

EXERCISE 8. Verb Tenses in Context

Fill in the blanks with the correct tense of the verb in parentheses.

Dear Susan,

Hi, how ❶ (be) _____ things at home? I
hope everything ❷ (be) _____ fine there. This
❸ (be) _____ my first time in Honolulu, and I
❹ (like) _____ it a lot. Today is such a beautiful
day. Right now I ❺ (sit) _____ outside by the
pool. The sun ❻ (shine) _____, and some birds
❼ (sing) _____ in the trees behind me. When I
❽ (arrive) _____ two days ago, it ❾ (be) _____
a little cloudy, but there ❿ (be, not) _____ any clouds in the sky today.
A little while ago, I ⓫ (go) _____ shopping, and tonight I
⓬ (eat) _____ some special Hawaiian food for dinner. I
⓭ (be) _____ here only two days so far, but wow, I love it! I am not
sure what I ⓮ (do) _____ tomorrow, but there are so many things
to do. What a great place! I ⓯ (miss) _____ you and the kids a lot.

Love, Wendy

EXERCISE 9. Verbs in Context

Read this information about proverbs. Fill in the blank with the correct form of the verb in parentheses.

What is a proverb? A proverb ❶ (be) _____ a special expression.

This special expression ❷ (have) _____ an important message.

Sometimes this message ❸ (be) _____ easy to see; other times you

❹ (have) _____ to think very hard about the meanings of the words

before you can understand the real message.

Many times the words in the proverbs ❺ (mean) [*negative*] _____

the literal or exact meaning of the word. For example, what ❻ (mean) [*question*]

_____ the proverb "When in Rome, do as the Romans do" _____? In

this case, ❼ (talk) [*question*] _____ we _____ about people from Rome?

❽ (talk) [*question*] _____ we _____ only about Romans?

The real meaning of this proverb is that when you are in a different place,

you should do what people there do. If you go to a country where everyone

❾ (arrive) _____ late, then you should arrive late. If you go to

someone's house where they ❿ (eat) [*negative*] _____ meat, you

should eat the food that they give you and not make any comments about not

having meat. The general meaning is that you should see what the people

around you are doing and follow their actions or customs.

Proverbs are interesting because they ⓫ (teach) _____ us things

about a country or culture. For example, in many English-speaking countries,

there are many proverbs about time and money. Therefore, one could argue that

time and money ⓬ (play) _____ a very important role in this culture.

ONE-MINUTE LESSON

To talk about a result, we can use the word **so**. We say, *The weather yesterday was bad*, **so** *we did not play football*. We can also use the word **therefore** for the same meaning, but we use **therefore** for more formal or academic examples. We say, *Families in that area of the world have large families.* **Therefore**, *it is common for someone to have eight or nine brothers and sisters.* When **therefore** begins a sentence, it is followed by a comma.

EXERCISE 10. Verbs in Proverbs

Identify the verb tense in these proverbs. Then write an explanation of what you think the proverb means. Pay attention to verb tenses in your explanations.

1. Money talks. **Verb form:** _____

   Meaning: _____

   _____

2. Curiosity killed the cat. **Verb form:** _____

   Meaning: _____

   _____

3. The first step is the hardest. **Verb form:** _____

   Meaning: _____

   _____

4. Old habits die hard. **Verb form:** _____

   Meaning: _____

   _____

5. The early bird gets the worm. **Verb form:** _____

   Meaning: _____

   _____

6. Practice makes perfect. **Verb form:** _____

   Meaning: _____

   _____

Appendix 1: Parts of Speech

Category	Definition	Examples
noun	a name of a person, place, or thing	*Maria, a store, a book*
verb	shows action or state of being	*eat, take, is*
pronoun	takes the place of a noun	*he, him*
adjective	describes a noun or pronoun	*good, delicious, green*
preposition	shows relationships	*in, with, for*
conjunction	connects	*and, because, if*
adverb	describes verbs, adjectives, or other adverbs	*quickly, very, extremely*
interjection	expresses strong emotion	*Wow! Oh! No!*

Appendix 2: Verb Tenses

Tense	Example
simple present	*I drive to my office every day.*
simple past	*I lived in an apartment in 2009.*
simple future	*I will help you with that job.*
present progressive	*I am reading these verbs right now.*
past progressive	*I was watching TV during the storm last night.*
future progressive	*I will be flying to Japan at midnight tonight.*
present perfect	*I have been here since 9 AM today.*
past perfect	*I had been in France twice before.*
future perfect	*I will have finished this work by midnight.*
present perfect progressive	*I have been living in Sacramento for two years.*
past perfect progressive	*I had been reading all night.*
future perfect progressive	*I will have been working here for thirty years.*

Appendix 3: 60 Irregular Verbs

All verbs in English have three basic forms: **present, past,** and **past participle**. The past and past participle forms of **regular verbs** use *-ed.* These two forms are the same.

Present	Past	Past Participle
play	played	played
work	worked	worked
react	reacted	reacted

The past and past participle forms of **irregular verbs** are different. Common endings for the past participle forms of irregular verbs include *-en, -ne,* or *-n*, but there are many possibilities. For some verbs, the irregular forms are the same for both past and past participle forms.

Present	Past	Past Participle
see	saw	seen
go	went	gone
wear	wore	worn
put	put	put

English has thousands of verbs, but only a small number are irregular. Students must memorize the irregular forms that are most commonly used.

Present	Past	Past Participle	Present	Past	Past Participle
1. be	was/were	been	31. leave	left	left
2. become	became	become	32. lend	lent	lent
3. begin	began	begun	33. let	let	let
4. break	broke	broken	34. lose	lost	lost
5. bring	brought	brought	35. make	made	made
6. build	built	built	36. meet	met	met
7. buy	bought	bought	37. put	put	put
8. catch	caught	caught	38. read	read	read
9. choose	chose	chosen	39. ride	rode	ridden
10. come	came	come	40. run	ran	run
11. cost	cost	cost	41. say	said	said
12. cut	cut	cut	42. see	saw	seen
13. drink	drank	drunk	43. sell	sold	sold
14. drive	drove	driven	44. send	sent	sent
15. do	did	done	45. show	showed	shown
16. eat	ate	eaten	46. sing	sang	sung
17. fall	fell	fallen	47. sit	sat	sat
18. feel	felt	felt	48. sleep	slept	slept
19. find	found	found	49. speak	spoke	spoken
20. fly	flew	flown	50. spend	spent	spent
21. forget	forgot	forgotten	51. steal	stole	stolen
22. freeze	froze	frozen	52. swim	swam	swum
23. get	got	gotten	53. take	took	taken
24. give	gave	given	54. teach	taught	taught
25. go	went	gone	55. tell	told	told
26. have	had	had	56. think	thought	thought
27. hit	hit	hit	57. understand	understood	understood
28. hold	held	held	58. wear	wore	worn
29. keep	kept	kept	59. win	won	won
30. know	knew	known	60. write	wrote	written

Appendix 4: 70 Common Prepositions [From *Keys to Teaching Grammar to English Language Learners*, 2009 © University of Michigan Press, pp. 164–167.]

This list contains 70 prepositions and example sentences. The alphabetical list is arranged in three groups: one-word prepositions (e.g., *about*), two-word prepositions (e.g., *due to*), and three-word prepositions (e.g., *on top of*).

One-word prepositions

1. *about*   This book is **about** a family who gets lost in the mountains.

2. *above*   I have a small reading lamp **above** my bed.

3. *across*   The Washington Bridge is the best way to go **across** the river.

4. *after*   I hope to have more free time **after** June 1st.

5. *against*   Why are you **against** the president's plan?

6. *along*   In the early morning, people run **along** the east bank of the river.

7. *among*   Laura Vinson is **among** the best tennis players in the world.

8. *around*   Two squirrels were running **around** the oak tree.

9. *as*   For Halloween, I'm dressing up **as** Dracula.

10. *at* (+ place) When I travel, I prefer to stay **at** the Hilton.

    (+ time)   The flight arrived promptly **at** 11:37.

11. *before*   The flights that leave **before** 9 AM are not full.

12. *behind*   The little girl is hiding **behind** that tree.

13. *below*   If your final score is **below** 70, you will not pass the course.

14. *beneath*   **Beneath** these rocks, you might find a spider or a snake.

15. *beside*   My cat usually sleeps **beside** my bed.

16. *between*   **Between** you and me, I don't think he is a good leader.

17. *beyond*   People who can't swim well shouldn't go **beyond** those rocks.

18. *but*   Most restaurants in this area are open every day **but** Monday.

19. *by* (+ time)   **By** noon, most of the seats had been taken.

    (+ -self)   Of course it is more expensive if you live **by** yourself.

    (+ place)   My car is parked **by** the train station.

20. *despite*   **Despite** my money problems, I am thinking about buying a car.

21. *down*   The rat ran **down** the tree.

22. *during*   **During** my last vacation, I spent two weeks in Mexico.

23. *except*   You can call me any day **except** Thursday.

24. *for* (+ person)	I believe that this gift is **for** you. Happy birthday!
(+ period)	My husband and I lived in Montreal **for** five years.
25. *from*	This gift is **from** my wife and me.
26. *in* (+ period)	The price of oil may double **in** the next five years.
(+ place)	Was George Washington born **in** Virginia?
(+ time)	My sister got married **in** 2005.
27. *inside*	If you look **inside** the refrigerator, you'll find some soft drinks.
28. *into*	Please put your coins **into** the machine if you want a sandwich.
29. *like*	I prefer subtle colors **like** tan and gray.
30. *near*	San Diego is not **near** Sacramento.
31. *of*	What is the title **of** your favorite book?
32. *off*	The little boy fell **off** the bed, but he was not hurt.
33. *on* (+ street)	Our house is **on** Jasmine Avenue.
(+ surface)	There is a map **on** the back wall in my classroom.
(+ day)	The store is closed **on** Sunday.
34. *onto*	The cat jumped **onto** the table where the meat was.
35. *opposite*	There are some apartments that are **opposite** the park.
36. *over*	The small plane had difficulty flying **over** the mountain.
37. *past*	If you walk **past** the lake, you will see dozens of ducks.
38. *since*	I have worked here **since** 1999.
39. *than*	Mexico City is larger **than** Toronto.
40. *through*	At dusk, hundreds of birds were flying **through** the trees.
41. *throughout*	**Throughout** her lifetime, my grandmother saw some huge changes in our society.
42. *till*	As a farmer, he worked from dawn **till** dusk.
43. *to*	Driving from here **to** Miami takes about six hours.
44. *toward*	We walked **toward** the park, but then we decided not to go there.
45. *under*	Your socks are **under** the bed.
46. *until*	To finish the project, we worked **until** 11 PM
47. *up*	We watched a squirrel run **up** the tree.
48. *upon*	The cat was sleeping **upon** the sofa.
49. *with*	The director asked me to go **with** him to the meeting.
50. *within*	Everyone must finish the test **within** the announced time limit.
51. *without*	**Without** any extra help, Josh managed to get an A in math.

Two-word prepositions

52.	*according to*	**According to** this dictionary, this word has multiple meanings.
53.	*ahead of*	If you need to hurry, you can get in line **ahead of** me.
54.	*as for*	Bill liked the book. **As for** me, I wasn't able to finish it.
55.	*because of*	We started eating here **because of** your recommendation.
56.	*close to*	Do you live **close to** the bank on Smith Street?
57.	*due to*	The flight was canceled **due to** the bad weather.
58.	*far from*	We walked an hour and were then **far from** our hotel.
59.	*instead of*	I'd like tea **instead of** coffee, please.
60.	*next to*	Who would like to live **next to** a cemetery?
61.	*prior to*	**Prior to** arrival, you should complete this tourist card.

Three-word prepositions

62.	*in addition to*	**In addition to** Monday, I can meet on Tuesday or Friday.
63.	*in back of*	There is a huge tree **in back of** our house.
64.	*in case of*	**In case of** emergency, call 911.
65.	*in front of*	Our house is the only one without a tree **in front of** it.
66.	*in lieu of*	For his birthday, he requested that we donate money to a local charity **in lieu of** giving him a gift.
67.	*in place of*	Would you mind giving me ten dimes **in place of** a dollar bill?
68.	*in spite of*	**In spite of** the cooler temperatures, we went to the beach.
69.	*on behalf of*	I'd like to thank you **on behalf of** my entire family.
70.	*on top of*	Your briefcase is **on top of** the coffee table.